PENGUIN BOOKS

MIXED BLESSINGS

Paul Collins was born in Melbourne in 1940. He is
a Catholic priest. He has had wide experience in the
ministry of the Catholic Church in both Australia and
the United States. A graduate of Harvard University,
he is at present a research scholar in the Department
of History, Research School of Social Sciences,
Australian National University, Canberra.

MIXED BLESSINGS

John Paul II and the Church of the eighties
Paul Collins

PENGUIN

Penguin Books Australia Ltd,
487 Maroondah Highway, P.O. Box 257
Ringwood, Victoria 3134, Australia
Penguin Books Ltd,
Harmondsworth, Middlesex, England
Penguin Books,
40 West 23rd Street, New York, N.Y. 10010, U.S.A.
Penguin Books Canada Limited,
2801 John Street, Markham, Ontario, Canada L3R 1B4
Penguin Books (N.Z.) Ltd,
182-190 Wairau Road, Auckland 10, New Zealand

First published by Penguin Books Australia, 1986

Typeset in Paladium by Midland Typesetters, Maryborough
Made and printed in Australia by The Dominion Press-Hedges & Bell

CIP

Collins, Paul, 1940-
Mixed blessings.

Bibliography.
Includes index.
ISBN 0 14 009752 X.

1. Catholic Church—History—1965-   . 2. Catholics
—Australia—History—20th century. I. Title.

282'.94

To

MICHAEL PATRICK COLLINS
and
VERONICA MARGARET COLLINS

and to

DIANE ODETTE
who never let up until
I set pen to paper

and to

MARY PESCOTT
who suggested the idea
of this book

CONTENTS

CONTENTS

ACKNOWLEDGEMENTS

Anyone who writes on the contemporary Catholic Church is in the debt of Peter Hebblethwaite, Vaticanologist extraordinary and expert on modern Catholicism. In a series of excellent books and a seemingly never-ending flow of articles in *The Tablet*, the *National Catholic Reporter*, and Australia's *National Outlook*, he has been a source of information and intelligent comment on all that has happened since the Council. His counterpart as a Vaticanologist in the United States is Father F.X. Murphy (reputed to be Xavier Rynne, author of four excellent books dealing with each session of the Second Vatican Council). Other authors to whom I am indebted are listed in the bibliography.

I owe a debt of gratitude to Weber Center in Adrian, Michigan, USA and to its Director, Sister Mary Sue Kennedy, where this book was first given a number of times as a course entitled 'The Catholic Church in the 1980s'. My thanks are also due to the staff and students of Ursula College in the Australian National University for putting up with me during the two-and-a-half months of writing this book. Thanks are also due to the Department of History, Research School of Social Sciences, the Australian National University, for giving me leave to write the book.

Finally, eternal thanks are due to Wolfgang Amadeus Mozart, to George Frederick Handel and to sundry composers of the renaissance and baroque who kept me company during the weeks of enforced seclusion while this book was being written. I have owed my sanity to them on more than one occasion!

PREFACE

Let me admit this right from the beginning – this book is self-opinionated and subjective. While it is factual, the facts are expressed in a way that helps *me* make sense out of the contemporary Catholic Church. No one, of course, is absolutely objective. I am not objective. I have a view on the Catholic Church. I am strongly committed to it and I believe that it will have to continue to adapt and develop if it is to be successful in the contemporary world. I recognise that there will be Catholics and others who will disagree with me. So be it! Life becomes interesting through our differences.

My own view is that the Catholic Church is one of the most dynamic and creative institutions in the world today. It is going through a period of revolutionary change. In order to understand this change we need a historical perspective. Our culture suffers from historical amnesia. While we pride ourselves on knowing so much about our world, we in fact know so little about our past. So often those who claim to be 'traditionalists' are in fact historical amnesiacs who want to resurrect mythical visions of a past that never existed. They do not understand Jesus' words: 'Leave the dead to bury their dead' (*Matthew 8:22*).

In this book I have tried to look consistently to the future. For a future to become a possibility we must be able to imagine it, to picture how it might be. For many, both inside and outside the Catholic community, the Church is a self-engrossed institution, concerned largely about its own maintenance. There is truth in this description, but the Church's creative and intelligent members are working to create a future where Jesus' words of reconciliation and peace have a chance to be realised. Such people see the Church as much more than a self-engrossed institution, for they have encountered within it a dynamic force for hope and renewal.

Canberra,
July, 1986.

xi

PART ONE

VATICAN II AND ITS CONSEQUENCES

1

THE CHURCH MUTANT

Most Catholic priests that I know prefer funerals to weddings. This is not because they are morbid or perverse, but because they feel that they can do more to touch the lives of people at funerals. Some well chosen words, appropriate readings from scripture and a well celebrated liturgy can really help those who suffer bereavement as well as those who are there as respectable spectators. At weddings the couple and the families might be serious, but the guests often indulge in a somewhat silly and forced jocularity that can inhibit celebrants; the seriousness of the occasion can be overshadowed by trivialisation.

This may seem a strange place to begin a discussion of contemporary Catholicism, but it is also at funerals and weddings that Catholics who only practise occasionally, and non-Catholics who do not know the Church at all, encounter it in operation. There are frequently comments to the priest afterwards on how much the Church has changed. Many are happy to see the change; others seem appalled that the Church isn't what it used to be.

It is often the occasional Catholic who notices the change in the Church most forcefully. Practising Catholics have become blasé about change. I have heard comments at weddings from 'occasional' Catholics (especially after the toasts have loosened their tongues). 'In the old days priests were real priests – remember Father So-and-So?' – and they often refer to a tough old parish priest who had driven curates and loyal parishioners to distraction. I have been told: 'Things were clearer in the past', 'I loved the Latin liturgy', 'We didn't have all this doubt before', 'Why is it now alright to eat meat on Friday?' No logical explanation can deal with this type of statement; they reflect inarticulated feelings about the Church and a pervasive sense of disjunction.

With practising Catholics the picture is less crude, more subtle and nuanced. The vast majority appreciate the changes in the Church, especially the relaxation of an over-rigid discipline. But many still experience confusion about the Church and question if it has a future. Younger people (in ecclesiastical terms this is everyone under 35) who have only known contemporary Catholicism, wonder what all the fuss is about. There certainly is a fuss: it has flowed over into the theatre and has inspired a couple of very good novels. David Lodge has described the experiences of a group of Catholics over the 20 years from the late 1950s to the late 1970s in *How Far Can You Go?* (1980). A number of plays have portrayed the 'old' style of Catholicism – in Australia *The Christian Brothers*, in the United States *Do Patent Leather Shoes Really Shine Up?* and *Sister Mary Ignatius Explains It All* and in England *Once A Catholic*. In Australia in 1981 there was a series of TV dramas entitled *Menotti* centring around the tensions generated by an old fashioned parish priest and a liberal young curate. The popularity of all these works does not originate only in nostalgia. They represent more or less successful attempts by some writers to integrate their past (often by laughing at it), and the works helped many people reflect on the difficult mutation through which they had passed in the process of renewal of Catholicism.

A man with the unlikely name of Leslie Rumble presented the longest running radio programme in Australia. It lasted from 1928 to 1968 on Sydney station 2SM. It was known as *Question Box* and was also published as a best-seller in Australia and the United

States entitled *Doctor Rumble's Radio Replies*. It sold over seven million copies. It was a religious question-and-answer programme and Father Leslie Rumble, a convert to Catholicism, replied to queries sent in by mail. The reason for his success as an apologist for Catholicism and as a radio presenter and author was his clarity and his ability to present simply, succinctly and unambiguously Catholic teaching and theology. He was also a past master at exposing the errors and inconsistencies of everyone else. But Rumble was no ignorant bigot. He was a first-class scholar with an extraordinarily wide knowledge of Protestantism, religious sects and secular philosophy. Yet he still spoke simply and directly in everyday language. He was one of the best of the old school of Catholic apologists.

Doctor Rumble would probably be amused by the comparison, but it is interesting to compare him with a contemporary apologist for Catholicism – Hans Küng. Here again is an author whose works are widely read: he must be the only serious theologian whose books are available at airport bookstalls! *On Being a Christian* (1976), *Does God Exist?* (1980) and *Eternal Life* (1984) have helped many persons, Christian and otherwise, to make sense of belief. Küng is also a man who writes with clarity and a wide knowledge of other churches and philosophies. But there the comparison ends. Küng is profoundly ecumenical in the widest sense. He is open to the truth in the position of others and he strives to integrate that truth into his own broad understanding of Catholicism. While Rumble spoke from the 'old' mainstream, Küng speaks from the perspective of contemporary liberal Catholicism. My own opinion is that history may well judge Küng to be the most important and successful apologist for Catholicism in the decades spanning the 1960s to the 1990s.

Rumble and Küng represent two aspects of the process through which Catholicism has passed over the last 25 years. The beginning of that process was the Second Vatican Council (1962-1965), although its origins go back much further. Küng participated in the Council as a key actor. Rumble retired from active ministry just after the end of it. Vatican II was the springboard which initiated a process which continues to develop within Catholicism.

But there are many Catholics who do not understand or even reject this process. Some Catholics still want the clarity, authority and precision of Rumble; others appreciate the ecumenical breadth of Küng. Between them are the vast majority of Catholics who are still committed in varying degrees to the Church, and who try to make some sense out of all that has happened over the last 25 years. The aim of this book is to try to help the reader sort out the complex process of change in which contemporary Catholicism has been involved.

The first thing that needs to be clarified is what is meant by change. For many Catholics the last 25 years have been traumatic. They have passed through the searing process of evaluating, sometimes abandoning and then re-discovering their meaning structure – the set of ideas, values and assumptions that gives cohesion to their lives. This was not an ordinary process of change. For the word change implies a gradual progression, a natural and prolonged transition from one state to another. Even large institutions like the Catholic Church are never static; they are in a constant process of change. I prefer to borrow a word from biology to describe what has happened to contemporary Catholicism – *mutation*. What the Catholic Church has experienced is a rapid and radical transformation, a sudden variation in its life. Old boundaries have been broken and something new has emerged. While there are obvious elements of continuity, the Catholic Church in the late 1980s is not what it was at the beginning of the 1960s. Twenty-five years is a long time in the life of an individual, but it is an exceptionally short period in the life of a Church with a 2000-year history. That is why I have chosen the word mutation to describe the process. It conveys a sense of both dramatic transformation and continuity. Biologically it refers to a genetic change. The evolution of a new reality, however, is deeply rooted in and is the result of all that has gone before. Those who have passed through a mutation have changed profoundly, but have done so on the solid basis of their past.

So it is not unusual that many Catholics feel a sense of disjunction. Anyone trying to understand contemporary Catholicism must be aware of this. There are several Catholic responses to this experience. Some want to go back, to return to the old times when all was clear and Doctor Rumble could provide an unequivocal answer. These are not all older people. Catholics born since the end of the 50s have experienced nothing but a Church in flux. Some of them long for stability and structure, for solid ground on which they can sort out their faith attitudes. Many of them took the full brunt of the chaos in religious education in the years immediately after the Council. They never knew the old and they learned little of the new (except insubstantial pap) and so these younger Catholics search for religious certainties that will underpin their life. Together with older conservatives, these young people look back romantically (and naively) to a more stable, less socially critical Church. It is here that they imagine that they will discover something more 'sacred'.

Then there are those who are happy with contemporary Catholicism, the satisfied liberals. They lead naturally to the *un*satisfied liberals who consider that the Church is still too immersed in past structures and attitudes, too cautious to commit itself to the important issues that trouble the people of our age. Some remain within the Church, others are on the periphery and a large group have ceased to practise but still retain interest in the Church.

Finally there are the majority of practising Catholics who appreciate many of the changes but who still experience disquiet about where the Church is going. Deep down you find both annoyance and anger with the Church. They will tell you the problem is poor liturgy, irrelevant preaching, lack of clear teaching and discipline ('One priest tells you one thing, another something else') and the dearth of firm and charismatic leadership – thus the popularity of Pope John Paul II. For some the problem is the socially critical role played by some clergy and laypeople. For instance many Catholics in Australia have been upset by the statements of the Catholic Commission for Justice and Peace. In the United States a whole group of Catholics have criticised the US bishops' pastoral letter on peace and the morality of war (*The Challenge of Peace: God's Promise and Our Response*, 1983). Probably even more will be upset by the US bishops' proposed pastoral letter on the ethics of capitalism. Such Catholics counsel the Church generally, and the clergy specifically, to stick to 'spiritual' things.

Let us try to analyse this disquiet and anger a little more deeply. It is a legitimate disquiet. It arises from a profound change in the way in which the Catholic religion interacts with the lives of people. An older Catholic said to me recently: 'My faith no longer comforts me, it disturbs me.' By considering this statement we can find one way of approaching the essence of the problem facing Catholics. Religion, traditionally, has been the bedrock upon which people built their lives, the structure that gave purpose to their existence. In this sense, religion is a 'comfort'. Emile Durkheim in *The Elementary Forms of the Religious Life* (1916) helps us to understand this. He argues that the role of religion in society is to provide a support for those values and beliefs which reflect the shared attitudes and perceptions of experience of a given culture. Religion's role is to provide solidarity, a kind of collective consciousness, a series of focal emotional points (expressed usually through worship) for participants in the culture. This, for instance, is the role that Catholicism plays in contemporary Polish culture. That is why it is such an important and potent force for Poles at the present. Solidarity within a culture is achieved through symbolising – a process through which persons and objects are given added significance beyond their normal personal or physical value. Durkheim argues that symbolism in religion bestows upon certain persons or objects power and moral strength, thereby creating the realm of the sacred.

I certainly do not accept this purely naturalistic explanation of the origin of religion. But it does help us understand the *dynamics* of how religion works in the lives of people. Religion normally acts as a means of social reinforcement. It sacralises roles, functions, places, actions. While seemingly a referrant for society, it draws its references from the social system of which it is the unconscious mirror. It reflects the participants' perception of their society. Thus religion is an essentially *conservative* force.

In this way religion 'comforts' people by giving them a feeling of security and solidarity with others who share their beliefs and values. It gives a sense of purpose and direction to life. It helps people feel at home in the universe and provides a structure of meaning that guides them in making sense out of the disparate elements of life.

As I indicated, I do not accept Durkheim's account of the origin of religion, but I do regard it as an accurate sociological analysis of the function of religion. My reason for referring to it is to emphasise the conservative role that religion normally plays in the lives of people. Thus Catholics (and other Christians) grew up expecting the Church to sustain those values, practices and beliefs which they had come to regard as sacred and unchangeable. Durkheim helps us understand the reason for the disquiet experienced by many Catholics. They encounter the disjunction of a Church that does not fulfil the role sociologically and psychologically assigned to it. The Church is perceived by some as proposing radically new values and beliefs to its adherents, and for most people this is very upsetting. Some Catholics, for example, will argue that when they grew up the Church was utterly opposed to communism and the possession of nuclear weapons was seen as the bulwark of freedom. Now they see the Church as soft on communism (and they will often refer to liberation theology) and they cannot understand why the Church says that the use (and even the threat to use) nuclear weapons is intrinsically immoral. At a deeper level Catholics become confused and angry when theologians or authority figures, such as priests and bishops, question teachings and practices which Catholic people had come to regard as inviolable and unchangeable. Some feel that there has been a tampering with the sacred.

But the fact is that Catholicism is far less authoritarian and rigid than people think it is. Catholics accept its authority, doctrine, liturgy and spirituality because they help them make sense out of life and opens up for them a way to the transcendent. But occasionally in the history of the Church this consensus breaks down, and the Church's expression of its belief no longer makes sense to its adherents. Contemporary Catholicism has experienced this. New and more plausible explanations of faith are emerging in the Church. The richness of the mystery of faith is never exhausted by one definition or explanation. Vatican II itself explained the faith in terms of some of these alternatives. A minority of Catholics have largely adopted these alternatives, but most have only done so superficially or not at all. Thus there is a real imbalance in the Church.

The problem is heightened by the fact that many of the elite (by this I mean those who do most of the Church's full-time ministerial work) have made the transition, but the ordinary Catholic in the pew is still struggling with it. The religious development of people is never the same across the board; many get left behind. Some of those left behind have suffered deep pain and the loss of a religious reality that was very sacred to them. As yet, they have discovered nothing to take its place.

Thus many Catholics are at sea without any way of symbolising or expressing their convictions and commitment. They are deeply troubled in their spiritual and religious lives. They are capable of growing and the convictions that will move them need to be both intellectual and spiritual. They will have to be helped to express their faith in a new way. The elite leads, explores, tries new ideas, but confirmation must come from the general body of the faithful. Contemporary Catholicism is still in the midst of this process.

Here I want to note that Durkheim's view only represents one element in the role religion plays in society – the conservative one. But religion also acts as an active agent of social change. This mode only rarely becomes predominant. It occurs when the symbiosis of authority, worship, spirituality and doctrine break down, and a new structure is there to take its place. Since the 1930s new ways of modelling the Church have emerged, coming to a head at Vatican II. It is worth noting that this revolutionary and prophetic mode is only possible for a supranational religion like Catholicism. Religions confined to one culture usually collapse with the culture they underpin.

It is at this level that we can come to understand why many Catholics have lost their sense of direction. The simple fact is that Catholicism is shifting modes – as it must to survive. From the conserving mode it is shifting to the *prophetic* mode (prophetic is a far more theological and traditional word than revolutionary or radical). In the Old Testament prophecy was usually linked to social and religious disquiet and criticism. Prophets were upsetting and they often made people very angry. They were generally opposed by the structure of established religion. When this type of shift occurs in a large institution like the Catholic Church, many people lose a sense of direction. Religion ceases to play the role traditionally assigned to it in society. Adherents become disoriented and angry.

For these reasons I prefer the word 'mutation' to 'change' to describe the process in which Catholicism is involved at the present moment. This process is not entirely new in the history of the Church. It has happened before. I think that at least four previous mutations can be distinguished in the experience of the Church:

• The first is found in the New Testament itself and in the period immediately following it. The Church emerged from its Jewish matrix to become adjusted to the reality of life in the gentile and Roman world. It sought and found a philosophy to underpin its theology – neo-platonism.

• The second was when Christianity emerged from being a persecuted minority to being the favoured and eventually the official religion of the late Roman Empire. This happened during and after the reign of Constantine (from 314 AD onwards). Christianity now had to adjust to being part of the real world of politics and secular affairs.

• The third was the 'Gregorian revolution' of the 11th century. In order to reform the Church of the corruptions engendered by feudalism, Pope Gregory VII (1073-1085) and his successors introduced a model of Church that was hierarchical and highly centralised. The power of local lay lords over the Church was broken. The hierarchical structure of the Church as we know it today finds its origin in this period.

• The fourth mutation was the Counter Reformation of the 16th century. A vast change swept over the Church in response to Protestantism. The Church adopted 'absolutist' models from political society. There was a major reform of liturgy, religious life and priesthood. A new more baroque spirituality emerged.

The mutation that we are experiencing at present might well be the most radical yet, especially in terms of the *rapidity of change*. A new type of Catholicism will emerge, in lineal continuity with the past, but characterised by a new form and with new qualities. Personally, I cannot see any way in which this process can be halted. It can be slowed down and tested by reactionaries, but I doubt if it can be turned around. Above all, one must recognise the work of the Spirit of God within this process.

By now it will be obvious to connoisseurs of Catholicism that I write from a specific viewpoint on the future of the Catholic Church. If labels must be applied, I am a liberal. Paradoxically, I have always thought of myself as a conservative, for it is my interest in Church history that has led to my concern with the future of the Church. Oddly, those who see themselves as conservative seem to seek answers in the past, or romanticise it by wanting to live in it or restore it. It is only when you know and have integrated your personal and communal past that you can begin to look honestly to the present and the future. I am a conservative in the sense that I know and respect the past – and I admire it – but I do not want to live in it or repeat it. The function of the past is to help us understand the present and to imagine the future.

This book asks the basic question, what is happening to the Catholic Church now and what is its future? This question can be put another way: is the Catholic Church at the present moment dying or rising? My answer is that it is both dying and rising at the same time. As one vision of the Church slowly dies, a new one is growing that will take its place. The Catholic Church most certainly has a future. But the Church of 1995 will be vastly different from that of 1965. Catholicism has emerged as one of the truly creative forces in the contemporary world. Capitalism and marxism have become increasingly stultified, unimaginative and shoddy as they struggle to adjust to the world of the late 20th century. Catholicism has a new lease on life and creativity.

2
A MIXED BLESSING

The contemporary Catholic Church cannot be understood without a knowledge of the Second Vatican Council. To understand the Council you must appreciate the attitudes of the two men who began it, developed it and brought it to its completion – Popes John XXIII (1958-1963) and Paul VI (1963-1978). Conflicting forces were at work within the Council and they deeply influenced the formulation of its documents, which were often the result of compromise. These compromises have continued to effect the Church in the 20 years since the Council. In this chapter I will describe what happened at the Council, the leading personalities and the major issues. I will especially note the compromises which have effected the Church so much during the subsequent years.

From the moment he announced the Council, John XXIII faced a wall of scepticism. He was disappointed when he spoke of it for the first time to a group of 17 cardinals in Rome at the church of St Paul Outside the Walls on 25 January 1959. They greeted his announcement with silence. The rest of the Church was more enthusiastic, but confused. Many leading churchmen thought that John had made a bad mistake and this was the standard opinion in the Roman Curia, the central bureaucracy of the Church. John was unclear about the aims and methods of the Council, but unlike many of the churchmen who surrounded him, he trusted in the Spirit of God at work in the Church. He was no fool either: he understood Church and Vatican politics. But he was also a simple Christian who believed that his intuition in calling an ecumenical council was guided by God's Spirit, and that despite his age (he was 77), he had the ability to carry it through.

Pope John XXIII was born Angelo Guiseppe Roncalli in the village of Sotto il Monte near the northern Italian city of Bergamo on 25 November 1881. His parents were farmers. He studied for the priesthood in the seminary of Bergamo from 1892 to 1900 and then went to Rome to study theology, was awarded a doctorate (granted almost automatically at the end of the course) and was ordained a priest on 10 August 1904. After a brief pilgrimage to Palestine, he returned to the diocese of Bergamo. Thus far his career was completely conventional.

His bishop, Giacomo Radini-Tadeschi, appointed Roncalli his secretary in October 1906. The years 1906 to 1914 were very difficult ones, the period of the so-called 'modernist' crisis. Pope Pius X (1903-1914) claimed that Catholicism was being subverted by internal heretics whom he labled modernists. It is clear now that the modernist scare was an over-reaction to those Catholic theologians who were trying to apply the findings of literary and historical scholarship to Catholic thought. But the Pope's attitude led to a paranoid search for modernists and the vast majority of the victims were entirely orthodox Catholics. Many were anonymously denounced to the Roman Inquisition and were sacked from their teaching posts. Roncalli's bishop, Radini-Tadeschi, was suspected in Rome of being one and Roncalli himself had to tread very carefully.

Pope Benedict XV (1914-1922) freed the Church from much of the anti-modernist paranoia, but he was unable to achieve a great deal because of the First World War and its aftermath. During the war Roncalli served in the Italian army as a chaplain and after the war he took charge of a student residence in Bergamo. In 1920 he was called to Rome to head the Italian section of the Society for the Propagation of the Faith (this organisation raised money for Catholic overseas missions) and he also became an official of the Roman Curia.

These were the years of the fascist take-over in Italy. In order to consolidate his power the fascist Duce, Mussolini, sought the support of the Church and he gained some sympathy from Pope Pius XI (1922-1939). Cardinal Pietro Gasparri, the Papal Secretary of State, said openly that he preferred negotiating with dictatorships; they were always more consistent and predictable than democracies! Secret negotiations were begun with Mussolini which eventually led to the Lateran Treaty (1929) and the establishment of the Vatican City State. As a consequence of this accommodation with fascism, the Vatican abandoned the Christian Democratic Movement led by the priest Luigi Sturzo.

Roncalli had felt much more comfortable in the open pontificate of Benedict XV. His position, however, demanded that he remain silent. It was a natural step for him to enter the diplomatic service of the Vatican. In March 1925 he was appointed Apostolic Visitor to Bulgaria and was ordained an Archbishop. The years in Sofia were difficult and lonely, but he developed close personal relationships with the powerful Orthodox Church. Thus Bulgaria served as an apprenticeship in ecumenism.

In November 1934 he left Sofia to become Apostolic Delegate to Turkey and Greece. Roncalli gained great diplomatic experience in Istanbul, especially during the Second World War. Turkey was neutral. It was a major contact point for both Allied and Axis powers. Through the German Ambassador, Franz von Papen, he tried to assist groups of Jews escaping from south-eastern Europe. His experience in Greece and Turkey was unique for a papal diplomat. In one sense, these were years of exile. In another, they provided a marvellous training in human experience and ecumenism.

In December 1944 Roncalli was moved to one of the most prestigious posts in the Vatican diplomatic service – Papal Nuncio in Paris. Charles De Gaulle and the Free French had just regained control of the government in the capital, and Roncalli was faced with the difficult problem of what to do with those Catholic bishops who had openly co-operated with the Vichy regime during the German occupation. The Vatican temporised, trying to find a 'face saving' solution. Roncalli was partially successful in negotiating this issue, although the final decision was made by Pius XII, the French bishops and De Gaulle, without consulting him as Nuncio.

He did, however, manage some personal triumphs. He became a close friend of the Soviet Ambassador at a time when the relationship between the Vatican and the Kremlin was at its worst. He also befriended Vincent Auriol, a non-believer, who was President of the Republic. It was Auriol who presented him with his cardinal's hat at the time of his appointment in 1953.

In France he found himself in the midst of two internal Church crises of great importance. The first was over the 'worker-priests'. This was a group of priests, founded by the Archbishop of Paris, Cardinal Suhard, who went as workers into the factories. Their purpose was to contact the urban proletariat who were lost to the Church. Regarded with suspicion by middle class and conservative Catholics, they were accused of becoming active in left-wing and communist politics and of betraying priestly lifestyle and spirituality. The Vatican was even more hostile. Pius XII condemned them in 1953.

The second crisis was over the *nouvelle théologie* – the revival of theology that centred around the Dominican faculty of theology in Paris, La Saulchoir, a group of Jesuit scholars and the theological reviews *Nouvelle révue théologique* and *Études*. The key figures in this intellectual renaissance were Henri de Lubac, Jean Daniélou, Yves Congar, Marie-Dominique Chenu and in the background the great Jesuit thinker Pierre Teilhard de Chardin. As Nuncio, Roncalli made no comment at the time, but in the long run the ideas generated by the *nouvelle théologie* must have permeated the mind of the future Pope. He remained silent, however, when these men lost their teaching posts and when some of their books were placed on the *Index of Forbidden Books.* The encyclical letter *Humani generis* (August 1950) also condemned the *nouvelle théologie.* The period resembled the modernist crisis of Roncalli's youth. The irony of it all was that these scholars were to become the leading theologians of the Second Vatican Council and they were to be eventually recognised as men whose thought changed the Church. Two of them became cardinals themselves—Daniélou and De Lubac.

Soon after Roncalli was made a cardinal he was appointed to Venice as Patriarch. He was sorry to leave Paris, but was glad to find his true métier in full-time pastoral work. As a pastoral cardinal-archbishop he was creative and open. He told the Venetians from the beginning that he came as a man ' . . . who simply wants to be your brother, amiable, approachable and understanding.' Thus before his election as Pope at the age of 77, he had experienced a wide range of people and places. There was a sense in which he was a contradictory mixture of the typically closed and insular attitudes of his Italian clerical generation and an openness that allowed him to live and let live. He never saw himself as an 'intellectual', but he was a competent historian and antiquarian. It is precisely the historian in him which permitted him to perceive the relativity of all things, including the structures of the Church. This may have been the key element in the liberation he seemed to experience as soon as he became Pope. His spirituality was traditional and simple, but it always remained humane and gentle. While he worked for much of his life for the Roman Curia, he was never a curialist in the traditional sense. He was far too human and pastoral in his attitudes for that. He came close to being a cural bureaucrat in Paris, although even here his warm humanity saved him. He never lost his common sense, rooted in his north Italian farming origins.

Pius XII died on 9 October 1958. His long illness and autocratic style had left the Roman Curia in disarray, yet still very much under the control of an old guard of career curalists. Roncalli emerged as one of the possible candidates, but it took 11 ballots to elect him. He was clearly perceived as a transitional Pope. His humanity, affability and humour were in sharp contrast to the austere Pius XII and he became popular with the media. People sensed in him a warmth, gentleness and genuinely evangelical spirituality. Right from the start the themes that were to typify his pontificate emerged: unity in the Church itself, a reaching out to separate Christians and peace in a world that spent enormous resources on the arms race while it ignored the needs of the poor and the dispossessed.

Immediately after his election Pope John talked to a number of non-Italian cardinals and the idea emerged of getting bishops together to talk about the world-wide problems of the Church. Slowly the idea of an ecumenical council emerged in his mind. He tested the idea out with a few close friends and attempted to discern God's guidance through prayer. He also became increasingly aware of the enormity of the task.

Right from the beginning people generally and the Pope specifically spoke about the Council as 'ecumenical' (the word means world-wide or universal). This was a normal way of speaking about councils of the Church, but the specific meaning in this context was that the Second Vatican Council would not only represent the Roman Church, but also Christians separated from Rome. Pope John issued ' . . . a friendly and renewed invitation to our brethren of the separated Christian Churches to share with us this feast of grace and fraternity.' This was a radical departure from the condemnation of all forms of ecumenism issued by the Holy Office for the previous 40 years. By the time the invitations were sent to the 'separated Christian Churches' (October 1959), it was clear that they would send observers not participants. But the ecumenical note was there.

Who, then, would participate? All of the bishops of the Catholic Church (there were 2594 of them in 1959) and the superiors-general of the religious orders of priests (156 of them). Suggestions for the agenda were sought from participants and Catholic universities and faculties of theology. The Curia kept control of the early process through handling the 2812 suggestions sent in from all over the world. They were sorted and sent to the different Curial Congregations and each Congregation set up a pre-conciliar commission. The Curia kept close control over each of these commissions and while some outsiders were invited in – bishops and major superiors who would have a vote at the Council – they were carefully vetted and very few represented views that differed from those of the Curia.

The aim of the Curia was a closed, in-house Council, approving – but not debating – previously prepared documents. The Curia simply presupposed that its views were the only possible ones. The Vatican had become increasingly self-enclosed during the 50s, and saw itself as the one and only norm of theological truth and ministerial policy in the Church. The men of the Curia were all similar: career bureaucrats of limited theological ability. Some were good canon lawyers and most were educated within the narrow confines of the Roman seminaries. Most were right-wing anti-communists with a mixture of moderates and a few neo-fascists.

But other powerful forces were at work in the Church. Pope John had set up the Secretariat for Christian Unity directed by the German Jesuit cardinal, Augustin Bea. He was a long-time Rome resident and a past-master at curial politics. He was also a first class scripture scholar. For him the gospels were the first norm of belief and the views of other Christians were to be taken seriously. Some of the bishops began to demand that the Council turn outward to the world and its needs. The French bishops, for instance, demanded that the Council address the problems faced by the developing world, an idea echoed by Cardinals Josef Frings (Cologne) and Alfrink (Utrecht) who also spoke of the need for decentralisation in the Church. Archbishop Lorenz Jaeger (Paterborn) asked for a broad ecumenical understanding and Cardinal Montini (Milan) said the Church must adapt to the needs of the age.

Throughout the period prior to the Council there was a parallel preparation carried on by theologians. Archbishop Jaeger, for instance, called for a council that would be democratic, collegial and open. He urged lay participation. But it was a young, outspoken Swiss theologian, Hans Küng, who succeeded in spelling out an alternative agenda from that of the Curia. In his book *The Council and Reunion* he outlined a programme for the Council and the Church. His programme was extraordinarily prophetic. He demanded:

• Reform of the Catholic Church leading to re-union with the separated Churches.

• Emphasis on the use of the Bible in theology and worship.

- Development of a vernacular liturgy.
- An emphasis on the universal priesthood of all believers.
- A dialogue with other religions and other cultures.
- A reform of the Roman Curia and the abolition of the *Index of Forbidden Books*.
- A de-politicisation of the papacy.

The book – and Küng's lectures all over the world – enjoyed enormous publicity and offered a real alternative programme to that of the Curia.

The theological foundations for the Council had been laid by scholars during the previous 30 years. In the field of history there had been Yves Congar, Jean Daniélou, Hugo Rahner and Marie-Dominique Chenu; in liturgy the big name was Josef Jungmann, but the work of scholars in Belgium, Germany, France and the United States was also important; in theology the leaders were Karl Rahner, Yves Congar, Henri De Lubac and John Courtney Murray. There were a growing number of Catholic scholars working in biblical studies; often they were deeply indebted to the pioneering work of Protestant scholars.

The groundwork was laid for a new view of the Church. The Curia did not have the field to themselves.

By August 1962 a set of procedural rules for the Council had been published. It is often forgotten that ecumenical councils only happen rarely in the history of the Church (the last was Vatican I in 1870). Thus setting up the Council was no easy task. One central problem was the relationship of the Pope to the Council. How and in what form would he make known his wishes to the bishops? How could he say something without pre-empting discussion and taking over the Council? One thing was clear: there were to be no condemnations of error, no 'anathemas'!

The Council opened on 11 October 1962. The number of participants made it the largest council in the history of the Church. There were 2640 voting members, the vast majority of whom were bishops. Europe was represented by 1041 bishops, North and South America 956, Asia and Oceania 300, and Africa 279. The numerical superiority of the Italians was lost; they had dominated the two previous councils of Trent and Vatican I. Present also throughout the sessions were the Orthodox and Protestant observers. At the opening session they numbered 47. Over the four sessions the numbers varied a little, but a broad cross-section remained represented. The presence and psychological influence of the observers was to be profoundly important.

On the opening day Pope John called the Church to look to the future without fear. He condemned the prophets of gloom who were always forecasting disaster. The Pope's remarks were clearly addressed to the critics of the Council from the religious and political right. His vision of 'Divine providence . . . leading us to a new order of human relations' whereby 'everything . . . leads to the greater good of the Church' was a vision of vast optimism. He spelt out an agenda for the Council. The Pope insisted that the Church ' . . . must look to the present, to the new conditions and new forms of life introduced into the modern world'. He told the Council that ' . . . the whole world expects a step toward a deeper penetration and a developing realisation of the faith in perfect conformity to authentic doctrine, which should be expounded through modern research and modern scholarly disciplines.' Statements like these would have been considered radical in 1962 even if uttered by Hans Küng! The Pope further shocked the pessimists by saying that ' . . . often errors vanish as quickly as they arise, like fog before the sun.' The historian in him could not resist turning upside down a statement of one of his papal predecessors: Gregory XVI (1832-1846) had said that a 'grand conspiracy of evildoers' had forced him to set aside 'the spirit of gentleness' and 'to employ the rod' (the reference is to *I Corinthians 4:21*). Pope John preferred 'to make use of the medicine of mercy rather than of severity.' The Pope concluded by praying for the achievement of Christian unity and the total unity of humankind.

It was strong stuff, but what were the assembled bishops to do with it? If you bring 2600 people together leaders soon begin to emerge and the Council soon began to assert its independence of the Curia. The bishops were to meet from 13 October to 8 December. The actual sessions were held in St Peter's basilica in the morning. After that there was lunch, siesta, and the afternoons

and evenings were increasingly taken up with meetings, conferences and lectures from theologians as participants tried to sort
out the issues for themselves.

The first test of conciliar independence came on the first day
with the election of members to the commissions. The Curia had
lists of candidates ready and tried to stampede the assembly. They
were stopped by the intervention of Cardinals Liénart (Lille) and
Frings (Cologne). Elections were not held for another three days
and resulted in a much broader representation. The bishops had
made it clear that they would set their own priorities, and the
Curia began to see the Council taken over by the bishops.

Here a note of caution needs to be mentioned. I am not suggesting that the main dynamic at the Council was the Curia versus
the rest. The real struggle was much more complex with coalitions forming around different issues. But there seems to have been
a determination by the leaders of the Curia to keep the Council
brief and to maintain control of its documents. They lost on both
scores. The bishops spent most of the first session finding their
way. Most of them were not professional theologians, aware of
the great issues of the world and the Church, but hard-working
pastoral priests, tied down by the minutiae of running a diocese,
many of them on a financial shoe-string in developing countries.
For them the Council was to be a marvellous exercise in in-service
training. They gradually became aware of each other's problems
and began to perceive what they had in common.

It was in this context that the introduction of the *Decree of the
Liturgy* as the first document for discussion was very sensible.
The pre-conciliar liturgy commission had put together a good
document which suggested the limited introduction of the vernacular (the local language) – remember that up to this point the
Church's entire worship was in Latin. For centuries the laity had
been excluded from participation in worship which had become
the exclusive preserve of the clergy. The giving of communion
'under both kinds' was also suggested (that is the laity could receive
both bread and wine). The debate revealed that the bishops would
divide along traditionalist (retain the liturgy as it is) and progres-

sive lines. The majority of bishops wanted a reform of the liturgy; their pastoral experience had taught them that changes were needed. Suggestions were proposed in the debate concerning the need for a better choice of scripture readings, changes in ecclesiastical music and art and a reform of the liturgical calendar. The schema was handed back to the liturgy commission for rewriting.

Like every large parliamentary gathering, the Council produced its fair share of bores. Speakers were limited to eight minutes but that did not prevent large numbers repeating over and over what had been said previously, wandering from the topic, or driving bishops away to the coffee bar that had been set up in the basilica. It was nicknamed Bar Jonah from St Peter's Aramaic name, Simon bar Jonah. It was difficult to control the dull speakers because of the guarantee of freedom of speech. The other problem was that all speeches were supposed to be in Latin. Most bishops were very rusty in this language – if they ever had any facility in it. So the majority of speakers were reduced to reading from prepared texts. Cardinal Cushing (Boston) became so disgruntled with listening to Latin speeches he did not understand that he offered to pay for a simultaneous translation service. By the middle of the second session the offer had not been taken up, so Cushing returned to Boston.

The liturgy was a practical pastoral issue which all bishops could comprehend. The next debate was on the complex theological issue of the sources of divine revelation. Many of the bishops were confused, but enough realised the importance of the issue for a major debate to occur. The pre-conciliar schema had been drawn up by the Dutch Jesuit, Sebastian Tromp. Some theologians tend to identify their views with 'absolute truth', giving them the right to demolish the views of those who disagree with them by identifying them with heresy and error. This was Tromp's tack. Much of the schema was taken up with an attack on the views of a German theologian, J.R. Geiselmann.

Let us try to sort out what is involved here. The whole issue presupposes *revelation*, that is that God communicates with human persons and the human community. The Christian understanding is that this occurs in a number of ways. The Church is the most important of these channels of communication. Protestants hold that God speaks in and to the Church only through scripture – thus Luther's cry: 'Sola scriptura'. Scripture alone is the Word of God and the sole source of all Christian truth. The Catholic view is more complex. The Council of Trent (April 1546) taught that the gospel of Christ is the fountainhead of all truth and moral conduct, and that this 'gospel' is contained in *both* the written works of scripture and the apostolic traditions of the Church. Both are inspired by the Spirit of God. Trent made no attempt to define how scripture and tradition are related to each other. Underlying this view is the conviction of the profound interaction of the Church and the Holy Spirit. In the period after Trent, Catholic theologians began to say that the 'gospel' was contained *partly* in scripture and *partly* in tradition.

In the years prior to Vatican II the view of J.R. Geiselmann became common. He said that there was no distinction between scripture and tradition, for tradition is the Church's on-going interpretation of scripture through its application in teaching and in everyday life. Thus scripture was not a second and independent source of revelation, but scripture and tradition are two sides of the same coin. This view was much more acceptable to Protestants. And Vatican II had aimed to be an ecumenical council.

It was, however, anathema to Tromp and the Council conservatives led by the aged Cardinal Ottaviani. The pre-conciliar schema rejected Geiselmann's view outright, insisted on a two-source theory and attempted to prevent the penetration of modern biblical scholarship into Catholic scripture studies. Tromp's schema was also an ecumenical disaster. It was rejected outright by the bishops. A string of cardinals attacked it: Frings (Cologne), Liénart (Lille), Léger (Montreal) Koenig (Vienna), Alfrink (Utrecht), Suenens (Brussels), Bea (Christian Unity), the Patriarch Maximos IV Saigh (Melkite, Antioch), and two Indonesian archbishops – and all in one morning! Bar Jonah was empty the whole time. Everyone wanted to witness the demolition of the schema. Only Cardinals Ruffini (Palermo) and Siri (Genoa) defended it. It was a historic day: for the first time for some centuries a Roman document was publically torn apart by a procession of bishops. It was to be an event often repeated at the Council and it has helped to develop among Catholics a more critical attitude to such material.

The names listed in the previous paragraph quickly emerged as the leaders of the Council and they will constantly reappear. The fight, however, was not over. The Ottaviani group, led by Archbishop Pietro Parente (Assessor of the Holy Office), argued that the Pope alone could determine what could be examined at a Council and that the schema was the product of the Pope's men. Those who wanted a new document were breaking the law. The President of the day, Cardinal Gilroy of Sydney, said that the Council rules allowed any bishop to express his opinion on the adoption, amendment or rejection of any schema. Ottaviani tried to protest, but Gilroy ignored him. As the debate dragged on over several days, Ottaviani tried to manoeuvre the Pope on to his side. It did not work. When it became clear that the schema would be rejected by the Council, Pope John set up a mixed commission, representing a range of theological views, to rewrite it. The co-presidents were Ottaviani and Bea.

I have outlined this debate in detail for it was a turning point at the first session. The bishops now felt free to reject the schema on the Eastern Churches and demand its complete revision. (Eastern Churches such as the Melkites, Maronites, Ukranians and others had their own liturgy and church polity but were in union with the Roman Church.)

As time was running out for the first session – and it was still not clear if there would be any further sessions – the schema *De Ecclesia* (On the Church) was brought forward. Ottaviani was obviously afraid of the surgery that awaited his text (all theological texts had been prepared by his pre-conciliar commission). At the end of November he tried to head off discussion by saying it was too long for the short time remaining and that the Council should rather discuss a text on the Virgin Mary. The suggestion was rejected and the Council turned its attention to the most important issue of all – the schema *De ecclesia* on the nature of the Church.

The Church had emerged from the 19th century with a very unbalanced conception of itself. Since the First Vatican Council (held in Rome in 1870), the 'Church' had come to be identified with the papacy. For Vatican I had defined the primacy and infallibility of the Pope. By primacy the Pope was not only declared the head bishop (the primate) of the Church, but he was also given total control over the whole Church without any real countervailing power. Infallibility meant that the Pope could not err when teaching officially as head of the Church ('ex cathedra') on faith or morals. All power in the Church quickly came to be centralised at the top, and the real function of bishops became obscured. Were they merely functionaries who represented the Pope in each diocese, or did they have a role that flowed essentially from episcopal ordination? What about the laity? Were they merely passive recipients in the Church or did they have a real ministerial function? Could the Church become less hierarchical and move more toward the separated Orthodox and Protestant Churches? The debate on the Church was the central issue of Vatican II.

The debate on *De ecclesia* lasted from 1 to 7 December. Ottaviani's speech was brief. He told the bishops: ' . . . I know what you will say about (the schema). You will say it is negative, scholastic, not pastoral, not ecumenical.' He was right. A succession of speakers described the document's short-comings: it reduced the Church to a set of laws, it was too triumphal and juridical, it ignored the role of lay people, it had too much on primacy and infallibility and not enough on bishops, it was theologically superficial, it was not ecumenical. Not that everyone was pro-ecumenical: one of the constant speakers of the Council was the tough conservative Bishop Luigi Carli of Segni (Italy). He voiced the reservations of many bishops in Italy, Spain and Portugal where Catholicism was the religion of the vast majority and the separated brethren were rare birds. Spain and Portugal were still ruled by dictators (Franco in Spain and Salazar in Portugal).

It was the greatest speaker of the Council, Bishop Emile Joseph de Smedt of Bruges (Belgium) who summed up the problems with Ottaviani's schema (whenever De Smedt spoke Bar Jonah was empty): De Smedt said the key problem was what he called 'Romanism', the tendency of the Vatican to assume that it owned the Church. He divided Romanism into three categories:

• Triumphalism: there is the tendency to present the history of the Church as if it were a succession of triumphs.

• Clericalism: the Church is seen as a pyramid with Pope, bishops and priests at the top while the laity occupied a secondary place. He spoke of the dangers of 'bishop-worship and pope-worship'.

• Juridicism: this is the tendency to define the Church in terms of *exclusion*. If a person does not keep this or that law, they are excluded from the Church. De Smedt said: 'What mother would ever say: "He is no longer a member of my family?" It is not fitting for Mother Church to speak this way either.'

The first session of the Council concluded on 8 December having achieved very little that was concrete. But the bishops had begun to think for themselves and to make their own decisions. It was now clear that this would not be a quick Council approving the pre-determined texts of the Curia. It had gained its own momentum. In December a co-ordinating commission was set up to establish priorities and to supervise the revision of the schemas.

Pope John XXIII died on 3 June 1963. He had succeeded in initiating a revolution in the Church. Things would never be the same again. Giovanni Battista Montini was elected Pope as Paul VI on 21 June 1963 after a conclave of only two days. He immediately announced the continuation of the Council.

The second session began on 29 September 1963 and Pope Paul set out four major tasks for the succeeding sessions. Firstly, he asked for a doctrinal presentation of the nature of the Church. Thus the schema *De ecclesia* was brought back into major focus. He stressed the importance of the collegiality of bishops. In other words, he was inviting the bishops to share with him in the government of the world-wide Church.

Secondly, he wanted an inner renewal of the Church to recall the community to the core of its spirituality.

Thirdly, he pledged the Church to work for Christian unity, and made the famous admission of guilt and responsibility on the part of the papacy for the scandal of Christian disunity: 'If any guilt in the separation is ours, we humbly ask God's pardon and also seek forgiveness from the brethren who should have felt themselves separated from us; for our part we are prepared to forgive the wrongs which have been done to the Catholic Church.'

Finally, he opened up the horizons of ecumenism to include dialogue with the wider world. This was to lead straight to the *Constitution on the Church in the Modern World*.

The revised schema on the Church was presented by the irrepressible Ottaviani and the dour Irish Dominican, Cardinal Browne. It had four chapters which included one on the hierarchical structure of the Church and one on the laity (the 'people of God'). Cardinal Frings moved to have the people of God put first and to add the proposed schema on Mary, the Mother of God, as a final chapter in the *De ecclesia* schema. This was eventually adopted but it did not please the Marian maximalists – those who wanted to give as much honour as possible to Mary. Most of these were opposed to ecumenism.

But this struggle was quickly overshadowed by a fierce debate over the chapter on the hierarchy and specifically on the question of the college of bishops. For a minority – mainly curialists – the idea that the Pope should share his authority with the bishops was anathema. They saw this as an encroachment on papal primacy and denied that collegiality was based in scripture or tradition. This view, of course, was self-interested given that most of them shared in papal power through their curial offices. Against them ranged the majority of the bishops.

The debate about the restoration of the permanent deaconate also revealed a range of different approaches. In the early Church the official ministry was carried on by bishops, priests and deacons – and in some places deaconesses. The work of deacons (celebration of baptisms, marriages, conducting of funerals and the offices of preaching and church administration) had been absorbed by priests. The proposal was to restore the deaconal order and to admit both married and single men to the ministry.

Many speakers saw this as a threat to the priesthood and specifically to celibacy. Who would choose to be celibate if they could be in the official ministry and marry? Most support came from missionary countries which were already short-staffed. The proposal also had the advantage of allowing missionary bishops to ordain as deacons their married catechists who carried on much of the ministry at basic level in developing countries. As locals these men were often natural leaders, spoke the language and were more in touch with the people than foreign missionaries. They were an emerging local leadership cadre.

It was a natural progression to the role of the laity. But the debate had dragged on for a month and bishops were becoming impatient. There was a feeling that the Council had become bogged down, participants were subjected to interminable speeches and some bishops had already left Rome. The only ones to profit from this state of affairs would be those who wanted the Council to achieve nothing. It was to their advantage to drag it out.

After much delay five questions were proposed to test the views of the bishops. The questions centred around the issues of collegiality and the restoration of the permanent deaconate. The results of the straw vote made it clear that both would gain the support of two-thirds of the bishops.

It was during this period that Cardinal Suenens made the suggestion that the lay 'auditors' (Catholic laymen who could listen to debates but not participate) be increased with the addition of some women. The right-wing press jeered Suenens for mentioning women and snide comments were made about the 'feminism of his Eminence'; he was referred to in the English Catholic press as 'the paladin of ecclesiastical neo-feminism'! The Cardinal emphasised that the gifts of God were given to all Christians, not just to the hierarchy. It was on this theology of gift that lay ministry was based. Suenens and a number of speakers gradually introduced these ideas into the debate on the schema which was again handed back to the theological commission.

Debate then turned to a schema on the pastoral office of bishops and the government of dioceses. This schema was presented by

Cardinal Paul Marella (Apostolic Delegate to Australia from 1948 to 1953, where he was famous for wearing dark-tinted glasses – no one could see where he was looking!). He stressed that the Curia had a precise knowledge of every diocese and that Rome had always respected local uniqueness. This was greeted with frank disbelief on the part of bishops who had long experience of the petty and centralised control exercised by the curial departments over every aspect of the Church's life. They had experienced the narrow Italianised attitude of many Roman officials. It is often forgotten that bishops used to need 'faculties' from Rome concerning the most trivial minutiae – such as giving nuns permission to wash the linen used by the priest to cleanse the chalice at Mass.

The schema was attacked as juridical and disjointed with too much insistence on the rights of the Curia and too little on those of bishops. Theologically it lacked any sense of the co-responsibility of bishops in the government of the Church. During the discussion of the schema the idea of a synod of bishops was suggested. Bishops from all over the world would meet periodically in Rome to assist the Pope in the government of the Church. The idea started to gain ground that the Curia needed reforming. It should be the servant of the Church, not its master.

It was at this point that one of the 'scenes' of the Council occurred. Cardinal Frings attacked the Holy Office. He said that it still acted inquisitorially by condemning people without a hearing, without clear charges and without giving them the opportunity to defend themselves. He spoke of ' . . . methods and behaviour . . . (which) are a cause of scandal to the world.' This was greeted with long applause. He went on to suggest that lay persons could qualify for many tasks of the Curia. Even though it was forbidden, there was more applause. Cardinal Ottaviani responded; he was obviously angry. He argued that such attacks were based on ignorance, that to attack the Holy Office was to attack the Pope ' . . . because he is its prefect'. He was followed by Cardinals Browne and Ruffini who warned of the dangers of collegiality. Collegiality would weaken the power of the Pope. Ruffini also defended the Curia: 'I have heard in this gathering a severe and offensive speech against the Roman Curia.' The gloves were off!

That afternoon Ottaviani tried to get the support of the Pope. He was rebuffed. He seems to have considered resigning. As though the debate in St Peter's were not enough, the Holy Office looked even more foolish that evening. For reasons known only to themselves, they had arranged for a showing of the movie version of Henry Morton Robinson's novel *The Cardinal*. Many bishops considered the film in poor taste. It was the story of a young American priest who worked his way through the bureaucracy to become a cardinal – and on the way he had a minor romance, appropriately in Vienna! It did nothing to lessen the tension on the Council floor. Problems such as the size of dioceses, the unequal distribution of priests, frictions between dioceses, a retirement age for bishops and the position and role of auxilary (assistant) bishops – 'parish priests in purple' as they were called – were discussed. It was a comprehensive survey of the problems of the world's bishops.

Despite frayed nerves and tension, the schema on ecumenism was introduced on 18 November. A major role in its introduction was played by Cardinal Bea and Archbishop Jaeger. Strong criticisms of the schema were voiced outside the Council by the Orthodox and Protestant observers. The debate showed that there was acceptance by Catholics of the need for ecumenism. The word had become part of the Catholic vocabulary. But the schema raised a number of new coalitions and new issues. Much of the early debate was taken up with two questions: the relationship of Judaism to Catholicism and the question of religious liberty. Both were important issues and were debated vigorously.

Cardinal Bea introduced chapter four of the schema entitled simply 'The Jews'. He dealt with the responsibility of the Jews for Christ's death. He spoke of Jesus' forgiveness ('Father forgive them for they know not what they do'). He spoke of the lineal continuity between ancient Israel and the Church, of the terrible consequences of anti-semitism, and of the fact that the Jews of our time can hardly be blamed for crimes committed against Christ 2000 years ago. Yet the Catholic liturgy was still speaking of 'perfidious Jews' and preachers were still overtly anti-semitic, especially on Good Friday. Bea concluded by warning the Council that it was considering a religious not a political question. The bishops should not get entangled in the question of the relationship of the Arabs to the contemporary state of Israel. This, of course, was precisely the area upon which the bishops focused.

The chapter entitled 'Religious Liberty' was introduced by the great De Smedt. He stated the core teaching of the chapter unequivocally: every person who follows his or her conscience in religious matters has a right to authentic religious freedom. No person or institution can take the place of a free judgement of individual conscience. This was radical talk for many of the bishops. The Catholic Church itself had had several varieties of inquisition, including the Spanish and Roman. In a number of countries where Catholicism was the majority religion, the state was still bound through concordats (treaties) with the Vatican to enforce the unique position of the Catholic Church. Certainly Catholicism had a tradition of claiming religious freedom for itself but it was often very unwilling to grant this to others when it had power. De Smedt did not run away from the problem: he quoted the encyclical *Quanta cura* (1864) of Pius IX where freedom of conscience and religion is described as *deliriamentum* (madness, delirium). He even managed to describe these strictures as though they supported religious liberty. It was a tour de force!

The reality was that the concept of religious liberty, in the sense it was being used at the Council, was based very much on modern democratic experience. Catholics had found that living in pluralist countries such as the United States, Canada, Australia and the Western European democracies was far preferable to the situation in countries where Church and State were united – Spain and Portugal were prime examples. The Church had held in the 19th century that union of Church and State was the norm and separation could be tolerated as an exception. This was questioned in the 20th century, especially by French philosopher Jacques Maritain and US Jesuit, John Courtney Murray. In the Council a counter-attack on the chapters on the Jews and religious liberty was soon mounted.

Naturally, those bishops whose dioceses were in predominantly Arab or Moslem countries were most concerned with the Jewish question, the Americans and Western Europeans with religious liberty. Strong speeches in favour of ecumenism were made by Cardinals Ritter (St Louis), Meyer (Chicago), Léger (Montreal), Archbishop Heenan (Westminster), Patriarch Maximos Saigh and Bishop Elchinger (Strasbourg), The Eastern bishops were opposed to the inclusion of any discussion of the Jews. Slowly, things seemed to be grinding to a halt again. Some of the promoters of ecumenism began to feel that the issues of religious liberty and the Jews should be separated from the schema on ecumenism. Religious liberty was considered more important than the Jewish question. The whole problem was complicated by the fact that the curial minority still had a stranglehold on the machinery of the Council through the Secretary General, Archbishop Pericle Felici. The two 'problem' chapters went into a temporary limbo.

At the beginning of December, elections were held for additional members for the different commissions. Enough bishops got together to be able to draw up an international list of those who represented the majority. Key figures such as Abbot Butler (Downside Abbey, England) joined the Theological Commission, and the Louvain University theologian, Gérard Philips, became its second secretary. It was he who largely wrote *Lumen gentium*.

Meanwhile some work had been brought to a conclusion. The Council finally adopted the *Constitution on the Sacred Liturgy* and the *Decree on Social Communications* on 4 December 1963. The *Constitution on the Liturgy* laid the foundation for the liturgical renewal of the Church, the most radical and far-reaching in its history. The schema had been well-prepared from the beginning. For most Catholics the introduction of the vernacular at Mass and in the celebration of the sacraments was the most obvious effect, together with the call for a full and active participation of the whole community. Concelebration of Mass by several priests was reintroduced. Much more power was given to local episcopal conferences over liturgy.

The *Decree on Social Communications* was seen by many as a retrograde document and it has had absolutely no subsequent impact. It was based on a pre-conciliar vision of the Church. The opportunity of addressing one of the key issues of the modern world was lost. The document is best left in the oblivion in which it is buried.

The closing address of Pope Paul conceded that there had been problems in the second session and that it did not correspond to all expectations. But some things had been accomplished. He concluded by announcing a pilgrimage to Jerusalem with a meeting with the Ecumenical Patriarch of Orthodoxy, Athenogoras. This took place in January 1964. This action strengthened the ecumenical thrust of the Council. As one of the first major papal journeys it had a world-wide impact.

To many, Pope Paul's role in the second session appeared ambivalent. He seemed unwilling to come down on one side or the other, unwilling to make a stand with the majority. But he had to guarantee the freedom of all, including the minority. Humiliation and direct confrontation is not the way of the Vatican in dealing with its own. Saving face is important. And Paul VI knew the Curia better than most. The Vatican way is summed up in the tag: *promoveatur ut amoveatur* – 'Let him be promoted that he may be removed'! Some saw in Paul an indecisiveness, a Hamlet-like quality which stymied action. There may have been elements of this in his personality, but a key factor for him would have been freedom for all to express their views and a willingness to allow things to take their course.

The third session lasted from 14 September to 21 November 1964. It brought both the climax and the major crisis of the Council. The co-ordinating commission had outlined in advance the areas for consideration:
- the nature of the Church
- revelation
- the episcopal office
- ecumenism
- Jews and religious liberty
- lay apostolate
- the Church in the modern world

The question of Church and world was a new one. It had been generated by Paul VI's concern with 'dialogue with the world'. The Pope made clear in his opening speech that the doctrine of the Church and the nature and function of the episcopate and its links to the primacy of the Pope were still the central issues. The Pope spoke of ' . . . the nature and function of the episcopate as [a] complement of the doctrine of the primacy.' This was a sign to the opponents of collegiality to back down. They did not. Pope Paul tried to keep the proceedings very focused.

Debate opened again on the re-written schema *On the Church* (as mentioned Gérard Philips was the major writer). The proposed text had eight chapters:

I The mystery of the Church
II The people of God
III Hierarchical structure of the Church and episcopate
IV The laity
V Universal call to holiness
VI Religious life
VII Eschatological nature of the Church
VIII On the Blessed Virgin Mary

Chapters three and eight ran into a lot of trouble. Collegiality was still the stumbling block. A strong speech in its favour by Archbishop Pietro Parente of the Curia (he had probably been encouraged by the Pope) brought over some waiverers, but there was still a solid core of resistance. Xavier Rynne describes the result of the key vote on collegiality:

The key votes on collegiality resulted in only 328 negative votes at most; this probably represented the full strength of those opposed to collegiality . . . the pattern of resistance had some hilarious results: 50 bishops voted against the divine origin of the episcopate . . 44 against the episcopate as a sacrament . . . 150 against the proposition that only bishops could confer ordination . . . when it was announced that 90 bishops had voted against the supreme authority of the Pope . . . the Council burst into laughter. Apparently some bishops had been instructed to vote against collegiality and did not know how to behave voting simply negative throughout. (Xavier Rynne: *The Third Session*, p 52)

The concession of the deaconate to mature married men also ran into more problems. The idea of conceding the order to young men without the obligation of celibacy was rejected. Chapters four, five and six passed without much comment (chapter four on the laity was a good one) and chapter seven – 'on the eschatological nature of the pilgrim Church' – was re-written as a result of the debate in mid-September. The mouth-filling word 'eschatological' (and also the word 'parousia') became clichés at this time: both words refer to the end of the world and the final consummation of all things. Given that all discussion of this reality must be in terms of symbols and poetry, both the romantics and the cynics had a great time!

The chapter on the Blessed Virgin Mary also ran into trouble. The Marian maximalists considered the chapter too weak, too minimalistic. Cardinal Stefan Wyszynski (Warsaw) and several Spanish and Italian bishops wanted (another) consecration of the world to Mary and the introduction of the titles 'Mother of the Church' and 'Mediatrix of Grace' introduced into the text. Such titles would not have helped ecumenism. These views were by-passed, but Paul VI was to proclaim Mary 'Mother of the Church'.

The schema on *The Pastoral Office of Bishops* was re-introduced but it too ran into more difficulties. On the one hand the tough little firebrand, Bishop Carli (Segni) insisted that collegiality was wrong; bishops were not competent to share with the Pope care for the universal Church. On the other hand Cardinal Léger (Montreal) and several French bishops still found the document too juridical and clerical. Some further problems emerged: the powerlessness of bishops in relationship to exempt religious orders (this was an old problem; it had come up at Trent and Vatican I). The problem referred to the exemption of religious orders of priests from the jurisdiction of the local bishop. This gave them a freedom shared by few others. Other problems concerned the distribution of priests and the fluctuation of population in dioceses. There were enough difficulties to send the text back to the commission.

Two major crises characterised the third session: the October crisis and the November crisis. Actually, there was an overture to the October crisis, what could be called the late September crisis: this centred again around the questions of religious freedom and the Jews. Concerning religious freedom, the fundamental question was freedom of conscience *even if the conscience was in error*. To allow the rights of an erroneous conscience was a decisive departure from the medieval and post-reformation legal system, which required the proscription of those in error as heretics by both Church and State. No account was taken of their subjective attitudes. Cardinal Ruffini (Palermo) asked: how can the Catholic Church, believing itself to be the true Church, allow people the freedom to ignore, abandon, reject or even attack this faith? It may be necessary for the State to help the Church to protect the truth. Toleration of error was permissible; freedom for error to thrive was not! Ottaviani expressed concern about the privileged position of the Church in countries with concordats with the Holy See. Would the Church repudiate its treaties?

It was the Americans, Cardinals Meyer (Chicago) and Ritter (St Louis) who defended the draft on religious freedom; they were supported by Archbishop Karol Wojtyla (Krakow) who defended religious liberty in the face of communist totalitarianism.

In early October the bishops opposed to religious liberty tried to deceive the Council through the machinations of Secretary General Felici; they unsuccessfully attempted to ease the draft out of the control of Bea's Christian Unity Secretariat by handing it over to a nominated commission. They were in flagrant violation of the rules of the Council. Again the Pope refused to act decisively.

The *Declaration on the Jews* had by now become a largely political issue. The text was weakened to appease Arab Christians, and Islam was now explicitly mentioned. Only contemporary Jews were absolved from the charge of 'deicide'. The stumbling block was Arab rejection of the state of Israel. Diplomatic pressure was exerted by Eastern rite bishops and Patriarch Maximos Saigh (Antioch in Syria) accused the framers of the *Declaration* of having been 'bought' by Israel. Again the document was sent back to the Secretariat for Christian Unity for rewriting.

The schema on *Divine Revelation* had been completely

rewritten by a group of theologians which included Karl Rahner, Yves Congar, the young German Josef Ratzinger (ironically now head of the Congregation of the Doctrine of the Faith, the new name for the Holy Office) and Gérard Philips of Louvain. By now the vast majority of bishops could see the deep inter-relationship between scripture and tradition and the importance of serious scriptural studies. But the minority again argued that the proposed schema departed from the teaching of Trent on scripture and tradition and so the schema went back to the commission to incorporate the suggestions from the Council floor.

Between 7 October and 20 November nine texts were presented to the Council. These concerned:
• the ministry and life of priests
• the missions
• the lay apostolate
• the religious life
• Christian education
• the Church in the modern world
• the sacrament of marriage
• the Eastern Churches
• the Church.
Here we will follow the fate of four of them: the schemas on the laity, the ministry and life of priests, the final debate on the Church and the new schema *The Church in the Modern World.*

The schema on the laity reflected the usual hierarchical clericalism. It was attacked by a number of speakers. The principal complaints were that no layperson had been consulted in its formulation and that it presented the ministry of the laity in terms of 'Catholic Action' dominated by the hierarchy. It lacked any discussion of laity achieving holiness in and through their work in the world. 'Catholic Action' was the product of the time of Pius XI (1922-1939). He defined Catholic Action as ' . . . the participation of the Catholic laity in the hierarchical apostolate.' The Pope said that the laity could participate in the apostolate because of lack of clergy. The ministry was the preserve of bishops. Thus it was only by delegation that the laity exercised a ministry. There was no appreciation of the fact that ministry flowed directly from baptism and that all Christians shared in the priesthood of Christ (*I Peter 2:9-10*).

For the first time for many centuries a layman spoke to the Council, naturally enough on the laity. He was Patrick Keegan, president of the International Young Christian Workers. He spoke in English and his speech was rather tame. It appeared to have been doctored and thus clericalised. The schema was sent back to the commission for revision.

The discussion on the ministry and life of priests began in mid-October. The text on priests had been reduced to a series of twelve propositions, most of a 'pious' kind. The Council had enhanced the power and position of bishops in the Church. The schema on priests gave the impression that they were second class and unimportant. A number of positive suggestions were put forward: bishops should see priests as collaborators, not as servants. Priests needed emotional and spiritual support. They also needed an explicitly priestly spirituality. In the background was the question of clerical celibacy. At the third session no one was brave enough to bring this to the floor of the Council. The schema on the priesthood was sent back to the commission for rewriting.

On 20 October the long-awaited schema on *The Church in the Modern World* was introduced. This became the most integrated and radical document produced by the Council. It almost failed to make it to the Council for there was pressure to end with the third session. But as Pope Paul was one of the prime movers of this schema it was soon made clear that the Council would continue for a fourth session. The schema came to the Council floor well prepared. Since the spring of 1963 it had been through several revisions and there had been wide input into the document. One of its major formulators was Bernard Häring, a German Redemptorist priest, who had spent most of the Second World War as a POW in Russia. The aim of the document was to shift the focus of the Church outward to the world which forms the context of the Church's ministry. The schema was presented to the Council by Bishop Emilio Guano (Livorno), who stressed the necessity of the Church entering into dialogue with the world on the pressing problems facing humankind.

The debate began tamely enough with compliments or mild criticisms, including a comment by Archbishop Wojtyla (who had been one of the committee that formulated the schema) that it would make sense to non-believers – presumably Marxists.

Archbishop Heenan (Westminster), however, attacked the document. In a passionate and somewhat confusing speech he said that it was full of 'sermonising platitudes' unworthy of a Council. This led him to attack the *periti*, the theological experts. He argued that the Church had suffered from the writings and speeches of a 'few specialists' who cared nothing for the teaching authority of the bishops and the Pope. The attack seemed to be directed against Bernard Häring who had annoyed Heenan earlier by his views on birth control – specifically the pill. This was a foretaste of things to come after the Council, especially in 1968 on publication of Pope Paul's encyclical *Humanae vitae*.

Discussion of the text included the need for dialogue with atheism, communism and philosophies opposed to Catholicism. The bishops wanted a renewed and positive vision of the world and of the place of human persons in it. The need to 'read the signs of the times' eventually became a cliché. The bishops also discussed the problem of poverty, modern science, human dignity and racism, feminism and the role of women, marriage and issues concerning procreation and contraception. The theologian, poet and scientist, Pierre Teilhard de Chardin, was mentioned; he, of course, was one of the sources of this optimistic reappraisal of the world.

The 87-year-old Patriarch Maximos Saigh was his usual outspoken self on the birth control issue. He highlighted the crisis of conscience faced by many Catholic couples: by using contraception they were denied the sacraments. He mentioned the terrible problem of over-population in many countries. He said bluntly that the Church's teaching on marriage and family was hopelessly out of date. He spoke of 'outmoded ideas', the 'bachelor psychosis' of the clergy, of ' . . . a Manichaean conception of the flesh' which led Catholics to think that the body was intrinsically bad. Cardinals Alfrink, Suenens and Léger reflected the same views.

Naturally enough, it was Cardinals Ottaviani, Browne and Ruffini who put the opposite view. Ottaviani stated flatly that the Church could never teach that married couples could determine the number of children that they would have. He said that he himself was the 11th of 12 children and that his father was a labourer in a bakery in the Trastevere, the poorest area of Rome. Browne set out the usual teaching about the primary (procreation) and secondary (love and fulfillment of the spouses) purposes of marriage. He said he would not mention the pill ' . . . because the Pope has reserved this to himself.' He did mention, however, 'sterile periods' which, he informed the bishops, were 'now being studied by true experts'. He was presumably referring to the research of Doctors John and Lyn Billings in Melbourne. It is good to know that Australia has produced some 'true experts'.

Apparently, far too many problems of sexuality were being aired for the debate on marriage was suddenly foreclosed.

The Council then turned to a discussion of world poverty. One of the lay Catholic auditors, James Norris, mounted a campaign for Barbara Ward, the English Catholic economist, to speak to the Council. For over 20 years she had been a recognised expert on poverty and population. But there was one problem – she was a woman! Archbishop Felici and his macho-clerical bureaucracy could not face the prospect of being addressed by a woman. So Norris himself spoke – in Latin – on 5 November 1964. It was a truly great speech. He spoke of a 'lopsided' world where 16 per cent of the world's people own 70 per cent of the world's wealth. ' . . . three-quarters of the human race live in a state of poverty bordering on or below the subsistence level.' He said:

Recently a bishop from one of these lands said to me, 'My people live not only in poverty but in permanent misery.' This type of utter poverty brings with it other human sufferings. The first is hunger – a constant gnawing hunger that is never satisfied day or night. Poverty brings diseases that can never be cured because there are no medical services. Poverty brings illiteracy in lands where the great majority of people cannot read or write. Poverty brings bad housing, slums that breed crime and sin. Poverty means that a mother looks at her new-born infant knowing that it will probably die before the year is out. For millions of people poverty means that life-expectancy is 35 years. For millions of people living in this kind of poverty, death is a sweet release.

Norris was followed by a host of speakers, many from the third world, who supported his views.

The bishops then turned to the questions of peace and modern war.

Here division ran along national lines: European bishops called for a total ban on nuclear weapons, while US and some English bishops spoke in favour of nuclear deterrence. A number of bishops, including Cardinal Feltin (Paris) said that the schema had retreated from the explicit condemnation of nuclear war by John XXIII in his encyclical *Pacem in terris*. Opposing this, Bishop Philip Hannan (then Auxilary in Washington, soon to be Archbishop of New Orleans) spoke of 'just war' theory and of the danger of slavery to materialistic atheism. He called for support for those who had defended freedom, especially those who had died for it. He was a former US paratroop chaplain. The debate closed on 9 November.

Dissatisfaction with the administration of the Council had been simmering under the surface throughout the third session, specifically with Secretary General Felici, who, it was felt, was manipulating the Council on behalf of the conservative minority. Feelings reached crisis point on 14 November when the revised text of the schema on the Church (*Lumen gentium*) was given to the bishops.

Chapter three on collegiality was again the storm centre. A *nota explicativa praevia* (a 'presupposed explicative note' is the literal if tortuous translation of the Latin) was appended to the chapter which was designed to exclude every encroachment on the primacy of the Pope by the doctrine of collegiality. Felici told the Council that it had come from a 'superior authority', whom everyone supposed to be Pope Paul VI. Confusion reigned: was the *nota* part of the text? 'No' said Felici. What was its purpose then? Felici said that the bishops had to understand the text and to vote in terms of the *nota*. Why had the Pope imposed the *nota* on the Council as a pre-condition for voting? The answer probably was that the Pope wanted moral unanimity when the text was voted on and he knew that the minority conservatives would never agree unless something like the *nota praevia* were imposed. It was to protect their views and, probably more importantly, their feelings and pride.

Many bishops were furious over this action which was considered arbitrary and unnecessary. The *nota* probably did not alter the sense of the text very much, but the question remained: did the Pope have the right to make his consent to the schema dependent on an interpretation determined in advance? This was debated. A somewhat gloomy Council eventually adopted the constitution *Lumen gentium* on 21 November 1964. It has been viewed by most as a theological highlight of the Council, but the unresolved problems inherent in the text still trouble Catholics today. We will examine these problems in the next chapter.

The last session of the Council went from 14 September to 8 December 1965. It was the smoothest session – in terms of dealing with and passing schemata – but it was not without its fireworks. Prior to the opening of the session Pope Paul had announced that he would reform the Roman Curia and that canon law (Church law) would be revised (24 June 1965). The question of mixed marriages (marriages between Catholics and non-Catholics) and birth control continued to be discussed. In his opening speech the Pope announced that he would summon a Synod of Bishops at regular intervals through which the episcopate could work with him for the welfare of the Church. But the synod would only be an advisory body – not like an ecumenical council with its own decision-making power.

The Council was under pressure; this had to be its last session. The *Declaration on Religious Freedom* was the first item on the agenda. Despite clarifications from De Smedt that the *Declaration* did not equate truth and error, and that all persons had a moral obligation to seek the truth, 249 bishops still voted *non placet* (not pleasing) to the *Declaration* at the final vote. The emphasis of the *Declaration* was that no human power can command conscience. (The Church, however, places itself outside this category by relying on 'the spiritual authority established by Christ'). But the Church can no longer call on secular authority to buttress its spiritual authority, for modern society is recognised as essentially pluralist. The natural right of a person to freedom of conscience cannot be impeded by civil authority. This was a decisive turning away – at least in theory – from the previous Catholic position. Tragically, it does not seem to have changed the attitudes of some highly placed clerics and laypersons whose closeness to oppressive regimes, especially of the right, is notorious. For instance, a number of the Argentinian bishops were very close to the murderous military junta that ruled the country from 1976 to 1984. Regimes of the right deny human rights on the grounds that they are defending 'Christian civilisation' from 'atheistic communism'. They use this to justify abduction, torture and murder. Even in recent years, the Church has not always been quick to distance itself from such regimes, and some Church organisations, such as the integralist organisation Opus Dei, actively support right wing regimes. The Church, of course, has always been a stout defender of human rights under oppressive regimes of the left.

Following the *Declaration on Religious Liberty* several reworked schemas moved swiftly through the Council to a final vote: the *Decree on the Pastoral Office of Bishops* and the *Decree on the Renewal of Religious Life* passed the Council without a great deal of trouble. As we shall see, few people took postconciliar renewal more seriously than many religious orders of sisters. The schema on the *Formation of Priests* left the traditional seminary more or less intact, but insisted that biblical, liturgical and practical pastoral studies be given more emphasis. Local bishops conferences were given more control over the course of studies and the regimen of the seminary.

Simmering under the surface of this discussion was the question of obligatory celibacy for priests. Pope Paul became quite emotional over this issue, so any discussion of it was dismissed as 'inopportune'. The basic problem was a sharp division in the

Latin-American hierarchy. Clerical concubinage had always been (and continues to be) a serious problem in Latin countries. There were also widespread rumours that thousands of priests from all over the world wished to be released from the obligation of celibacy. The intended speech of Bishop Paul Koop (Lins, Brazil – he was a Dutchman belonging to a missionary order) on this topic was leaked to the press and published in *Le Monde* (12 October 1965). His proposal was quite modest: he was not suggesting the abolition of celibacy, but the ordination of married men to serve beside the celibate clergy in areas (like Brazil) where there was an acute shortage of priests. It is a view still held by many bishops today, especially those from Third World countries.

A *Declaration on Christian Education* was passed in mid-October. It is a weak document that has subsequently been largely ignored.

The revised *Declaration on Relations With Non-Christian Religions* (an expansion of the *Declaration on the Jews*) came before the Council again in mid-October. The issue was as divisive as ever. Bishops from Arab countries were still convinced that a declaration on the Jews would imply recognition of the State of Israel. Despite the fact that the *Declaration* was addressed to Buddhists, Hindus, Moslems and to other religions, it was the section on the Jews that received most attention. This section tried to: abolish the charge of 'deicide' against the Jewish people in the killing of Jesus; extinguish anti-semitism among Christians and stress the ties that Jews and Christians had in common. A new Secretariat for Relations with Non-Christian Religions had already been set up under Cardinal Marella (soon to be taken over by Cardinal Koenig of Vienna). The Council aimed to promote a 'wider ecumenism' – in other words to attempt dialogue with non-Christian religions.

But there still was a sizeable group of bishops – and they were not all Arabs – who were determined to oppose the section of the *Declaration* on the Jews. There was a real note of anti-semitism in this opposition. Bishop Carli's *Coetus Internationalis Patrum* (International Committee of Fathers) continued its opposition and a number of anti-semitic pamphlets were distributed among the bishops. Most were probably the product of cranks. A bomb threat on 14 October did not delay the voting. But 250 bishops opposed the document to the end. The *Declaration* described what it saw as the positive aspects of Hinduism, Buddhism and Islam. 'The Catholic Church rejects nothing that is true and holy in these religions . . . the reflection of the ray of that truth which enlightens all people.'

The rewritten constitution *On Divine Revelation* was still opposed by a minority. They were again mollified by the Pope who asked that the relationship of scripture and tradition be more clearly stated and that the doctrine of the divine inspiration of scripture be strengthened. But the text retained the idea that God speaks through human persons in a human way. On 10 November the decree *On the Apostolate of the Laity* was passed. A schema on indulgences was abandoned. The decrees *On the Missionary Activity of The Church* and *The Ministry and Life of Priests* were passed after further debate in mid-November. The decree on the priesthood is a poor document, but it does make the comment that celibacy is 'not demanded by the nature of the priesthood'. There are married priests in the Eastern Churches in union with Rome. There is also a small group of convert clergy from the Anglican and Protestant Churches in Australia and the United States who have remained married after their ordination as Catholic priests. The document does say that celibacy is 'appropriate' to the priesthood.

The last big problem for the Council to surmount was the schema on the *Church in the Modern World*. Despite enormous work on the document by ten sub-committees, there were still many problems to be resolved when it was presented to the Council on 21 September. Criticism came from the whole spectrum of bishops. Some said the schema was too general and unfocused – Bishop Elchinger (Strasbourg); it lacked clarity – Frings (Cologne); its evaluation of the world was 'too optimistic' – Bishop Höffner (Münster). Four-hundred-and-fifty bishops said that it was soft on atheism, especially atheistic communism. The document was originally written in French; it was then translated into Latin. The speed of its translation may have effected its clarity.

When the Council examined the schema in detail, a number of issues were highlighted. There was a long discussion of marriage and sexuality, but the question of birth control was skirted at the Pope's request. Only one speaker, Archbishop Zoghby (Melkite Vicar for Egypt), confronted the question of divorce; he said that he considered this a more serious problem for Catholics than birth control. Subsequent history has proved him right. Immediately before the discussion of the issues of war, peace and justice, Pope Paul VI made his famous trip to the United Nations (4 October). His presence was a signal to right-wing Catholics – who constantly sniped at the United Nations – that the organisation had his support. It was at the UN that he issued his passionate plea for peace: 'No more war; war never again! Peace, it is peace that must guide the destinies of peoples.'

The schema before the Council, however, was much more cautious. It permitted the use of force against an unjust aggressor. Presumably, it would allow nuclear force to be used. The bishops reacted strongly against this view. A number of bishops pointed out that it was a pretence to argue (as the US still does) that nuclear weapons were possessed merely as a deterrent to the other side. If you have them, you clearly intend to use them. As Abbot Butler (Downside) said: 'No one thinks that the great powers merely *possess* such arms . . . there is a system of preparation for the use of these arms – and for their illegitimate use in indiscriminate warfare.' The constant Catholic teaching has been that 'indiscriminate warfare' is intrinsically immoral. Butler argued that nations do not just 'possess' nuclear weapons. You possess them in order to threaten the other side with their use. But to threaten to do something intrinsically immoral is in itself an immoral action. This view was supported by Cardinals Alfrink, Liénart, Archbishop Martin (Rouen) and Bishop Rausch (Innsbruck). Everyone was surprised when Cardinal Ottaviani firmly supported the anti-war position. Many had forgotten that he had taught international law for many years. In his speech Ottaviani went much further and suggested the establishment of a world republic. A number of bishops stressed the right of conscientious objection. For instance, Bishop Gordon Wheeler (then Auxilary of Middlesborough) said that the conscientious objector was no 'milksop'. Such a person was ' . . . a witness of the Christian vocation to bring about peace.' Some Spanish and Italian bishops were opposed to conscientious objection. The final text was weakened in deference to the Latins and to some Americans – such as Cardinal Spellman (New York). These were the days of the escalation of the Vietnam war.

The world population problem was highlighted by Bishop Marling (Jefferson City). He examined the demographic explosion in the light of the inequalities between rich and poor nations. The theme of birth control and its relationship to population was discussed by Bishop Simons (Indore, India). He bluntly said that the Church's views were out of date. The traditional arguments against birth control were not convincing. In the light of the discussion the schema was sent back to the sub-commissions for further revision.

From mid-November onwards most of the political manoeuvring went on in the sub-commissions revising the text. Bishop Carli and his *Coetus Internationalis Patrum* worked hard to get the Council to condemn communism, even though both Popes John XXIII and Paul VI had made it clear that they opposed the Council engaging in outright condemnation of anyone. It is significant that Archbishop Marcel Lefebvre (formerly Archbishop of Dakar, Senegal; during the Council he was made a titular archbishop and Superior General of the Holy Ghost Fathers, a missionary order) was one of Carli's closest collaborators. Lefebvre, of course, is now the leader of the so-called 'traditionalist' schism. Lefebvre's schismatics accuse the Church of having surrendered to 'modernism', of celebrating 'invalid' eucharists and of generally abandoning the faith. A group of priests called the 'Society of St Pius X' have followed Lefebvre and there are tiny groups of lay people who have joined the schism in English-speaking countries. I will return to these 'ultra-traditionalists' in a later chapter.

The bishops who opposed any change on the birth control question were also busy manoeuvring to have every form of artificial contraception condemned. Among those most opposed to any change was the US moralist, Father John C. Ford. Ford will reappear when we consider the encyclical *Humanae vitae*. He was part of a group that tried to use the Pope's name to introduce their views into the schema. Their machinations were not successful and the contraception issue was shelved for a later decision.

The issue of war and peace emerged again just before the schema was finalised. Archbishop Hannan (New Orleans) considered that the comdemnation of nuclear weapons was insulting to the United States. He argued that nuclear weapons ' . . . had preserved freedom in a large part of the world. The defense of a large part of the world against aggression is not a crime, but a great service.' Hannan's views were circulated through a letter which was signed by ten bishops including Cardinal Spellman (New York) and Australia's Archbishop Guilford Young (Hobart). Many of the American bishops were embarrassed by the letter.

The schema on *The Church in the Modern World* was approved on 7 December 1965 with 2319 for, 75 against and 7 invalid votes. The same day the Pope and the Orthodox Patriarch Athenogoras 'consigned to oblivion' the mutual excommunications that had poisoned the relationship between Catholic and Orthodox since 1054. By 8 December 1965 the Council was over.

3

REFORMATION OR RENAISSANCE?

For many of the bishops who attended the Council it was a 'conversion'. But they returned to their dioceses to the practical problems of implementing radical and far-reaching change. Catholics look back on this period of implementation and recall experiences that were both painful and funny. Ordinary Catholics were confronted with change most dramatically in worship. Latin was rapidly phased out and the vernacular introduced. No one was asked how they felt about this, nor what was the best way to do it. It was simply decreed.

Ecumenism became one of a number of new clichés and Catholics had suddenly to recognise that people they had known for years as non-Catholics, might have more in common with them as Christians than had ever been realised. In fact for a short time among the liberal avant garde it was fashionable for some Catholics to insist that they were Christian rather than Catholic.

David Lodge's excellent novel *How Far Can You Go?* (1981) is one of the best introductions to the pain and exhilaration of Catholics in this period after the Council. The novel traces the inter-connecting life histories of a group of English Catholics from the mid-50s to the late 1970s. It vividly illustrates the close relationship between the contraception debate, which culminated in *Humanae vitae* (1968), and the renewal of the Church. As we review the results of Vatican II, I will refer to several incidents in the novel to illustrate the range of reactions to renewal.

The Second Vatican Council and the years following it changed the face of the Catholic Church. Radical change was needed. For much of the 19th and the first half of the 20th century, the Catholic Church had become a self-absorbed institution, defining itself over and against the world. There were, of course, exceptional people, like Dorothy Day or Joseph Cardijn or Pierre Teilhard de Chardin, who looked outward to the world and its needs. But mainstream Catholicism, as exemplified by its suspicion of 'modernism', had defined itself in terms of a narrow and static orthodoxy. Therefore the sudden changes to this mainstream naturally caused trauma.

The critics of the Council pointed to some of the consequences: the 'simple faithful' were perplexed by theological pluralism; many religious and priests left their vocation; the Church became 'democratised' and the power of the pope and bishops was weakened. The critics stressed the decline in Mass attendance, the 'new' sexual morality, confusion in catechetical teaching and the decline of 'traditional spirituality'. For 20 years after the Council, however, the liberals came into the ascendant in the Church, and it was they who pushed the Catholic community more or less successfully into the implementation of Vatican II.

Not that everything the progressives did was right. Some terrible mistakes were made, and I will touch on some of these. But much of the criticism of the Council is misdirected. The drop-off in Mass attendance in Western countries, for instance, is the result of a range of other issues, some sociological, some religious. In this chapter I will focus specifically on the results of the Council and on issues that arose from its documents. In a later chapter I will look at the other important questions the Church has faced since the early 1960s.

Many of the difficulties and contradictions confronting Catholics now result from compromises made at the Council and from deficiencies in the conciliar texts.

The first, and for institutional Catholicism the most important, result of the Council was a far-reaching shift in understanding the nature of the Church itself. This is marvellously illustrated in *How Far Can You Go?*. The situation concerns Father Austin Brierley, a sincere but somewhat naive curate and Father Mc-Gahern, the Irish parish priest. The parish was on the north side of London:

Aggiornamento came very slowly to Father Austin Brierley's parish at the end of the Northern Line, where the Parish Priest regarded Vatican II and the whole movement for Catholic Renewal as an irritating distraction from the serious business of raising money . . . Parochial life was one long round of bingo, raffles, whist-drives, dances, football pools, spot-the-ball competitions, sweepstakes, bazaars, jumble sales, outdoor collections, covenant schemes and planned givings. His addresses from the pulpit consisted of one part homily to three parts accountancy . . . The pastoral side of things he left pretty well to Austin Brierley, who could scarcely cope with all the work. (p 85)

In other words, Father McGahern's view of the Church was unequivocally institutional. The parishioners obviously shared their pastor's views: ' . . . the parishioners did not seem to object to this constant harping on the theme of money. The active ones worked in the fund-raising campaigns and . . . the apathetic majority paid up regularly and uncomplainingly.' So Father Brierley complained to the Chancery: 'I can't stand another week in that madhouse . . . counting house I should say.' The Monsignor from the Chancery offered him the opportunity to go on a renewal course and Father Brierley opted for an 'updating' in New Testament studies. He was astonished, shocked and fascinated by what he discovered:

Austin Brierley almost rubbed his eyes in disbelief sometimes. He read the professional theological journals with much the same feelings of shock and liberation as (others) read *Lady Chatterley's Lover* and the sexually explicit fiction that was published in its wake. Of course the theologians and exegetes were generally more discreet than novelists. They expressed themselves with elaborate caution in learned journals of tiny circulation, or exchanged ideas with like-minded scholars in private. It was understood that one did not flaunt the ideas before the laity, or for that matter before the ordinary clergy, most of whom were deplorably ill-educated and still virtually fundamentalists when it came to the interpretation of the New Testament. (p 89)

But Austin Brierley was not going to keep his scholarship to himself, so when he returned to parish life at the end of the Northern Line, he began to expound some of his new-found ideas from the pulpit. The result was predictable: 'After a few sermons . . . like this, the parishioners complained to Father McGahern, and Father McGahern to Archbishop's House, and Austin Brierley was seconded to another diocese in the Midlands that was allegedly short of priests' (p 90). Out in the real Church many sincere and well educated clergy ran into similar problems. Sometimes they were foolish and undiplomatic in their approach. A number, unfortunately, were pushed right out of the active ministry.

This same conflict was also vividly shown in a TV drama series produced and presented in Australia by the ABC. It was entitled *Menotti* after Father Jack Menotti, recently returned from a renewal course in the United States. He worked with – or more precisely for – and sometimes against – Monsignor Donnelly, a shrewd, tough pastor of the old school. The series showed that the essential conflict between the two men was their different understandings of the nature of the Church. Menotti saw it as an open ministerial community, Donnelly as a closed hierarchical structure. Flowing from this conflict was a more practical difference: their views of ministry were opposed. Menotti saw it as a missionary outreach beyond the Church. For Donnelly it was a matter of caring for those who lived within the structures of the Church. The series was remarkably true to life.

Both of these fictional situations illustrate one of the basic conflicts of the contemporary Church. Lurking just under the surface today are two mutually exclusive ideas of what the Church is and what it is all about. The origin of this disjunction is to be found in *Lumen gentium*, the dogmatic Constitution on the Church. Here two views of the Church are presented which are much more mutually exclusive than the Council realised. The Church is described in chapter three of *Lumen gentium* essentially as a hierarchy. In the first two chapters it is described essentially as a sacramental community.

To understand the hierarchical model let us go back briefly to the period of the Reformation. In the 16th century Roman Catholicism reacted against the Protestant reformers who argued that the Church was an inner, hidden reality, a Church of the predestined. In response to this the Council of Trent and the Catholic theologians of the baroque era emphasised that the Church was visible and hierarchical, a perfect and self-sufficient society. They presented it as a militant Church that was on the march against Protestantism. This pre-Vatican II image of the Church as a 'perfect society' is described with typical clarity by Australian theologian, Frank Sheed:

A society of men . . . has to have officials and they have to have authority. Christ has given his society officials with authority. It is through them that He gives the gifts of life and truth and preserves the unity of the society. As ultimate custodian of the sacraments which convey life, and the teachings which convey truth and the ultimate authority for the preservation of unity, Christ uses the Pope . . . The officials represent Christ. And in so far as they represent Christ, there is no defect in them. F. J. Sheed: *Theology and Sanity*, (p 219)

Flowing from this hierarchical and sacerdotal-papal conception of the Church is a specific conception of the ministry as the duty, preserve and privilege of the clergy, who in various grades share in the hierarchy of the Church. They are the pastors and they alone, through the power of orders and jurisdiction, exercise a ministry in the proper sense. This model reflects the absolutist and monarchical conceptions of society that were current. In civil society such views were destroyed by the French Revolution and the liberal movement in 19th century Europe. But the reactionary efforts of the 19th century Popes, especially Pius IX (1846-1878), preserved the 16th century model of Church government well into the 20th century. Many perceptive Catholics of the 19th century had challenged the Church's espousal of absolutism and foresaw the disastrous consequences of not listening to 'the signs of the times'. At Vatican Council I (1870) the

Church was defined in terms of papo-centrism: all authority in the Church was focused on the Pope through papal primacy and all teaching power (*magisterium*) was focused on him through the definition of papal infallability.

In contrast to this hierarchical view of the Church, chapters one and two of *Lumen gentium* develop images of the Church as a sacramental mystery and a community. The word *mysterium* comes from both the New Testament and the early theologians of the Church. It refers to the Church as a profound symbolic reality – like a great artistic masterpiece – that can be progressively explored but never exhausted. It always has something new to offer the person who perceptively participates in its reality. The Church is a sacrament in the sense that it is a sign: it shows that God is active in the world to save and fulfill those persons who hunger for justice, who work for integrity and who seek the meaning of human existence. Karl Rahner calls it the *ursakrament* – the primal or basic sacrament. As Pope Paul VI said: 'The Church is imbued with the hidden presence of God. It lies, therefore, within the very nature of the Church to be always open to new and greater exploration.'

The second chapter of *Lumen gentium* also concentrates on images of the Church taken from scripture. It is seen as a community, a people drawn together by the choice of God's Spirit. Each member of the people of God has specific gifts and these are meant to be used for both the sake of the Church and the world. The whole community is called to proclaim the good news of the person and message of Jesus Christ. No longer is the emphasis to be on hierarchy or sacerdotal or juridical power. Rather the Church community is to be a sign and the active ingredient of the continuing presence of Christ in history. In this conception the Church is not a 'perfect society' that has already arrived at a state of static perfection, but a people on the pilgrimage of life, often confused but always trusting in the power of the Spirit of God. It is a conception of the Church that begins not at the top with the hierarchy, but at the bottom with the people.

Thus chapter two of *Lumen gentium* presents a communal model of the Church, a model which does not sit easily or comfortably with the concept of the Church as a self-enclosed hierarchical institution. Yet chapter three presents the Church as an essentially hierarchical institution, and develops this model of Church almost as though the two previous chapters did not exist.

Most contemporary Catholics argue that the two views of the Church are complementary and that the hierarchy exercise a genuine leadership in a community Church. This might work if all popes, bishops and priests exercised a Christ-like type of leadership. The fact is that they do not. Catholics are discovering that the two models are not only not complementary, but that their side-by-side existence has created an enormous tension. Many Catholics (including some in the hierarchy) view the Church *fundamentally* as a community. Many others (including a lot of laity) view the Church *fundamentally* as a hierarchy. It cannot be *fundamentally* both. Father J. Rémy has said correctly that these two models are 'mutually exclusive' and 'mutually corrosive'.

Enormous tension has been generated in the Church by this ecclesiological conflict. One of the most blatant examples of this was the regime of the late Cardinal John Patrick Cody in Chicago. The whole story is told in Charles Dahm's book *Power and Authority in the Church: Cardinal Cody in Chicago* (1981).

Catholic Chicago had been ahead of its time under Cardinal Meyer, a leader of the progressive majority at Vatican II. For years priests and people had built a real commitment to social justice and to widespread Catholic action. Many lay people were involved. The elite of Catholic Chicago firmly supported Martin Luther King and the civil rights movement. Into this generous and lively Archdiocese (one of the largest in the world) strode Archbishop (soon to be Cardinal) John Patrick Cody. The story of the guerilla warfare that characterised his regime is detailed in Dahm's book. It lasted from 1965 to Cody's death in 1983.

Just one incident will have to serve to sum up Cody's hierarchical autocracy. Chicago pastors had developed a strong commitment to maintaining parochial schools in areas on the south side of the city that had become black ghettos. In 1974 Cody suddenly announced the closure of four lightly attended black south side schools – to the total surprise of the concerned pastors, parishioners and parents. The Priests Senate and the Archdiocescan School Board tried to conciliate. Cody emasculated the School Board, rescinded its right to review decisions and made himself its president. He told his critics bluntly: 'In the law of the Catholic Church there is only one authority – the bishop.' This parallelled a similar statement he had made earlier: 'In Chicago I am the Church.'

Chicago and Cody may seem remote to Australian situations, but the problem is that Catholics in many countries have experienced bishops whose behaviour resembles that of Cody. The problem is that Cody was right. His behaviour was simply a logical extension of the hierarchical conception of the Church. His destructive autocracy is only an extreme example of the behaviour possible for any episcopal despot.

Such behaviour is not isolated to bishops. Priests are also capable of it. Take the example of the parish that develops programmes that involve the people in decision making, in religious education and in the liturgy. The parish priest who encourages and supports this is replaced by the type of man who is threatened by lay participation or by one who has not emerged into the post-Vatican II Church. The laity are pulled back into line and often emerge bitter and disappointed. They had come to appreciate a participative Church and had come to a sense of ownership of their community.

Tragically one could go on and on with examples like this. Catholics tend to shrug their shoulders and say 'Well, that is the way priests and bishops act.' The problem is that many people have already integrated a participative and co-operative model of Church – as had many priests and people in Chicago – and when they encounter an ecclesiastical autocrat operating out of a hierarchical model in their own community, their pain and frustration is doubled. They have internalised one model of Church and see themselves as the 'people of God'; but out there, in ecclesiastical reality, they find an entirely different model in operation.

That is why Father Rémy refers to the present situation of Catholicism as 'corrosive'. Many Catholics experience a real tension from the dichotomy between their internalised conception of what the Church should be and what they experience at the level of the institution. Several inescapable conclusions seem for me to follow from this situation:

• *The two models are incompatible* – one or other has to be chosen to avoid the danger of two parallel organisations.

• Vatican II clearly opts for the communial model, thus breaking with the past and *bringing to an end an era in the Church*. But a small minority at the Council were never reconciled with the renewed ecclesiology.

• *Do not expect a rapid change* from one model to the other. The hierarchical model has been with us for many centuries and is not just going to go away.

• The change is so fundamental *that you must expect considerable resistance.* Old authorities will defend the power that they will lose and the change runs counter to the most sacred convictions of some people.

• Switching models will be even more difficult because many of *the people entrusted with the process of change are often the ones most opposed to it.* Thus there will be considerable pressure to block change and to return to former models – but always using the jargon of the Council.

• Finally, a community model of Church does not allow its supporters *to use constraints or threats* in order to remove obstacles and to ensure their success. This is not a problem in the hierarchical model.

Contemporary Catholicism thus faces an ecclesiological mutation that is generating tremendous tension in the Church.

Flowing directly from this is what can be called a *ministerial mutation.* In the Catholic Church two models of ministry are operative at the present. In the hierarchical understanding ministry is the preserve of the Pope and bishops who share it with the clergy (priests and deacons) through jurisdiction (this is the authority to celebrate the sacraments and to preach). Bishops, priests and deacons share in the priesthood of Christ through the sacrament of orders. In this conception the laity have no ministry of their own. They are simply there to share in and to buttress the ministry of the clergy.

Ministry in the participatory model of Church is quite different: the Church is a people drawn together by the choice of God's Spirit, each one organically united to the person of Jesus through the sacraments, each one given specific gifts to use for the sake of the Church and the world. In this model ministry flows directly from baptism. It does not come by delegation. The role of bishops and priests is to give unity and a sense of direction to the gifts of the community. Their task is to exercise leadership through facilitating the work of the community.

The US Jesuit, Father John Coleman, points to the significance of the change of words used by Catholics to describe what the Church does. Up until about 12 years ago Catholics always talked about apostolate (as in the statement 'The apostolate of the Church is to save souls'). Without anyone really noticing it, the word ministry replaced apostolate and there is an increasing emphasis on ministries (plural). Coleman says:

The appearance of a new language system is always significant. For language defines for us our world. New language focuses our attention in different places and frees our imagination to see reality in a new light. A shift in language usage raises fresh questions and new problems . . . The collapse of one language system and its replacement by another which does not justify current institutional arrangements is always a sign of crisis in ideological legitimacy. (John A. Coleman: 'The Future of Ministry' in *America* 144/12 (1981), p 244)

In other words there is real significance behind a language change. In this case it points to a shift of emphasis from ordained episcopal and priestly ministry as the norm, to a situation where lay ministry becomes the norm with ordained ministry as a development of it. Underlying this is a shift of emphasis from the sacrament of orders to the sacrament of baptism. Flowing from this shift of emphasis is a movement away from a focus on Church office (which results from ordination) to a focus on gift or charism (which results from baptism and the action of God's Spirit).

Certain conclusions can be drawn from this. The most

important is that all members of the Church are radically equal. 'For as many of you were baptised into Christ have put on Christ. There is neither Jew nor Greek, there is neither slave nor free, there is neither male nor female; for you are all one in Christ Jesus' (*Galatians 3:27-28*). St Paul is saying that all divisions based on race, economic or social status, or gender are broken down in Christ. All are equal. On the basis of this equality the Christian community has always recognised functional diversity – that is that different people have different gifts, and flowing from these gifts carry out different roles and functions in the Church. The Letter to the Ephesians says: 'And his gifts were that some should be apostles, some prophets, some pastors and teachers, to equip the saints for the work of ministry, for building up the body of Christ' (*Ephesians 4:11-12*). Thus it is on the basis of specific gifts that functional diversity emerges.

But the constant danger is that equality is swallowed up and functional diversity assumes the dominant role in Church life. This is exactly what happened in the 4th and 5th centuries when the ordained and professional clergy cornered more and more of the Church's ministry.

The division between cleric and layperson has no basis in the New Testament. It emerged in the late Roman period and it has led to the clergy subsuming the whole of ministry to themselves. Saint Augustine's warning to his clergy in Hippo was soon forgotten: 'Let not the priest in you swallow up the Christian'. From this clerical/lay division it is a short step to deny equality. This inequality was eventually enshrined in medieval canon law.

Unfortunately, the Church still suffers from an inbred clericalism whereby lay*men* who wish to exercise a liturgical ministry have to become clericalised as deacons or acolytes. Of course, this clericalisation totally excludes women.

I want to conclude this treatment of *Lumen gentium* by referring to an issue that will constantly recur in the rest of the book – the need to encapsulate in structures the insights of Vatican II. The Council, naturally enough, caught most Catholics unaware. They were simply not prepared for change and were unskilled in achieving it. Over the last twenty years those most

concerned with and committed to change were generally somewhat cerebral and politically naive. There were, of course,
exceptions to this, such as the women who led many of the United
States' religious orders of sisters. Most people interested in
renewal, however, seemed to think that it could be brought about
by talking. At times those interested in renewal made the mistake of assuming good will on the part of Church authorities and
forgot how much self-interest was (and is) invested in the old structures. It was simply assumed that if personal renewal occurred,
structural renewal would follow.

But human beings do not exist in a vacuum but within the context of structures, and if renewal is to be both deep and
far-reaching, it must have foundations in renewed structures.
Catholics have been unwilling to face this aspect of renewal; somehow it seems too 'Marxist'. Yet unless institutional structures are
renewed or removed, they will become a choking, dead weight
which will destroy all efforts at personal renewal.

This structural renewal will, in my opinion, prove a lot more
difficult than the renewal of persons. Structures tend to become
immovable and are tied to our very deep need for security. Therefore, renewal of the ministry will require not only a re-education
of personnel, but also a renewal of structures and strategies. This
needs to be carried out in the context of the concrete socio-
economic situation.

I will turn next to a consideration of what has happened to the
worship of the Catholic Church since Vatican II. Before I do, I
want to emphasise again that the ecclesiological mutation is basic
to the conflicts that still trouble the Church. It will appear again
and again under various guises as our treatment of contemporary
Catholicism proceeds.

Again, in *How Far Can You Go?* there is a marvellous description of the 'trendy' worship of the late 1960s and the early 1970s.
The particular performance that David Lodge describes was
celebrated on Sunday mornings at a university chapel. The priest
'tolerated a liturgy that would have lifted the back hairs on the
red necks of the local parish priests had they known what was

going on in their midst.' The students chose the readings from scripture and from here, there and everywhere. The music at Mass was similarly eclectic in style and accompanied by guitar and perhaps flute, violin, Indian bells, bongo drums . . . .' They sang folk hymns and pop classics. At the prayers of petition participants might end up praying for anything from the success of the Viet Cong to the rediscovery of someone's missing pet. 'At the offertory, the bread and wine were brought up to the altar by two students, usually a courting couple holding hands and exchanging fond looks, and it wasn't only married couples who warmly embraced at the kiss of peace.' There was public discussion and criticism of the sermon. Maximum participation was ensured because those there never knew what would happen next. This liturgical style contrasted vividly with the stodgy and unimaginative worship that was to be found in most parishes.

Lodge makes a telling comment about the 'trendy' liturgy: in order to participate you had to suspend your sense of irony (and, in some cases, your sense of taste). Personally I will never forget some of the tasteless folk hymns, one of which had the line 'Eat his body, drink his blood', sung to an appalling and childishly inappropriate tune. Some of the worst of these hymns have, thankfully, dropped out of current usage, although many of the current crop of popular hymns are not much better. This type of trendy liturgy is less common now. Its spontaneity can easily degenerate into sentimental kitsch.

At the other end of the spectrum was the Catholic conservative. *How Far Can You Go?* has a typical English conservative – a convert bachelor named Miles. Lodge describes his predicament:

Miles certainly felt spiritually orphaned by the times. The Catholic Church he had joined was fast disappearing, and he did not like the new one he saw appearing in its place, with its concert-party liturgy, its undiscriminating radicalism, its rather smug air of uxorious sexual liberation. (p 137)

Miles attempted to diagnose the problem:

The trouble with Catholics is . . . that they have absolutely no taste, no aesthetic sense whatsoever, so that as soon as they begin to meddle with the . . . worship that they inherited from the Counter-Reformation, as soon as they try and go 'modern', God help us, they make the most terrible dog's breakfast of it, a hideous jumble of the old and the new, incompatible styles and idioms, that postively sets one's teeth on edge. (p 83)

In between the trendy liturgy and Miles are the vast majority of Catholics and their varying experiences of liturgical reform. The liturgy schema was well prepared before the Council. It was one area where the progressives were well ahead of the reactionaries and the Roman Curia. The *Constitution on the Liturgy* was only a first stage in liturgical renewal. Beyond it was the adaptation of all of the worship of the Church and much of this was carried out by a post-conciliar Commission.

One of the key people in this post-conciliar Commission was its secretary, Archbishop Annibale Bugnini. It was he who supervised and co-ordinated the revision of the entire liturgy of the Catholic Church. On a number of occasions he was viciously attacked by the right-wing press, especially in Italy, as a barbaric philistine who wrecked the artistic work of centuries by his 'mindless reform'. But as Peter Hebblethwaite points out, the post-conciliar Commission was

aiming at something wholly new in the Roman Catholic Church: a liturgy that would be valid for the *present* though in obvious continuity with the past; a liturgy for the *people*, not an elitist consolation for aesthetes. And since the way Christians worship reflects the way they think about the Church, the conflict was partly one between an 'elitist' and a 'populist' understanding of the Christian community. (Peter Hebblethwaite: *The Runaway Church*, p 32)

Archbishop Bugnini received little reward for his work. He was appointed Apostolic Delegate to Turkey and Iran and he had the unenviable task of acting as the representative of Pope John Paul II in Iran during the American hostage crisis. He died in 1985.

There can be no doubt that the reform was needed. The essential nature of Christian worship had become obscured and lost under the historical accretions of the medieval, post-reformation, baroque and romantic periods. At the core of the renewed liturgy is an emphasis on the celebration of the Easter mystery – the death, resurrection and second coming of Christ. In the old liturgy the emphasis was on the priest as celebrant. In the renewed liturgy the community is the primal focus of the celebration. The celebrant acts primarily as the leader of the community.

There has been a restoration of the importance of the reading of scripture. The Word of God is there to nourish the faith of the participants. The *Constitution on the Liturgy* certainly reflects the conflicting opinions of the bishops at the Council. But the post-conciliar reform was less ambivalent and left little room for conservative manouvering. Extreme conservatives, like rebel Archbishop Marcel Lefebvre, were unable to get around it, so they were forced to reject it out of hand and were cornered into retaining the so-called Tridentine liturgy.

People now have a chance to follow the Word of God and all the prayers in their own language. Certainly, some still express a nostalgia for the Latin, but I suspect that this betrays a deeper dislocation than the question of language. There is a much greater sense of participation and Catholics can begin to feel that they are part of the people of God and that they share in the priesthood of all believers. The simplified liturgy is much more expressive of the core of Christian faith. As the role of the rest of the community is stressed there is a healthy dimunition of a clerico-centric conception of worship. Catholics have come to realise that worship is not unchangeably sacrosanct. This realisation is, of course, double edged. There is a real security in permanent and predictable liturgical forms. An unchanging worship symbolised an unchanging God and the stability and universality of the Church. A changing liturgy is the symbol of a changing Church.

This brings us to some of the problems that have emerged over the last 20 years. Miles in *How Far Can You Go?* puts his finger indirectly on the most basic difficulty: he speaks of the banal tastelessness of much worship. It lacks power as symbol; it does not point beyond itself or conjure up in participants a deeper sense of the transcendant. The very fact that people could not understand the Latin accidentally created for them a sense of the numinous nature of liturgical action. The change to the vernacular and the adaptation of liturgical forms has had one serious but unarticulated result: the dislocation brought about in the spiritual lives of many Catholics. Miles again is typical: he feels a real spiritual orphan in the contemporary Church. In the past many Catholics unconsciously linked their spiritual identity to the old liturgy. It gave expression to their spiritual essence. At Mass and the sacraments they experienced the numinous – the deep mysterious presence of God. For some it was akin to an artistic experience.

While it is true that the liturgy is primarily for the congregation, it is also an act of worship of God and therefore must be expressive of the sheer mystery of God's presence. It is still an encounter with God through sacramental symbols. Many Catholics experience a subconscious but palpable loss of the sense of God's presence. It is a reinforcement for them of the feeling that God is absent from the world. Such people are often written off by liberals as too conservative. In my view their disquiet should be taken more seriously for it points to a basic lack in much contemporary worship.

The liturgy is both a traditional and prophetic action. For most people the traditional element is the one they experience. For most Catholics worship is expressive of the search for the constant and unchanging elements in human existence, symbolised by an unchanging God:

My God is a fortress and a rock,
In Him I am safe.

Because their search is for permanency, most worshippers prefer liturgical and spiritual forms whose age and rootedness in the past convey security. It is significant that Catholicism has hardly ever departed from the classical liturgical forms developed in the late Roman world. Most Catholics are still medieval in their spirituality for this style symbolises for them a sense of rootedness and permanency. It should not be forgotten that most liturgy still occurs in buildings designed precisely for a medieval/baroque form of celebration. In most congregations the 17th century baroque concept that liturgy is a performance still holds sway. At a performance the people are passive spectators. Even avant-garde liturgies and some of the better folk Masses are still performances by individual clerics and musical professionals who have developed a following. Thus for many Catholics worship is still a very traditional activity.

Only a handful of Catholics have begun to enter into the other side of the liturgical coin: the prophetic nature of worship. The liturgy is not just seeking the security of an unchanging God. It should also be a confrontation with a dynamic challenging God who demands that those who enter the divine presence be changed themselves and be agents of change for others. In this sense the liturgy is not meant to soothe but to upset; it is not meant to confirm the present but to call to the future. If it is to do this it will have to be celebrated by a community of persons who are willing to challenge each other and on the basis of that to go out to confront the world. This style of liturgy demands a much more fluid structure – although to maintain a sense of shape and discipline it also needs a basic form which is usually followed. Catholics are only beginning to explore this aspect of liturgy and it will take considerable time to develop ways of worship that are expressive of this prophetic element.

Tragically in many places the liturgy is just plain bad. The first and most obvious problem is that priests are poor celebrants. Part of this is lack of training, but there are deeper issues involved. Priests trained before the Council were never prepared for the liturgical revolution which they have had to face. In their training the stress was on the immutability of liturgical forms. The Mass was 'their' prayer on behalf of the community. The priest was the one who went up on behalf of the congregation to approach God. The celebrant's back was turned to the people and his concentration was focused on the sacramental action itself. Except for the sermon and for the occasional greeting to the people (when he turned and said *Dominus vobiscum*), the priest acted almost as though the congregation were not there. An insistence on the observance of the minutiae of rubrics sometimes trapped individual priests into scrupulosity. Moral textbooks listed all the venial and mortal sins that could be committed by the careless priest in the celebration of Mass! Suddenly, after the Council, priests had to learn a whole new way of doing things. They now faced the people and scrupulous observance of rubrics was not so important. Overnight they were expected to become facilitators and leaders of public prayer. Awkward and sometimes ungainly males were told that their ritual gestures were as important as their ritual words. There was a terrible period just after the Council (from about 1966 to 1975) when there were no missals containing all the prayers and readings. Priests and congregations had to juggle three and sometimes four separate books as they struggled to find the appropriate place.

But many priests trained during and after the Council have also failed, but in another way. The celebrant can now dominate the liturgy by focusing everything on himself. Because the form is more fluid there is also the danger of the constant interjection of comments, little sermons and ad lib prayers, so that the community is drowned in words, words, words. There are some celebrants who give a brief homily (sometimes of two to three minutes) at the start of Mass, an introduction to each of the readings, a homily (15 minutes – sometimes longer), and then interrupt various parts of the rest of the Mass with further ad lib comments.

A further problem has emerged in the ignorance and lack of training of the laity. I have already noted that many people come to the liturgy with a very traditional attitude: they expect to be 'entertained' and instructed. Many priests experience the sheer frustration of the dead weight of a non-participative congregation. The lack of participation and apparent apathy of many flows from the fact that they do not really understand their active role as part of the congregation. They come from a world of spectators where passive TV viewing is the universal pastime.

Many laity, of course, want to participate. In some parishes they are encouraged to do so. But there needs to be a careful discernment of gifts. It is a question of who can do what competently. There is nothing worse than a lector who cannot read, a preacher who cannot preach, a cantor who cannot sing.

Of course, one whole group of people are almost totally

excluded – women! Catholicism still excludes women from virtually all active participation in the liturgy. They are only permitted to act as lectors and 'extraordinary ministers' of the eucharist. The exclusion of women from so many ministerial roles is one of the great scandals of contemporary Catholicism. The liturgy remains a male and clerical stronghold, where even little girls are officially excluded from the relatively minor role of serving at Mass.

Thirdly, there is the suspicion, especially in Rome, of allowing the liturgy to develop along local lines. To give an example: a large number of Australian Aborigines are Catholics. They are much less verbal people than whites. They communicate through dance and symbol. But there is no Aboriginal liturgy. They (like white Australians) are drowned in words: at Sunday Mass there is an Old Testament reading, a psalm, a New Testament reading, the gospel, a sermon, the creed, petitions, eucharistic prayer – all are spoken with a minimum of symbol. At the same time the congregation is cooped up in a pew. Liturgical dance is still an odd business engaged in largely by pubescent girls. In Latin America where Catholics form a large part of the population, and in Africa where Catholics are a sizeable minority, as well as in the Pacific and in countries like Papua New Guinea, the Church will eventually have to allow the emergence of liturgical forms expressive of each cultural framework.

In western countries like Australia, on-going liturgical change will involve a return to a more simple celebration with a community where people are at least known to each other and are involved in some form of personal interaction. Catholics are coming to realise that worship is the action of a group of people who are rooted in human reality, but who open themselves to levels of existence beyond the merely tangible. It is a symbolic sacramental action that both gives them a foundation in the past and points them prophetically to the future. The forms that this type of celebration will involve are just beginning to emerge. Thus Catholics find themselves in another mutation as they struggle with the future of worship.

I will now turn to the question of leadership in the Church and more specifically to episcopal leadership. There is a sense that bishops emerged from Vatican II with their position more enhanced than any other group in the Church. *Lumen gentium* teaches that they are the successors of the apostles and that episcopal ordination is the apex of the sacred ministry and the fullness of sacramental orders. The doctrine of collegiality insists that bishops are specifically called to assume responsibility not only for their own dioceses but for the wider local Church. They do this through national conferences of bishops. Collegiality also means that they are called to assume a degree of responsibility for the universal Church.

Countries like Australia, England, the United States and Canada have, generally speaking, much more practical pastoral bishops than those of 20 or 30 years ago. In some countries – such as Brazil, Bolivia and the Philippines – bishops have assumed the role of leading the people against oppressive dictatorial and military regimes. In the United States, particularly, there are large numbers of excellent pastoral bishops.

Technically, all bishops are appointed by the Pope. Since he cannot possibly know the details of every diocese, he chooses from a list of three names submitted to him by the Roman Curia. But how are the three names arrived at in the first place? Here things get complex.

Let us say that the bishop in diocese A is getting old and needs an auxiliary or assistant bishop. The Papal Nuncio (nuncios act as papal ambassadors in countries with formal diplomatic relationships with the Vatican) consults various carefully chosen people (in secret) asking them to submit the names of priests they think suitable for the episcopate, or asks them to comment on lists of names already submitted. Needless to say the other bishops of the country or region are the most important of those consulted. Various names are canvassed. Rome wants to make sure that there are no financial or personal scandals concerning the person under discussion. Their 'orthodoxy' is also checked. Under John Paul II this orthodoxy question has become increasingly important. There is evidence that in the United States, and probably

Australia, candidates are checked to see if they hold the papal line on sexual ethics, the ordination of women, the *magisterium* (the Pope's teaching power) and social justice.

The danger with this secret process is that natural leaders can be eliminated on the say-so of some unknown person who might well have a grudge or unfounded suspicion against the candidate under consideration. The process generally brings to the surface the most cautious people, those unlikely to rock the boat. From these consultations the Nuncio draws up a list of three names (called a *terna*) which is then sent to Rome. It is from this list that Rome chooses the new bishop. Much obviously depends on the papal representative, most of whom are conservative career diplomats.

Generally, bishops have failed to take the initiative in assuming responsibility for the local Church. Bishops conferences still look to Rome for far too many permissions and allow the Vatican a strangle-hold over decisions that should be taken at the local level. This situation is often made worse by the fact that conservative pressure groups often go over the head of the local bishops and appeal directly to Rome. The Vatican has been only too happy to listen to them.

In Australia this interference still remains at a less public level. There is, for instance, some evidence that pressure has been put on Australian bishops by the Vatican to refuse employment to priests who have left the active ministry. How much notice is taken of this varies from diocese to diocese, but where discrimination does occur there is usually very little that the individual former priest can do. Civil authorities, such as equal opportunity boards and ombudsmen, are usually loathe to take on the Church. Another aspect of papal interference is manifested in papal visits. The Vatican attempts to vet all speeches in advance and the Pope comes to lecture the local bishops and Church.

At the international level Paul VI tried to make collegiality real by the institution of the Synod of Bishops. The Synod was to be a representative group of bishops from all over the world who would meet every three years to discuss a topic of importance to the life of the universal Church. It was hoped that the pooled experience of the bishops would assist the Pope in the evolution of the Church's attitude toward difficult and contraverted questions. The meeting in 1969 was by far the best. That Synod focused on the issues of justice in the world and the ministerial priesthood. The document on justice is one of the best issued by the Church since the Council. Since 1969 the Synod has become an increasingly ineffective body. Since the mid-1970s the Synod has left it to the Pope to issue a document summarising conclusions and recommendations. These have increasingly represented what the Pope wanted the Synod to say rather than what was actually said at the meeting.

Part of the problem lies in the constitution of the Synod and the papal restrictions that limit its range of discussion. It was a creature of Paul VI and it has been kept in dependence on the Pope. It would have been much freer if it had been set up by the Council itself. It only meets intermittently and lacks a coherence and spirit of its own. It tends to avoid those issues that the Pope wants kept out of discussion. French theologian, Father René Laurentin, speaks of 'the unbelievable accumulation of restrictions' placed on the Synod. The cause for these lies in:

. . . the ancient fear . . . (of) any organs of a democratic type which might limit papal power . . . These restrictions may also be traced to the personal temperament of Paul VI, given to disquiet as he was with all that might interfere with papal power and papal psychology . . . he barricaded his power. He would not accept dialogue with others of divergent views unless he were at first assured of their agreement on whatever fundamentals were at stake in the meeting. (R. Laurentin: 'Synod and Curia' in P. Huizing and K. Walf: *The Roman Curia and the Communion of Churches*, 1979, p 96)

Despite his protestations of support for collegiality, John Paul II also wants a tame Synod. It has become a rubber-stamp body, unwilling to express views contrary to those prevailing in Rome. This was clearly demonstrated in the Synod on the family, where the actual deliberations were by-passed in the subsequent Synodal document which was written by John Paul himself.

A surprise was sprung on the Church by Pope John Paul II in

January 1986. He called an Extraordinary Synod to ' . . . discuss the worldwide application of the Council and to deepen that application in the light of new needs.' The proposed Synod was seen by many liberals as another scheme of the Vatican to try to turn the clock backwards and to undo the effects of the Council. This suspicion was deepened by the publication of the *Ratzinger Report*, the pessimistic ruminations of Cardinal Josef Ratzinger. Suspicion of skullduggery was deepened again when it was discovered that there was a plan afoot to 'reform' the Curia, involving the abolition of the conciliar and post-conciliar bodies. The Secretariat for Christian Unity, for instance, was to become a study commission in the Congregation of the Doctrine of the Faith. However, the worst expectations of the liberals were not realised. The Cardinals rejected the plan proposed for the reform of the Curia and the Synod was able to modulate the pathological pessimism of Ratzinger into a more optimistic key. The bishops felt that the Church was not headed for disaster. Nevertheless, the best that can be said about the Extraordinary Synod is that it faithfully reflected the real Church – it ended in stalemate. In 1988 the topic for the Synod is the laity.

I mentioned that some bishops conferences have begun to take collegiality seriously. The United States' episcopal conference is one. In 1983, despite strong pressure from the Reagan administration, Catholic right-wingers and the Vatican, the American bishops issued a powerful pastoral letter on war and peace. I will examine the letter in detail in a later chapter.

What then is Christian leadership? I must admit that I am always apprehensive when the gospel of the good shepherd is read (*John 10:1-15*). For in Australia we know that sheep are stupid animals moving in large flocks herded by sheep dogs that snap at the heels of any that dares to go off in an independent direction. Many Australian parish priests in the past behaved like sheep dogs, snapping at the strays! Now the approach is likely to be a little more subtle, but some priests still think that they can assume the role of 'director' of the moral and Christian development of their fellow Catholics and there are still very few priests who have integrated a genuinely Christian approach to leadership.

True Christian leadership is that discussed and lived out by Christ in the gospels. Saint Peter advises his fellow presbyters: 'Never be a dictator over any group that is put in your charge, but be an example' (*I Peter 5:3*). Thus the leader of the Catholic community (whether he be Pope, bishop or priest) is faced with the self-effacing task of helping others to discern their gifts, creating an ambience for their use, supporting them in their ministries and drawing the whole together to give a sense of unity and direction to the work of the Church. This is no small task. Increasingly Church leadership will need training in process and facilitation. Persons who are uncertain about their own identity, or who have low levels of tolerance of frustration, or who tend to dominate others, or who are psycho-sexually immature are unsuited to any leadership role.

It is easy to talk about Christian leadership, but as I myself found during a brief stint as a pastor in a large urban parish, the institution has a way of possessing you. Christian leadership so often becomes bogged down with details concerning the maintenance of the institutional structures of the Church and bishops and pastors are more often the slaves of the Church than its dictators. Many of them have good will toward the implementation of participatory structures but they become so immersed in ad hoc details and crises, in day to day administration, that they lose both the focus and the energy required for a more truly Christian form of leadership.

If love, the service of others, joy, peace, a critical openness to reality, strength and courage are integral to faith, then the Christian leader must symbolically incorporate something of each of these virtues. Consensus involves the discernment of God's will for the community. The Church is not a democracy, nor is it a dictatorship. The basic task of the community is to decide the way in which God is leading. Votes will be taken, but the real task is to obtain as inclusive a decision as possible. Discernment, however, does not mean accommodating the lowest common denominator. At times leadership will be forced to take hard decisions in the face of a majority whose views represent mediocrity. The leader in this case acts as prophet.

It is within the context of this idea of leadership that we can begin to examine the role of priests in the contemporary Church. Priests were badly neglected at Vatican II. The document on the *Ministry and Life of Priests* is a poor one. The emergence of the laity has meant that many aspects of ministry that were previously exclusive to priests have been taken over by unordained persons. I refer here to ministries such as taking communion to the sick, counselling couples preparing for marriage or parents preparing for their child's baptism, as well as routine administrative tasks. Are priests, then, merely appendages of the bishop? What is their unique role in the Church? Many are quite demoralised. I remember an older priest complaining 'I would never have become a priest if I thought that these jobs could be done by laypeople.'

While the number of laity has increased, the number of priests has decreased. Thus priests are faced not only with ever-increasing workloads (especially the generous and talented ones), but they are also faced with the struggle to redefine their identity which seems to be challenged from all sides. They are often unconsciously on the defensive because they feel that they are blamed for every problem in the Church. They are of course to blame for some of the problems, but more often the blame accrues to them because they are the accessible ecclesiastical figures. They are easy to get at! Pope and bishops are walled in behind a phalanx of bureaucrats and secretaries. But the parish priest often answers his own phone or door. You have got him! Most priests are ill-prepared for a community model of Church, for their seminary training created an institutional mentality.

What is the 'typical' priest like? Obviously there is a danger in generalisation, for priests differ from each other as much as any ordinary group of mortals. The hard evidence we do have comes from the US bishops' study *The Catholic Priest in the United States. Psychological Investigations*. While this material comes from the late 1960s my impression is that it still reflects the 'typical' priest:

These studies have shown the priest to be an ordinary man, much like his fellow citizens in the scale of psychological growth, and therefore fitting into the largest category of adult American males of comparable background, that of emotionally underdeveloped adults. This does not mean that he is a disturbed person, but that his growth index follows the majority of his secular counterparts and that he suffers arrested development on some points. Ernest E. Larkin and Gerald T. Broccolo: *Spiritual Renewal of the American Priesthood*, 1973, p 1)

Thus the problem lies for most priests in emotional and interpersonal underdevelopment. Ronald Conway has consistently claimed that underdevelopment is a basic characteristic of Australian males. So priests are not all that different. Australian priests tend to undersell themselves. Beyond superficial convention there is considerable tolerance among them. They are wary of speaking about their own (often very real) spirituality, which inhibits them in helping the laity in their struggle to articulate their spirituality. Many priests are hard-working and caring. Deep down, however, one senses a profound existential loneliness.

Here, of course, one must face the problem of celibacy. I say 'problem' purposely for it is a major difficulty for the Catholic clergy. This is not to claim that emotional under-development would be immediately solved by marriage, or that celibacy cannot lead to a full life. The problem with celibacy is the link between it and the priesthood. It is incorrect to state, as does John Paul II in his *Letter to Priests* (Holy Thursday 1979), that celibacy is an essential feature of the priesthood. His own predecessor Saint Peter was married, as were a number of other early Popes and the Western clergy for almost 1000 years! Priests of the Eastern rite, both Catholic and Orthodox, are still married. Pope Paul VI permitted the priestly ordination of several convert clergymen in Australia and John Paul himself has also allowed the ordination of married convert clergy in the United States. To make the priestly promise of celibacy the equivalent of the marriage vow – as John Paul does in his *Letter* – is to push theology to the point of absurdity. Marriage is a free sacramental commitment, rooted in the nature of the human person. Celibacy is a gift given, Saint Paul says, to few, yet is now a legal requirement for ordination.

The law of celibacy for priests has been imposed for a thousand years in the Western Church, and it has not worked well.

In Latin countries and increasingly in Africa and the Pacific, celibacy is not observed by many priests. This is increasingly the case in other countries. Recently the novel and TV special *The Thorn Birds* superficially but nevertheless publicly aired this problem. However unreal Archbishop Ralph de Bricassart's assignation with Meggie Cleary on a tropical island in Australia's Barrier Reef might be, the story highlighted an unspoken problem in the Church. The novel also showed up the real dishonesty in the Church's attitude to this issue. And it also should be noted that the relationship with Meggie was the one humanising reality in the life of this ruthlessly ambitious cleric. Theologically it was the 'happy fault' that saved De Bricassart from his own deadly ambition.

Much more important than the problem of celibacy is the critical shortage of priests. Numerous Catholics are deprived of the eucharist without which there cannot be an authentic Church community. Large numbers of bishops from all over the world have petitioned Rome to allow married men to serve beside the celibate clergy. Often in Third World countries the bulk of the ministry is carried on by married catechists who are the natural leaders of their communities. These established family men teach, preach, conduct funerals, marriages, baptisms and form the heart of the local community, but they cannot celebrate the eucharist. They form the nucleus of the community, while the indigenous clergy, often inexperienced younger men, trained in a Western-style seminary and in a lifestyle and theology that alienates them from the local people, find it difficult to adjust to the lifestyle of the local parish.

Papua-New Guinea is an example of this. Here the seminaries and theological colleges were the first to offer a top class education to talented young local men. But the Western bias of this education often drove a wedge between the expectations of the young clergy who received the education, and their own people and culture. A number became unsatisfied with ministry in the local area and either left the priesthood for the more financially rewarding profession of politics or public service, or have become very disgruntled in ministry.

The law of celibacy will not be altered from the top but from the bottom. One or more local bishops, driven by the shortage of clergy and the absence of the eucharist, will simply begin ordaining married men. One would hope that these were experienced catechists who had not been ruined by a seminary education!

Underlying Rome's insistence on celibacy is the question of power. The celibate man is the Church's man with no other focus to his life except the Church. The Church tries to make itself his entire world. He has no other emotional or human home. In most countries he is dependent on the Church for his economic security and even for his residence. The priest has no offspring or progeny, thus there is a need to build an 'immortality project' in and through the Church. Economically, psychologically and spiritually he is the Church's man, tied to it through a network of dependency. For many priests celibacy has meant existential impotence. They work in and for a hierarchical Church which is utterly impervious to all their attempts to change it.

In the old seminary system women were usually presented to students as innocent, slightly neurotic and basically manipulative; they 'wanted' the priest in an ill-defined but sexually threatening way. This 'desire for the priest', of course, was a male sexual projection. I was trained in a relatively enlightened seminary where women were actually discussed. In some seminaries they did not rate a mention for they were unconsciously linked to sexuality and uncleanness. There is a great scene in Thomas Keneally's novel *Three Cheers for the Paraclete.* Father Maitland, the hero, has invited his young cousin and his wife to stay the night in his room at the local seminary. Monsignor Nolan, the Rector, is most upset when he discovers this. He tells Maitland:

You know James, I don't even let my sisters stay in this house, though they're both widows. I have them stay up the hill at the convent . . . Can you understand you have introduced something new into this place? . . . But worse than new. Alien . . . This has been a celibate house since its foundations were laid. That is a matter of eighty years . . . I think that given the fact that they travelled throughout last night, and given their youth and various other condign circumstances, then we must make certain assumptions, James . . You will see to it that your sheets are changed tomorrow, won't you, James?

For Nolan sexuality is linked to femininity and therefore must be expunged from the seminary.

But clerical celibacy is as important for some lay Catholics as it is for the hierarchy. This is shown by conservative Catholics who get angry with priests and sisters who 'do not wear their garb' or who do not fulfill the expectations projected onto them. Unconsciously, some people in the Church have a deep-felt need for a person who incarnates the sacred as separate, a person who symbolises sacrality as a mysterious yet potent force. This is what Durkheim refers to as the need for a sharman. Priests have fulfilled this role for Catholics whose spirituality is dualistic and who conceive of the sacred as something totally separate and divorced from experienced reality. By refusing to play out the sacred role, many contemporary priests and religious sisters have angered conservative Catholics who feel the need for symbols of the other world. This, of course, is changing with a growing majority of Catholics and priests and sisters beginning to be recognised as human beings.

Linked to the question of the role of the priest is that of the full admission of women to the ministry of the Church. The question of women and ministry was vividly illustrated in the famous encounter between Sister of Mercy Theresa Kane, President of the Leadership Conference of Women Religious, and Pope John Paul II at the national shrine of the Immaculate Conception in Washington D.C. (October 1978). Sister Kane spoke of 'the excruciating suffering of countless women, particularly sisters and nuns, who felt the Church treated them as second-class citizens in the Kingdom of God.' She insisted that women be granted entry to all the ministries of the Church. John Paul also could not help seeing the sisters who stood throughout the ceremony in the shrine as a protest against his attitude toward women. His answer was that Mary, the Mother of Jesus, was not among the apostles at the last supper (the first eucharist) and that she played no part in the hierarchy of the early Church. It was the encounter of two mutually exclusive views of the Church and ministry: for Sister

Theresa Kane ministry was the right of every member of the people of God – and half of them were women. For the Pope, ministry was a possession of the hierarchy to be exercised only by those to whom this privilege was granted – and this does not include women.

In the past the Church simply excluded women. The 1917 *Code of Canon Law* equated women with minors and systematically excluded them from holding any office in the Church. Some slight improvements have occurred: the *Constitution on the Church in the Modern World* noted with approval women's efforts to attain equality with men. John XXIII in *Pacem in terris* saw the liberation of women as one of the signs of God's saving presence. Even the Vatican's *Declaration on the Admission of Women to the Ministerial Priesthood* (15 October 1976) gives cautious approval to the entry of women into the ministry. But on the question of the ordination of women to the priesthood, the *Declaration* is negative.

The Sacred Congregation for the Doctrine of the Faith judges it necessary to recall that the Church, in fidelity to the example of the Lord, does not consider herself authorised to admit women to priestly ordination . . . It is a position which will perhaps cause pain but whose positive value will become apparent in the long run since it can be of help in deepening understanding of the respective roles of men and women.

Abstracting from the Freudian slip of using the feminine pronoun to describe a Church which excludes women from ordination, several other things can be noted about the *Declaration*. First, it is not a personal statement of the Pope but of a Roman Congregation. As such, it has no doctrinal binding force. Secondly, Rome is wedded to the idea of roles for men and women. While being prepared to admit that women have, in fact, emerged into many new roles, the Vatican still sees women as homemakers.

Thirdly, the *Declaration* cites the Church's constant exclusion of women from priestly ministry. This is not entirely accurate. Women did have important liturgical roles in the early Church – and the priesthood as we know it today did not emerge as a separate ministry in the Church until the fourth century. The

Declaration admits the mysogony of the early theologians of the Church (which it describes as 'prejudices unfavourable to women' – an understatement!) but then adds the curious conclusion: 'It should be noted that these prejudices had hardly any influence on (the early theologian's) pastoral activity, still less on their spiritual direction.' Apparently the clergymen of the Congregation of the Doctrine of the Faith are unacquainted with the writings and activities of Tertullian and Saint Jerome!

The *Declaration* has been roundly criticised by many scholars; it is a most unsatisfactory document. It never once attempts to face the basic ministerial question: does the Church need women in its ministry? It talks much of male priests as 'signs of Christ' but never confronts the fact that many of these same clerics are very ineffective signs of the caring and humane ministry of Jesus. It is ironic that while saying that only a male priest can 'image' a male Jesus, Pope John Paul II in his Holy Thursday *Letter to Priests* says that in celibacy the priest 'seeks another fatherhood and even another motherhood'. The *Declaration* had argued strongly that because of 'symbols imprinted on human psychology' women could not image a male Jesus. Paradoxically, male priests can apparently transcend the imprinted 'symbols' to image motherhood!

Although it has never been admitted, the basis of discrimination against women playing any part in the Church's liturgical ministry lies largely in the concept of ritual purity. Cultic purity is basic to the development of clerical celibacy. While I have no doubt that the Church must eventually admit women to all levels of the ministry, I think that the psychological and sociological difficulties will be considerable. Further it would be a mistake for women to enter the clerical priesthood as it now stands. What women need to do is to create a liturgical leadership style that is uniquely theirs, not simply to ape a male model. This may be a most important contribution to the renewal of the Church – to image a new and more truly Christ-like model of leadership.

No group in the Church took the Council more seriously than women's religious orders. The Council document on religious life (*Perfectae caritatis*) was uninspiring. But religious women, with typical generosity, immediately tried to apply the Council's teaching to themselves. In the first half of the 20th century their lifestyle had become static and legalistic, their spirituality individualistic and self-engrossed. But because their structures were authoritarian they were able to achieve an enormous amount in terms of maintaining the institutional ministry of the Church. For instance, in countries like Australia and the United States, they carried the heavy burden of the Catholic education and hospital systems right up until after the Council. Their contributions to education and health service only began to break down in the 1960s. Prior to the Council women religious especially had stressed higher education. So when Vatican II came there were enough educated women in many of the orders to realise the Council's significance and to assume leadership.

The early days of renewal were tough for both young and old in religious orders and some terrible mistakes were made. *How Far Can You Go?* describes both the pain and the exhilaration:

The mood in the convent in those days were comparable to the French National Assembly in '89. The older generation was fearful and sometimes appalled at the rate of change; the younger and more progressive nuns were drunk on liberty, equality and sorority. (p 93)

Lodge puts his finger on the reason for this revolutionary change. Sisters began to see that the rules and regulations of the order, which they had been taught were essential for holiness and which governed the minutest detail of their lives, were in fact 'the fossilised remains of obsolete manners and customs'. Male religious, especially priests, had always been freer than women religious, but their lives too were often regulated in minute detail. Among the sisters there was a long-drawn-out war of attrition on the question of dress. The 1960s was, of course, the era of the miniskirt, and as one of David Lodge's sisters remarked: 'After all, a nun does take a vow of chastity and I don't really think you should be able to see the tops of her stockings when she sits down.'

Most 'progressive' sisters began with a compromise habit of black, dark blue or brown with a short veil. Some wore it with a style that was innate. Others had no sense of style or had lost it through years of repression. Only the 'radical' orders broke out into full lay dress. The question of dress still seems to trouble some today. Even now there is talk of the 'witness value' of the habit. I heard it suggested recently that a return to the habit would 'Put God back on the streets'!

The debate over the habit was symptomatic of deeper changes. From 1965 to 1975 radical and far-reaching changes swept through religious orders. At first there was great optimism about the future: dress changed, former structures of prayer (such as community mediation, rosary, examination of conscience) were swept away and new forms of prayer were tried, experimental communities were set up and religious were encouraged to assume responsibility for their own lives. But the euphoria soon disintegrated. Many left religious life, those ill-prepared for freedom acted irresponsibly, experimental communities collapsed and abrasive confrontations between progressives and conservatives occurred.

Out of this chaos some religious orders (mainly of women) began to sort out revolutionary new approaches to religious life. These approaches were often based on a return to the real intentions of the founder of the order. What emerged from all of this was that there is no one perennial essence of religious life, normative for all persons and for all ages. Women religious particularly have used the experience of the last 20 years to develop new forms of community, ministry and above all a commitment to work for justice and for the poor.

But they have run into problems with Rome. Recently John Paul II has expressed 'grave concern' over the sharp drop in numbers in religious orders in the Western world. This decrease has brought about a situation where some orders face the possibility of extinction. In terms of numerical decline the Pope is right. But the question of numbers and of the future of individual religious orders needs to be looked at more carefully. The Belgian Jesuit, Father Raymond Hostie, has made an exhaustive historical study of the foundation, growth and disintegration of male religious orders in his *The Life and Death of Religious Orders* (English trans. 1983). The book also gives a very complete survey of historical statistics for religious orders.

The first thing that should be noted is the inflation in the number of religious from the beginning of this century. The following table illustrates this:

Year	Male Religious
1900	135,000
1965	335,000
1970	310,740
1980	248,051

Between 1900 and 1965 there was a 240% increase. It is interesting to compare these figures with the 18th and 19th centuries. In 1770 there were 300,500 male religious in Europe and the Americas. As a result of the French Revolution this number had dropped to 83,000 in 1850. It was during the 19th century that a large number of new religious orders were founded. Their focus was mainly missionary and they were largely responsible for the tremendous growth in the number of religious in the first part of the 20th century. Let us take a number of well known and typical male religious orders and review the fluctuation in their membership from 1770 to 1980.

Order	Foundation Date	1775	1850	1900	1930	1965	1980
Benedictines (OSB)	529 AD	15,000	2,500	6,200	9,070	12,500	9,522
Christian Brothers	1802		161	826	1,707	3,900	2,801
Dominicans	1216	20,000	4,560	4,350	6,137	9,946	7,164
Jesuits	1540	23,000	4,600	15,070	21,678	36,038	26,905
Marist Fathers	1816		348	814	1,167	2,343	1,930
Salesians	1859			3,526	8,496	22,383	16,915
Trappists	1664	90	1,284	3,586	3,302	3,912	3,045

Several conclusions can be drawn from these statistics. The French Revolution (1789) brought a catastrophic decline in the number of religious men in Europe. Many orders simply ceased to exist at this time. But those with strong traditions did survive after going through a process of re-foundation. The period since 1965 has also seen a sharp drop in absolute numbers. But many of the orders listed have had a marked increase in the number of those entering in Third World countries. For instance, India is the fastest growing province of the Jesuits. Yet in Europe, North America and Australia numbers have dropped dramatically and the average age has risen sharply.

There is a sense in which some of the international religious orders are being re-founded in the developing world. In these countries they are forced to take innovative stands and revolutionary approaches to ministry. In most places they are committed to the poor and the marginalised. Under a number of right-wing dictatorships it is the priests who have been the victims of death squads. Some international orders are dying in the west, but coming to life through revolutionary change in the Third World. They are part of the great hope for the Church.

Also I think that genuine new forms of religious life are already emerging, especially among the laity. This new form of lay religious life is more flexible, has less need for or dependence upon Church authority, is more tolerant of different levels of commitment, includes single and married people, is more fluid in structure and reflects a spirituality that is more honestly contemporary.

This brings us to a consideration of the laity since Vatican II. In one sense the laity were so subservient in the Church prior to Vatican II that they had nothing to lose but their chains! The only officially sanctioned ministerial outlet for them was Catholic Action. I have already mentioned that this was under the complete control of the local hierarchy. Catholic Action was often politicised. In Italy it was strongly anti-Fascist, and provided the foundation for the post-war development of the Christian Democratic Party which has dominated Italian politics until now. In Spain Catholic Action became pro-Fascist. In France, it split along ideological lines: Christian democracy and later the worker priests emerged from the left. The right established strong links with *Action Francais* of Charles Maurras. It is from powerful right-wing Catholics in the tradition of Maurras that rebel Archbishop Marcel Lefèbvre gains financial support.

The *Decree on the Laity* of Vatican II takes *Lumen gentium* as its basis. It stresses that all members of the Church are called to ministry. The laity's fundamental task is evangelisation through Christian social action and practical charity. There is a stress on laypeople exercising this mission in the temporal order. The task of pastors is to facilitate and co-ordinate the gifts of the members of the community. The spirituality of the laity grows through life in the world, not through aping the spirituality of religious life or monasticism. The final chapter of the *Decree* is significant for it de-emphasises the need for clerical control. While maintaining the need for Church approval before an organisation can call itself 'Catholic', the *Decree* admits that 'in the Church there are many undertakings which are established by the free choice of the laity and regulated by their prudent judgement' (para 24). This is a radical departure from pre-conciliar views and it opens the way for independent lay organisations.

Since the Council, tremendous strides have been taken in trying to develop the consciousness of the laity. There is now a whole group who have come to a conscious and articulated faith. They have achieved this through programmes such as Marriage Encounter, Cursillo, the charismatic movement and a whole range of adult education programmes. Underpinning and impregnating this whole programme of lay formation has been the renewed emphasis on the reading and study of sacred scripture. The way in which the Bible has returned to the centre of Roman Catholicism in the last 25 years has been extraordinary.

In the United States there has been much emphasis on theological education at a tertiary level for Catholics. This has been able to be provided through the college and university system. There is now a sizeable group of lay Catholics in North America with advanced theological degrees. In Australia and the United Kingdom there has been little chance for this level of training to develop. The Catholic teachers colleges are the only places providing undergraduates with theological education. Some of the theological consortiums have lay students, but they are still a small group. I stress the need for this tertiary level of education for it is from this group of theologically educated laity that a leadership with a real Christian vision can emerge.

But the layperson who has come to conscious and articulated faith confronts one major snag. Faith always seeks to express itself through ministry – as Saint Paul said, 'I believed, therefore I spoke'. It was easy for Saint Paul for there were no structures that prevented him speaking! It is a lot more difficult for the layperson of today for there has been little or no structural change in the Church to incorporate this renewed consciousness of ministry. The Catholic Church has a lot of renewed people all dressed up with nowhere to go. Ministry has become the central question for the renewed elite of modern Catholicism, for it is the fundamental expression of the new spirit of Catholic people. There is a whole group of people who are no longer willing to accept a passive role in the Church, to do 'whatever Father wants'. But the structures for their participation in ministry are only just beginning to develop. The Church is still geared to a ministry dominated by priests.

It has always struck me as stupid to speak about a crisis resulting from a shortage of priests, when there are so many laypersons ready and willing to serve. The problem is that Catholics are insufficiently imaginative to be able to adjust Church structures to incorporate laity in ministry. Already laity have taken over some structures: Catholic schools in Australia are now substantially run by laypersons. Many have lay principals. There is a distinct advantage in young Catholics seeing their teachers model a lay commitment to faith. The Catholic community, of course, must monitor the ongoing commitment of Catholic schools to those values which are explicitly Catholic and the Church community has the right to ascertain that those who teach Catholicism have a serious commitment themselves to that faith.

But laity have had more difficulty penetrating other aspects of the Church's ministry. Laypeople with various forms of expertise are often invited to join advisory bodies. I know of situations where people have invested energy in researching a topic, writing a report, making recommendations – in their own time and at their own expense – to find that ecclesiastical authorities have ignored them. Take the example of the parish council that has spent months investigating the financial viability of a parish building project, only to find that the pastor has made a decision independent of them and already raised the bank loan. Or the example of the bishop who had protracted negotiations with a parish about the 'profile' of the pastor they wanted (and needed), but who then foisted on them a priest with a diametrically opposite 'profile'.

Church leadership is ill-prepared to accept advice and does not deal well with a participatory model of Church. Church leaders use the words, jargon and images of Vatican II, but they are still hierarchical in their thinking. All of this is what Jesus called 'new wine in old wineskins' (*Luke 5:36-39*).

This has resulted in the loss of many excellent laypeople (and also a number of priests and religious) from the ministry. People leave disappointed and cynical. Others respond positively by stepping outside the official Church to initiate new forms of ministry. There are already many people doing this. Some groups have focused on specific issues such as peace work, social justice, women's ordination or working on a specific ministerial need. A number of these groups are ecumenical in structure and membership. They strive through their living and ministry to incorporate union between the Churches. There are, of course, many individuals who strive to find new ways of ministering. Often they have to do this without support from the Church or community, either material or spiritual.

Thus as a result of Vatican II the Church is passing through a searing process of renewal. As in all human affairs the effects are mixed. The Church has been both reborn and reformed.

4
NEW MOVEMENTS

I was once giving some talks in a parish in a small town in the Midwest of the United States. Among those at the talks was a group of anxious Catholic parents. Their children had recently gone off to the state university and, as impressionable young people do, they had joined a lively and friendly religious group at the university that claimed to be Catholic. But the parents complained that the group had alienated the youngsters from their families. This so-called Catholic group was dominated by a couple of male 'leaders' in their mid-20s. As sects so often do, they had exploited the loneliness and insecurity of the young undergraduates living away from home for the first time. The university had an excellent and well-organised Catholic campus chaplaincy. But the youngsters had been gulled into joining a fringe charismatic group that had broken off from the Catholic Church to become a sect of its own.

It is often hard to tell what a group represents: for there are a large number of new groups springing up within the fold of Christianity, some healthy, others decidedly unhealthy. In this chapter I want to examine the most important of these new movements, especially those that effect Catholicism. Before I do that

I want to say something about fundamentalism in general.

I begin in the United States because North America is the fountainhead of the modern fundamentalist phenomena. We speak today about the 'new' religious right in the United States particularly. This is inaccurate, for the right has been a powerful force in United States religion from the beginning of US history. The alliance of reactionary politics and religious fundamentalism did not begin with Reverend Jerry Falwell and the foundation of the Moral Majority in 1979. Its roots go back to the foundation of America as a refuge for Protestant dissenters in the 17th century. The Puritans who came to Massachusetts between 1620 and 1650 saw themselves as a righteous remnant escaping the moral corruption of English society and the 'diabolical heresies' of the high Anglican Church. John Winthrop preached to them about the covenant and God's blessing on those who worked industriously and honestly. Idleness was a sin. A good successful life was sign of election. Failure was a sign of predestination to damnation. It was frightening, literal Calvinism. But it was also the pervasive social force upon which the capitalist ethos of the United States was built.

The Puritans came to subdue and use the land. In the 18th and 19th centuries, Americans saw themselves as the instruments of God in the wilderness. The native Americans stood in their way. They were massacred as savages, as were the Aborigines in Australia, who were swept aside by land-grabbing whites inspired by a secularised puritanism. In American puritanism we also find the origins of revivalism. Massachusetts experienced the Great Awakening in the 1740s with the sermons of Jonathan Edwards. A second Great Awakening occurred at the beginning of the 19th century. Puritanism is a religion perfectly adapted to the practical task of the foundation of a new nation. But it is badly adapted to dealing with complex and intractable social problems and with failure. The Vietnam war was a terrible failure for the United States and it has deeply scarred the American psyche. It was followed by depressing economic and social consequences.

A message that has always been close to the surface in American social and religious history is that when economic downturns come, they are moral judgements and precise punishment for the nation's sins. Setbacks of any kind, in fact, are related to failures of moral rectitude . . . In times of insecurity, when old certitudes are shaken and unanswerable questions are posed, people in this tradition look for simple answers, for visible enemies and assurance that they are right. (Ralph Clark Chandler : 'The New Religious Right: Worshipping a Past That Never Was' in *Christianity and Crisis*, 15 February 1982, p 25)

Of course, Reverend Jerry Falwell and his contemporaries have distorted and vulgarised the great puritan tradition and they cannot be compared with Cotton Mather or Jonathan Edwards. And their medium is more blatantly vulgar – television! A large part of their influence is that they reinforce the prejudices that their viewers already have. But the new religious right is not confined to the United States. Fundamentalism is becoming a widespread phenomenon and it is affecting the Catholic Church.

Fundamentalism is basically reductionism – the conversion of complex realities to simple ones. It is the tendency to see everything in terms of absolutes; relativity plays no part in the fundamentalist worldview. It is authoritarian: it appeals constantly to a superior power to support its claims, whether that power be divine, biblical or papal. It is anti-intellectual in that it abstracts from the historical context of all reality, especially the Bible. Its structures are usually either individualistic or sectarian rather than communitarian. It is also paternalistic and sexist. Its whole attitude is exclusive rather than inclusive.

Fundamentalism is a generic term and it can be applied with more or less accuracy to a number of organisations within the Catholic Church. My own view is that some Catholic charismatics are fundamentalist; there is a sense in which we might call these left-wing fundamentalists. At the same time the integralist Catholic organisation, Opus Dei, is an expression of right-wing fundamentalism. Both these groups of Catholics often have more in common with Protestant fundamentalists than is generally recognised.

The most well-known line of division between mainline Christians and fundamentalists is in the area of biblical and doctrinal interpretation. Here mainline Christians are contextualists; fundamentalists are literalists.

Literalists see the Bible (and Church documents) as directly dictated by God, each word guaranteed in its historical accuracy, each sentence a description of real persons and real events. The human author acts merely as an instrument. God dictates directly. The word is absolute. It is in no way relative to the time and milieu of its composition. Conservative literalists have the same attitude to papal and conciliar writings. Contextualists see the Bible and Church documents as literary works written by a human being from a particular culture and milieu – but these human words are inspired by God. Thus each work of scripture can be understood and assimilated more deeply by study and the application of literary, historical and critical methods. These two positions are irreconcilable for they presuppose two different ways of knowing.

Classical fundamentalism is a form of conservative Protestant Christianity. It began as a reaction to liberal Protestantism and a critical approach to biblical interpretation. Father Michael Trainor of Adelaide in an excellent article 'Fundamentalism: A Growing Concern for the Australian Catholic Church' (*Compass Theology Review* 2/19, 1985, pp 7-14) distinguishes several characteristics of fundamentalism. It begins in a personal experience of salvation, it believes in the infallability of scripture, it is strongly missionary and wages war against 'liberals' and 'modernists' and it is anti-ecumenical and sectarian. It has always been opposed to the Darwinian concept of evolution. This explains its contemporary promotion of so-called 'creation science'. Today fundamentalism is undergoing a powerful revival and is characterised by a political commitment to conservative causes (especially in the US), concerted action to maintain conservative social stances and the use of television as a way of spreading its message. Paradoxically, it was a Catholic, Bishop Fulton Sheen, who in the United States was the first to use TV as a way of proclaiming the Christian message.

Fundamentalism does affect the Catholic Church. Many young Catholics are influenced by or even join evangelical Churches. This seems to affect university students and graduates even more than ordinary young people. Many that join these Churches have no developed critical sense and are ignorant of their faith, even though they are the products of Catholic schools. A few Catholics are influenced by fundamentalist views in scriptural interpretation. A number of Catholics maintain a form of fundamentalism and literalism while remaining in the Church.

Father Trainor gives five reasons why Catholics adopt a fundamentalist approach or join an evangelical sect. Firstly, they are people whose Catholic affiliation is minimal. They lack a developed faith and are biblically illiterate. Tragically they are often the products of the Catholic school system. Secondly, some are attracted because of their difficulties with modern critical, theological, biblical and social scholarship. Thirdly, since Vatican II many Catholics have replaced one fundamentalism with another. These people lack self-direction in their lives. They have replaced the authoritarianism of the past with the 'paper pope' of the Bible. Fourthly, fundamentalism seems to arise especially in times of change, either in people's personal lives or in the life of society. Change brings personal insecurity, instability and dislocation. Many people cannot deal with this and they seek easy and certain answers to complex and difficult problems. Finally, fundamentalist groups offer security and a sense of company to those who experience alienation, loneliness and personal isolation. The sheer size and impersonality of most Australian Catholic parishes prevents them from being able to meet people at the level of their need.

Father Gilbert Padilla (in the *National Catholic Reporter*, 1 November 1985) says that there are three characteristics of fundamentalism: lack of scholarship, lack of faith and lack of compassion. It is no use talking to fundamentalists; you will never change them. Not all of them are stupid. Some are highly intelligent, but they are narrow and limited in vision. They scorn higher learning, and they have locked themselves into an attitude that protects them from having to budge from their pre-established certainties. Their ignorance is crass and stubborn. They are always right, you are always wrong and they have an answer for everything. Their certainty is based on a presumed access to divine knowledge: 'God has told me and what God says is IT'. It manifests a pride that covers a terrible insecurity.

Fundamentalists lack faith. Genuine faith is not certainty; it is a commitment to the unseen God. Faith often involves moving on into the dark unknown of the future.

Fundamentalists do not believe. They have their whole religious structure centered on the printed word, the word they can read and read literally as though the word had dropped out of the sky written in English . . . they have replaced Christ with the printed word. (Gilbert Padilla)

Because they can find nothing about nuclear weapons in scripture, they work happily for corporations that manufacture the weapons of mass destruction. In one parish in the north-east United States I knew a leading Catholic charismatic who happily worked as a successful salesman of napalm to developing countries! Fundamentalists lack compassion. They have no sensitivity to suffering. They are quite happy to see the oppressed people of the world destroyed, starved or exploited as long as their own security is not challenged. Their spirituality is self-centred. There is something fanatical about fundamentalism which is usually disguised under a smug self-rightousness.

I want to turn now to the influence of the charismatic movement on the Catholic Church. Although one finds elements of fundamentalism in some charismatics, this is not necessarily a general characteristic. Certainly the origins of the movement lie in enthusiastic fundamentalist Protestant sects and many non-Catholic charismatics are fundamentalist. Actually Catholicism has had many charismatic manifestations in its long history. Monsignor Ronald Knox has called these manifestations 'enthusiastic'. They were especially strong in the medieval Church where they provided one of the few ways of social deviance.

Within Catholicism the historical origins of these enthusiastic movements lie in the desire to return to a simpler and more primitive Christian religiosity and in the need for a more experiential form of Christian living. Paradoxically, there were very few charismatic manifestations in the Catholicism of the 19th and early 20th centuries. Much of the psychic energy of the time was channelled off into the romantic movement or suppressed by rigid papal or episcopal control of the Church. This psychic energy probably expressed itself in the many apparitions of the Blessed Virgin Mary and the psycho-physical phenomena associated with the cruder forms of mysticism. For instance, there were more stigmatists in the 19th century than in all the rest of Church history. (Stigmatism is the appearance in the body of an individual of the physical marks of Jesus' suffering on the cross.)

Within Catholicism the modern charismatic renewal got its start on US campuses in the late 1960s. It began in February 1967 at Duquesne University in Pittsburg and quickly spread to the University of Michigan, Michigan State University and to Notre Dame University in South Bend, Indiana. It is significant that the movement began in the universities. It was a response to the weariness of young Catholics who had been involved in the civil rights movement, social activism, attempts to renew the liturgy and to develop ecumenism. Kevin and Dorothy Ranaghan, who were among the founders of the movement, explain it this way: they maintain that in the 60s young Catholics

. . . felt that there was something lacking in their Christian lives. They couldn't quite put their finger on it but somehow there was an emptiness, a lack of dynamism, a sapping of strength in their lives of prayer and action. It was as if their lives as Christians were too much their own creation, as if they were moving forward under their own power and of their own will. It seemed to them that the Christian life wasn't meant to be a purely human achievement. (K. and D. Ranaghan: *Catholic Pentecostals*, 1969, p 7)

The movement spread quickly. All over the English-speaking world prayer groups sprang up in parishes, convents and universities. The movement spread to Australia where it had a significant impact. Many of the prayer groups developed into weekly gatherings, often of hundreds of people. At its best the charismatic renewal has interacted with the retreat movement to encourage a profound experience of faith in the lives of thousands of people. The renewal has also led to the establishment of communities, mainly of laypeople, one of the first of which was the 'Word of

God' community in Ann Arbor, Michigan (I will comment later on what has happened to this community). In Australia there are examples of charismatic communities. The Uniting Church parish in the Canberra suburb of O'Connor is a charismatic parish, as is the Catholic parish of Bardon in Brisbane.

The Emmanuel Covenant Community (also in Brisbane) has developed out of the charismatic renewal. It began in 1975 as a Catholic charismatic group and in 1986 has 1100 members. Members make a public commitment to support each other in prayer and fellowship and in the lifestyle of the community. Membership is open to families and single people. Members remain within their normal vocations but meet together regularly for prayer and teaching. Although the Community is ecumenical almost 95% of its membership is Catholic. The Community seems to have guarded against the sectarian tendency by insisting that members continue to worship in their own parishes; they are encouraged to 'belong' to the wider Church. For support members do live in clusters of houses in a specific geographical area. Brisbane is divided into seven geographical areas and each has a lay elder with pastoral oversight. The constitutions of the Community are approved by the Archdiocese of Brisbane.

The charismatic movement spread throughout the English-speaking world very quickly for a number of interconnected reasons. There was a real sense of psychic and spiritual exhaustion in Catholicism after the effects of the Council began to be felt and after a period of unprecedented change in the secular community. As the movement developed, other reasons for its growth began to emerge. Many felt the need for a biblically based spirituality. People were no longer satisfied with the arid moralism and rigorism which characterised so much pre-conciliar religiosity. Many were looking for an experience of faith, something that would bring their religion alive and give it emotional verve. Catholics needed to discover that faith was not an arid rationalism but an experience of the living God. The charismatic movement provided a caring community where participants could share their faith and give mutual support.

Added to these deeper reasons are the spectacular aspects of the charismatic movement: speaking in tongues, miraculous cures, prophecy. Charismatic liturgy is never dull (like so much ordinary Church worship), even though it is sometimes tasteless. I will never forget seeing a charismatic crocodile of dancing priests – in full vestments – gyrating around the sanctuary as a symbol of thanksgiving after communion at a renewal Mass. The liturgy was presided over by an unmoved (and unmoving) poker-faced Cardinal Archbishop, whose opinion of the spectacle going on before him could only be guessed at!

Cardinal Leon Joseph Suenens in his book *A New Pentecost?* (1975) emphasises that the charismatic movement brought hope to many Catholics who were sinking into despair as a result of the many negative things that followed Vatican II. Suenens describes his own 'dark night of hope' as he tried to implement the Council. It was the time of so-called theology of the 'death of God', the denial of Jesus, a period of moral decadence.

Every local Church knew its trials. With heavy heart I watched many priests, and men and women who had been in religious life, abandon their vocations. The conversations I had with some were deeply painful: breaks of this kind hurt a lot and leave their scars. (C. L. J. Suenens, *A New Pentecost?*, p 214)

It was the charismatic revival that rekindled his trust in God's Spirit. For many people it was the same. Their participation in the charismatic movement brought them alive, gave them a new experience of faith.

The wider Church has reacted very well to the charismatic movement. Bishops have not rushed in and condemned it – as did so many of their episcopal predecessors during past charismatic manifestations in history. The Church seems to have unconsciously realised that the movement has helped many people and has replaced the old popular devotions which also attempted to involve people in mass movements with a strong sense of participation. I am thinking here of manifestations like the Father Patrick Peyton Rosary Crusade of the 50s.

But some problems have also emerged with the charismatic movement. It should be a process through which people pass. In this sense it would be an experience of renewal of faith that will lead them back to participation in the wider Church. For many it has been precisely this. It is not, nor can it be, an end in itself. But tragically some people tend to become fixated. It becomes the be all and end all of their religion. It is among these people that the charismatic movement takes on sectarian tendencies. And once the sectarian mentality becomes predominant in a group, the wider community is rejected as uninitiated and uncommitted. This was rather amusingly illustrated for me when a lady came up to me after Mass and said: 'Father, you must be in the Renewal. You seem so happy and say Mass so nicely!' I thanked her for the compliment, and hastened to assure her that there were happy and even nice people outside the Renewal. 'Not in my experience!' she replied.

Some who remain permanently in the charismatic movement manifest a kind of religious schizophrenia. In normal life situations they are intelligent and controlled individuals but they seem to attain a real emotional release in charismatic gatherings. Others in ordinary life are emotionally undisciplined, so being carried away in charismatic prayer does not seem unusual for them. The claim is sometimes made by charismatics that because their experience is one of faith, it is no longer subject to the usual processes of human psychology. They claim that faith transcends empirical science. This seems to me a very dangerous claim, for it immediately drives a wedge between the traditional Catholic insistence on the union of faith and reason. It tends to make God a master manipulator who apparently suspends His own law of nature at a whim. Young people are particularly susceptible to this split between faith and reason. While it is good that the charismatic movement brings them to a real commitment to faith, one wonders what will happen when they come down from this high. There is a danger that they will identify faith with enthusiasm and religious experience, especially if they are not well rooted in normal Catholic life. The young are the ones likely to be gulled by groups with sectarian tendencies, especially those that are led by powerful (usually male) figures, who either consciously or unconsciously pose as gurus.

There is a tendency among some Catholic charismatics to become increasingly fundamentalist, not only in scriptural exegesis but also in theology. The naive adscription to God or Satan of human and psychological phenomena that are easily explained in other terms, trivialises the transcendent. My fundamental problem with such an attitude is rooted in theology. The constant seeking of tangible experiences of faith seems to me to evacuate the radical core of belief, which is a commitment to a God whose face is not seen, to a God who far transcends the human condition. Faith is to be found in the darkness of the struggle to make sense out of life. The assertion of God's constant and trivial intervention in human affairs through speaking in tongues, miracles, cures, prophecies seems to me to trivialise God into a kind of master magician.

The sectarian tendencies of the charismatic movement are well illustrated in the Word of God Community in Ann Arbor, Michigan. In 1974 Cardinal Suenens was very enthusiastic about the community which he said aimed 'to live a life true to the spirit of the gospel and to give witness of this in the world' (p 76). Anyone acquainted with the history of the community between 1975 and 1986 might come to another conclusion. The Word of God Community has very little to do with the wider Catholic Church in Ann Arbor or with the diocese of Lansing in which it is situated. The community has its own parish. The people involved in it have bought clusters of houses close together (many of them are professionals or academics and technocrats at the University of Michigan). They have their own religious education programme. They are very censorious of the 'ordinary' Catholic community with which they will not associate. They do not have anything to do with the local parishes. The community is dominated by a number of strong male figures. Their theological attitudes are very conservative and their social mores patriarchical. Their mentor is Ralph Martin whose book *A Crisis of Truth: The attack on Faith, Morality and Mission in the Catholic Church* (1983) contains a wholesale attack on liberal Catholic theologians, whom he accuses of unorthodoxy, heresy and disloyalty to the Church. The community manifests the characteristics of a sect

in the classical sociological sense. It is a sad parody of the ideal-
ism of ten years ago when the community aimed to transform
the Church.

The charismatic movement has been a two-sided phenomenon:
for most it has been a way back to a renewed and fuller spirituality. It has made them more deeply committed to the ministry of
the wider Church. However, it has turned some people into narrow sectarians, divorced from the mainstream of life in the
Church.

I want to turn now to several other movements of importance
in the life of the Church. Like the charismatic movement, these
also brought people to a living faith. The *Christian Family Movement* (CFM) began in Chicago before the Council, but it spread
to Australia in the years after it and it was one of the first movements to emphasise the use of discussion groups of Catholics that
were locally based. It had great value in itself, but it was eventually supplanted by Marriage Encounter.

The *Cursillo* began in Spain, also before Vatican II, and it
spread throughout the United States and from there to Australia
in the 1960s. It worked through an intense and highly charged
weekend wherein priests, religious and laity came together for an
experience that laid heavy emphasis on the communitarian nature
of Catholicism. Like the charismatic movement, it was rather emotional.

Another Spanish import via the United States is *Marriage
Encounter*. It came to Australia in the early 1970s. It aims to help
married couples and, more recently, engaged couples, rediscover
and strengthen their love for each other.

An even more recent spin-off from Marriage Encounter is
Antioch, a youth movement. Again, there is much emphasis on
an emotionally felt and experienced religion. While having some
characteristics in common with the charismatic movement,
Antioch is more family and parish based. Marriage Encounter has
been successful in bringing large numbers of couples together to
renew their commitment to each other. Some have criticised the
movement for turning couples inward in a self-absorbed way.

While this is true, it has also done undoubted good for many. Marriage Encounter is limited in so far as it really only works when the couples already have a well-founded relationship.

Finally, I want to describe the renewal of spirituality that has swept through the religious orders and from them spread to the laity. Associated with this has been the development of an emphasis on retreats and spiritual direction. It is not that there was no spirituality before the Council. There were many well-established retreat houses for laity as well as clergy and religious. The spirituality that characterised these establishments was generally moralistic. At best it offered an emphasis on methodical meditation and the laity were offered a watered-down generic clerico-religious piety.

After the Council, a number of religious orders, led by the Jesuits, began to develop a new approach to spirituality, drawing on their own traditions and the inspirations of their founders. Most of these religious orders had long spiritual traditions and much to offer from their experience. The Carmelites, Franciscans and Dominicans all participated in this movement. The Jesuits, for instance, emphasised the *Spiritual Exercises* of Saint Ignatius Loyola and the Carmelites the mystical spirituality of Saints Teresa and John of the Cross. Many women religious, as they began to discover the original inspiration of their orders – what in religious rhetoric was called the 'charism of the founder' – began to try to live their own unique spirituality. But the problem for many of the more recent orders is the superficiality of their inspiration and the brevity of their tradition. The purpose for the foundation of many 19th century orders was pragmatic. Many tried to discover an inspiration that was not really there. A number of people were trained in the spirituality of the older clerical orders, especially the Jesuits. Centres were set up to train people in spiritual guidance – Guelph, Ontario (Canada), the Jesuit Center for Religious Development in Cambridge, Massachusetts, Father Matthew Fox's Institute for Creation Centered Spirituality in Oakland, California. In Australia there are the Missionaries of the Sacred Heart's centre at Douglas Park (NSW) and the Jesuit Ignatian Centre of

Spirituality, at Canisius College, Pymble (NSW). The Archdiocese of Sydney has set up the Centre for Christian Spirituality in Randwick.

Linked with this emphasis on spirituality is the development of retreat houses. More and more religious orders have turned over empty novitiates, monasteries and convents to the 'retreat apostolate'. Many of these establishments have helped religious and laity to internalise the renewal that was generated by Vatican II. If this is not linked, however, to structural realignment of religious institutions, one wonders how far the renewal will go? Also nowadays the market is so saturated with retreat houses that many of them are marginal operations. A further problem is that a number of people have 'gone into spirituality' who are quite unsuited. It can be a refuge for inadequate people. A division is emerging within religious orders between the spiritualists and the pragmatists. The spiritualists emphasise the inner life of members and use spiritual direction as the model for the government of religious orders. Such people tend to focus on the individual religious and his or her spiritual growth. The pragmatists emphasise the need for the realignment of the institutional structures of religious life and they are concerned more about the ministry than the inner life of the members. Another important issue facing spirituality is how to integrate it with social justice.

Spiritual direction refers to the guidance that is given to a person who seeks help from another (who is normally seen as a kind of guru or spiritual father or mother – there are a number of women spiritual directors now) in objectifying and discerning the meaning of their spiritual experience. While it is true that much spiritual direction today concentrates on the call to ministry, this is not necessarily true of all of it. I perceive in many religious and in people generally an excessive concern with their own subjectivity and a turning away from broader social concerns. This seems to me counter-productive when the avowed aim of spirituality is to help people integrate life in the spirit and life in the world.

In all of this, the development of a unique lay spirituality tends to be neglected. The laity usually do not have the time or leisure for retreats. Spiritual development for laypersons cannot involve withdrawal from the world. They are not called to a watered down monastic spirituality, but to the development of their own spirituality. The laity must confront the reality of life in the body. Christianity and specifically Catholicism have a long history of dealing badly with sexuality which is a primal expression of life in the body. Both Protestantism and Catholicism have a minimal theology of marriage, even though this is the state in which the vast majority of Christians have always lived. The reason for this is that the Churches have an inadequate dualistic anthropology: the person is defined as an amalgam of body and soul. The Christian tradition has split the body off as an autonomous force essentially in conflict with higher spiritual and cultural aspirations. The body is seen as enemy of the soul.

Thus the Church faces the task of developing a spirituality which reintegrates the person, one which sees the human person as a psycho-somatic unity, not as a temporary union of two disparate parts. Our bodies not only root us within the fabric of human society and in relationship with other persons, but the body also constitutes the individuality of each of us. The body makes us separate persons. A fundamental human craving is for unity, for a breaking down of the barriers that divide us from each other. It is the body which posits our fundamental separateness, our inability to fulfill the longing for unity. Just as it grounds us in the totality of the material and social process, so it separates us from other individual beings. Both these realities must be held in tandem. One important reason for the Christian alienation from the body is that it is rooted in the process that leads to death. Because of an unconscious fear of death we repress the fact of bodily existence.

How should the Catholic Church face the task before it of developing a renewed spirituality, especially for laypersons? Firstly, there has to be an honest admission that the Church faces this challenge. While the Church must integrate its spiritual tradition, it also must abandon the idea that the answers to contemporary questions are always found in the past. Answers to modern questions are not found in this or that spirituality or saint. By this I do not mean that Catholics should not know or study their spiritual heritage. The creative nature of the Catholic tradition demands that it constantly build new possibilities. The task is to discover new solutions to contemporary issues.

I will turn now to a new phenomenon in Catholicism – *Opus Dei*. Let me begin with a story. A few years ago I knew a young man in the parish in which I worked who was open, intelligent and committed to the Church. He put in a lot of time helping unemployed and homeless people. He was well educated and came from an excellent Catholic family. Then he began to put me right about my sermons. He told me that I had some quite unorthodox tendencies! His attitude seemed to me to be quite out of character. I tried to discuss my unorthodox tendencies with him, but we did not get too far. He suddenly left the parish and the excellent work that he was doing and it was only later that I found out that he had joined Opus Dei. (I will refer to it as either Opus Dei or The Work – the Latin means 'Work of God'.)

What is Opus Dei? It is very hard to answer that question because of the secrecy that surrounds the organisation. We can say what it is *not*. It is not a religious order; it is not a secular or lay institute. 'Opus Dei is a new phenomenon in the Church and no juridical situation that fits it had been foreseen earlier' (Monsignor Alvaro del Portillo, Prelate of Opus Dei). In other words it fits into a unique legal category in the Church. Since November 1982, Opus Dei has been a 'Personal Prelature' with the title of Prelature of the Holy Cross and Opus Dei. It is all very confusing. In Australia, The Work runs two residential colleges at the University of New South Wales. They are strictly segregated. Warrane College is for male students, the much smaller Creston is for females. The Work has made attempts to open a foundation in Melbourne, but there has been opposition from a considerable number of clergy. There is no debate that The Work is a right-wing organisation or that it has been patronised and supported by John Paul II and by powerful elements in the Roman Curia. Nor is there any doubt that many moderate Catholics, including prelates in the Roman Curia and among the bishops, are suspicious of Opus Dei and its intentions. The Spanish bishops, for instance, opposed the erection of Opus Dei into a personal prelature, and they, after all, have had more experience of The Work than anyone else. It has been suggested that the Pope sees Opus Dei taking over the role of the Jesuits, whom he sees as too liberal. This seems to me a stupid suggestion. Part of the strength of the Jesuits is their tradition – the fact that they have served the Church for just on 500 years. The spirituality of Saint Ignatius Loyola was revolutionary and the structure of his religious order a radical departure from what had gone before. The spirituality of The Work is conventional (I will discuss it below) and its structure adapted merely to a newly invented canonical category. There is nothing all that new about it.

The Work has been widely criticised. It has been referred to as the 'holy mafia' and 'octopus Dei' with tentacles all over the Church. It has been accused of maintaining totalitarian control of its members; of involvement in right wing politics, especially during the regime of Francesco Franco in Spain and more recently on behalf of military regimes in Latin America; of involvement in the scandal surrounding the Vatican Bank and the collapse of the Italian Banco Ambrosiano and even more recently in the collapse of a large Spanish bank; of the recruitment of young people without parental consent; of discrimination against women; and of elitest tendencies whereby only those with influence, university education or money are recruited. Opus Dei constantly denies these allegations, but contrary evidence is never forthcoming. Its secretiveness is the cause of the rumours. Information has to be prised out of it.

Let us try to sort things out by getting the organisational details first. Opus Dei has both priest and lay members. It claims to have 73,000 members from 87 nationalities. Membership is divided into several categories:

• Priests – about 1000 worldwide (these are always recruited from the ranks of Opus Dei members). There are eight in Australia.
• Numeraries – men and women who are bound to celibacy and to the strict living of Opus Dei spirituality. The number of these is uncertain, but is probably about half the total membership. These are the elite of Opus Dei.

- Associates – fully committed working-class members.
- Super-numeraries – married laypeople committed to the ideals and spirituality of Opus Dei.
- Co-operators – laypeople who receive the spiritual benefits of Opus Dei and who help to pay for and foster its activities.
- Diocescan priests who wish to follow the spirituality of Opus Dei can join the Sacerdotal Society of the Holy Cross.

Despite the emphasis on lay people joining, the key members are obviously the numeraries. Among the numeraries, the lay-men contribute all their earnings to The Work (most are professionals of one sort or another) and some live in commu-nity. Women celibate members are largely engaged in domestic tasks or they work among non-celibate women members and co-operators. 'Women need not be scholars; it is enough for them to be prudent' (Monsignor Escriva, founder of Opus Dei). The priests are obviously the most important members. It is they who direct the lives of other members through the confessional and spiritual direction. Clergy who belong to the Prelature are drawn from the ranks of the laity who are incorporated into Opus Dei. Incorporation comes about through a 'contract'. Opus Dei avoids the use of the term vow because this would make it seem like a religious order. Yet the Opus Dei member promises poverty, chastity and obedience 'according to the spirit of Opus Dei for the rest of my life'. Most people would see this as a vow, but The Work always stresses its uniqueness.

Opus Dei began as a secular institute, but after the foundation of several other secular institutes The Work began seeking another canonical category. They got this from John Paul II. Members are largely divorced from the control of the local bishop and are subject to the prelate (the head priest) of Opus Dei. It is precisely this independence from local supervision that is resented by many. The Work is not under the supervision of the Roman curial Con-gregation of Religious and Secular Institutes, but it is under the Congregation for Bishops. The former Prefect of the Bishops Con-gregation, Cardinal Sebastino Baggio, is a patron of Opus Dei. The Work has gained influence in the Church precisely through the use of powerful patronage.

The founder of Opus Dei was Josemaria Escriva de Balaguer

(1902-1975) – always referred to by members as The Father – who was born in Barbastro, Spain. He was ordained in 1925. His parents were aristocrats fallen on bad times, but he always retained an aristocratic snobbishness. Escriva claimed that on 2 October 1928 he was inspired to found The Work. The time and place of foundation tells us much about Opus Dei. Spain in 1928 was heading toward eventual civil war. Intransigent Catholics supported autocracy; liberals supported anti-clericalism. When the civil war did break out (1936-1939), the Church underwent a persecution in Republican areas. Opus Dei reflects the Spain of the civil war and Franco. There is evidence of The Work eventually gaining considerable influence in the generalissimo's regime. Its spirituality is characterised by a siege mentality, its government is autocratic and secretive and its mentality and methodology manipulative. No one would doubt the sincerity of most of its members. But we have to ask whether it is an organisation that advances or hinders the contemporary Church.

Intellectually, Escriva was a narrow, pious, simple man, certainly not the intellectual giant that the Opus Dei legend makes him out to be. His anti-intellectualism is illustrated in the chapter on Study in his spiritual work *The Way*. (*The Way* is a collection of 999 aphorisms, first published in 1934.) Three aphorisms illustrate this:

Books. Don't buy them without advice from a Catholic who has real knowledge and discernment. It is so easy to buy something useless or harmful. How often a man thinks he is carrying a book under his arm, and it turns out to be a load of trash! (339)

Culture, culture! Don't let anyone get ahead of us in striving for it and possessing it. But remember that culture is a means, not an end. (345)

You worry only about building up your culture. But what you really need to build up is your soul. (347)

He obviously has a circumscribed view of knowledge and culture. In its own institutions The Work only allows members and students to read approved authors – and they run universities in Spain, Mexico, Colombia and Peru as well as schools and university student residences. Henry Kamm of the *New York Times* (8

January 1984) reports that at the Opus Dei University of Navarra in Pamplona, Spain, students are not permitted to read Marx or Marxist writers, Sartre, Kierkegaard or Schopenhauer. Kamm comments on his visit to the university library:

In a very small collection of French literature, the works of Dumas, Lamartine, Molière, Balzac and Diderot are not for general student use. Twentieth century writers are massively absent. The philosophy shelves are almost evenly divided between the permitted and the forbidden, the latter including Spinoza, Kant, Hegel, Kierkegaard, Nietzsche, Heidegger, John Stuart Mill and William James.

Opus Dei aims to provide a spirituality for those living a secular life in the world. It tries to achieve this by emphasising that all are called to holiness through the circumstances of their ordinary lives. There is nothing new about this. Thomas à Kempis attempted the same thing in the 15th century in *The Imitation of Christ*. Specifically, there is nothing revolutionary about the methodology suggested by Escriva. What Opus Dei tries to do is to set up a kind of monastic life-style or cordon sanitaire in the world to protect its members from the infection of worldliness or unorthodoxy.

Opus Dei's spirituality is linked to an equally traditional asceticism. Members must attend Mass daily, spend half an hour in meditation twice a day, say the rosary and the special Opus Dei prayer, the *Preces*, and spend 15 minutes daily in spiritual reading. Members are required to go to confession once a week to an Opus Dei priest. Confession to another priest is frowned on. Each member has a specific spiritual director. They are expected to reveal all aspects of their lives to this person in what are called 'confidences'. Physical penances are also part of the Opus Dei regimen: use of the discipline (a small whip for self-flagellation), cold showers, sleeping on a wooden plank (especially recommended for younger women!) and other forms of bodily asceticism are recommended. Escriva himself says:

Blessed be pain. Loved be pain. Sanctified be pain . . . glorified be pain! (*The Way*, 208)
If you realise that your body is your enemy, and an enemy of God's glory

since it is an enemy of your sanctification, why do you treat it so softly? (227)

Even allowing for the fact that *The Way* was written in the Spanish ecclesiastical milieu of the 1930s, one cannot avoid the masochistic overtones of these statements. The present Prelate, Monsignor Alvaro del Portillo, seems to reflect a similar attitude when discussing the use of the discipline:

It is a normal thing for those who want to follow Christ's path faithfully. It is not a terrible thing – a small mortification. It is ridiculous . . . it is so little. It is much worse what the husband does to the wife, and the wife to the husband. (Quoted in the *New York Times Magazine*, 8 January 1984)

Anyone who entered a religious order 30 years ago might well have been presented with a discipline, but physical penances were generally not encouraged or were tightly controlled. And even in the most oppressive days of religious life, members had a guaranteed freedom to speak to any priest they chose. Since the early 1960s the Church has moved right away from autocratic and dictatorial regimes. There is nothing particularly modern or revolutionary about Opus Dei spirituality. It is obviously rather dated.

Who are the people who join Opus Dei? The Work shows an interest in people with professional backgrounds. Many of its members are technocrats – the type of people who easily split off technical training from their religious development. It often tries to attract promising young people (some as young as 14 or 15). In 1983, after many complaints from parents, the minimum age for becoming a numerary was raised to 16½ years. At 17 a candidate can make an annual contract with Opus Dei until permanent commitment at the age of 22. There have been constant complaints that young people have been estranged from their parents. In 1981 Cardinal Basil Hume (Westminster) refused to allow Opus Dei to recruit young people without discussion with their parents and freedom to choose their own spiritual director.

Why have I emphasised Opus Dei so much? Because, in my view, it is dangerous to the future growth of the Church. It is opposed to renewal and ultimately to Vatican II. Its power is increasing, especially in the Latin countries. For instance, in Peru almost half the bishops are now Opus Dei members. It is patronised by John Paul II. Soon after his election to the papacy, he visited the tomb of Escriva at the imposing mansion which serves as Opus Dei's headquarters in Rome on the Viale Bruno Bozzi. The Work has recently opened a theology faculty in Rome to train its own priests. The Pope has approved the establishment of an Opus Dei university in Rome despite opposition from the other pontifical universities in the city. The Pope also ignored the advice of the Spanish bishops who were opposed to raising The Work to the status of a Personal Prelature. The Work is using its power in Latin America to oppose liberation theology. While its main strength still lies in the Latin countries – Italy, Spain and South America – it has already made inroads into the English-speaking world. Numbers of Opus Dei members are to be found in media and business. Membership in the United States, for instance, is estimated at about 3000.

The Work strongly objects to non-members writing about it. For instance, in preparation at the present moment is an encyclopedia of religious orders. The article on Opus Dei was written by Father Giancarlo Rocca. Opus Dei tried to prevent the publication of the article by using the Roman Congregation of Religious to put pressure on the publisher. Father Rocca was eventually forced to publish his article separately. People resent the way The Work tries to white ant and control other organisations.

Similar to Opus Dei is a right-wing Italian youth movement called *Communione e Liberazione.* This organisation began in 1954. It was founded in Milan by Father Luigi Guissani. The movement took off in the 1970s. It aims to inspire young people with high ideals and a sense of mission. But its theology is, like Opus Dei's, integralist. It has a political arm, the *Movimento Popolare*, which is a kind of youthful Italian moral majority. The Italian bishops are suspicious of Communione e Liberazione because of its divisive ideological attitudes in a country that is learning to live with pluralism. Pope John Paul II is a supporter of this movement, as is Cardinal Ugo Poletti, whom the Pope recently imposed as President on the Italian bishops conference.

From this survey, one would have to conclude that the new movements are a mixed blessing for the Church. There is no doubt that much good has been done for many people, especially when these movements have been a means to bring people to a fuller participation in the life of the Church. The problem largely arises when the movement becomes an end in itself and the focus on the wider Church is blurred. It is then that there is a danger that these movements can become sects.

PART TWO

THE EIGHTIES AND THE NEW POPE

5

PROBLEMS OF THE EIGHTIES

I often talk to Catholics who are unhappy with the Church because they experience it as stultified and conservative. Yet when you explore their objections you discover that their experience of Catholicism is confined to their own parish or to their own local area. They lack the consciousness of belonging to a world Church. One of the recurring themes in this book is the creativity of contemporary Catholicism. In countries all over the world the Church is emerging as a force for renewal in the lives of many people. Catholic thought is currently characterised by intellectual vigour and Catholic life by a search on the part of many people for the meaning of Christian existence in the contemporary world. The problem for many Australian Catholics is that they have become so bogged down in the narrowness of their own experience of Catholicism that they seem unaware of the wider creativity at work in their Church.

This chapter focuses on Catholicism as a world-wide Church. It looks firstly at those issues which have effected the universal Church during the three most recent pontificates – those of Popes Paul VI (1963-1978), John Paul I (1978) and John Paul II (1978-). It then focuses on Catholicism in a number of different areas in the world.

Pope Paul VI had a bad press during his lifetime and this has continued since his death. In the minds of most people he is the Pope of *Humanae vitae* (1968), the encyclical against artificial contraception. It is forgotten that he is also the Pope of *Populorum progressio* (1967), an encyclical that called for a vast social reform by which the advanced and rich countries of the world would discharge their moral responsibility to help poor and underdeveloped nations. He spoke in *Populorum progressio* of a world '. . . where every man, no matter what his race, religion or nationality, can live a fully human life, free from servitude imposed on him by other men or natural forces over which he has not sufficient control; a world where freedom is not an empty word and where the poor man Lazarus can sit down with the rich man' (47). But it is not Pope Paul's social radicalism that is remembered, but his moral conservatism.

The encyclical *Humanae vitae* was certainly a turning point in the modern history of Catholicism. So much of the power of the Church over its adherents was exercised through its role as a moral arbiter. This power was applied to individuals through the confessional. Obedience to the Church's moral teaching, especially in the area of sexuality, was considered a precondition of belonging to and participating in the Church in a full sense. Because the Church claimed so much control, it stood to lose an enormous amount of influence if that control was ever questioned or called into doubt. *Humanae vitae* brought on that moment of doubt and question. And as the doubt was in the area of sexuality and fertility it could not be side-stepped by Catholics.

Let us try to sort out the facts surrounding *Humanae vitae*. Firstly, it needs to be remembered that oral contraceptives are a very recent invention. The use of the pill only became widespread in the early 1960s. Prior to that all other forms of artificial contraception had been condemned by Pius XI in the encyclical *Casti conubii* (1932). The only method of birth control permitted for Catholics was the Ogino-Knaus method, or what was popularly called the rhythm or safe-period method, and cynically referred to as Vatican roulette. The introduction of oral contraceptives created confusion among some Catholic moralists

who said that the use of the pill was morally permissible. Many
Catholic couples, for whom the issue was more than theoretical,
began to use the pill. The issue came up at Vatican II, but was
side-stepped and handed back to the Pope. Paul VI, in a remark-
able interview published in Milan's *Corriera della Sera* confessed
that he was completely flummoxed by the issue. Vatican conservatives were thunder-struck by this admission and mounted a
counter-attack to explain what the Pope really meant. Progressive moralists applied the adage *Lex dubium non obligat* (A
doubtful law does not oblige). Married couples, they argued, were
free to use oral contraceptives.

Prior to this the Pope had set up a Papal Commission of laypeople, moralists and doctors to study the issue and report their
findings to him. They were to examine the whole question of the
control of fertility and specifically the question of oral contraceptives. The large majority of the members of the Commission were
for granting permission to Catholics to use oral contraceptives.
The opposition to this in the Commission was made up of four
priests: the American Jesuit John C. Ford, the Dutch Redemptorist Jan Visser, the Franciscan Emenegildo Lio and the Jesuit
Marcellino Zalba. These priests were supported by the Holy Office
and by Cardinals Ottaviani, Browne, Samore and Cicognani.
Cardinals Heenan (Westminster) and Doepfner (Munich), the co-
presidents of the Birth Control Commission, held the majority
position. The Commission made its report and went home. But
the minority of four priests submitted a separate report – even
though their views had been taken into account in the majority
report. The Curia put the Pope under pressure to uphold the traditional position against all forms of contraception. Father John Ford
may well have been the one who tipped the balance. He argued
strongly to Pope Paul that any change would gravely weaken
papal teaching authority. It would contradict the condemnation
of all forms of contraception by Pius XI. After months of agonis-
ing, Pope Paul began work on an encyclical with the French Jesuit,
Father Gustave Martelet. It was published on 24 July 1968 as
Humanae vitae.

The Pope had it explicitly stated that this was not an infallible document. It was an exercise of the 'ordinary magisterium'; in the Pope's view, it was a serious and binding solution to a contemporary moral problem. In the encyclical the Pope based his teaching on the binding nature of Pius XI's decisions in *Casti conubii* and on an appeal to the natural law. Conception was a natural result of intercourse and the processes of nature could not be artificially vitiated. 'Every conjugal act must be open to the transmission of life.'

The Pope's teaching was greeted with a storm of protest from all over the world, especially in developed countries where the use of contraceptives was already widespread. Catholics could not avoid the issue. Of course, they could, and did, ignore the Pope's revolutionary teaching of the year before on social reform. Although *Humanae vitae* was an exercise of ordinary magisterium – and thus was not infallible – the teaching was crudely presented by some bishops and priests as 'almost infallible'. In Australia most priests who publicly tried to explain the encyclical in terms of ordinary magisterium and the rights of conscience were summarily dealt with: four priests, for instance, wrote to the *Canberra Times* on 3 August 1968 stating that the encyclical was not infallible (which even the Pope had asserted) and that 'A person is not rejecting his Catholic faith by not submitting to the Pope's judgement in this matter.' Speaking to the Catholic Women's League the next day the then Archbishop of Canberra-Goulburn, Archbishop Thomas Vincent Cahill, made the (to put it mildly) un-nuanced statement: 'You can't belong to the Church if you refuse to obey the Pope . . . No one in this diocese has any authority to teach other than what the Pope and I teach' (*Canberra Times*, 5 August 1968). Such archepiscopal nonsense in the daily newspaper simply exacerbated an already difficult situation and failed to address the carefully thought out letter of the four priests. Two of them, Fathers Michael Fallon and Barry Brundell, are now recognised as important Australian theologians. The moralist, Father Nicholas Crotty was suspended by Cardinal Knox, Archbishop of Melbourne, after a series of articles in the *Australian*. Crotty spent a brief time in Hobart, and then left for that Australian *refugium peccatorum* – the United States.

The majority of priests in Australia said nothing for or against the teaching publicly, but they tacitly accepted the fact that many, if not most couples, continued to use the pill. A minority of priests advised against its use. While many Australian priests shared the agony that laypeople went through in making decisions about this issue, the official Catholic Church settled down and hoped that the problem would go away. After initial token support for the teaching of the encyclical, the official Catholic Church lapsed into silence. This was probably the most pragmatic way of dealing with the issue. It probably had the unintended but good effect of allowing people space to make up their own minds. In other countries, however, the teaching was widely challenged.

While not actually confronting the Pope, bishops conferences in the Netherlands, Canada, France, Scandinavia and Italy told their people that the Pope had proposed a high ideal but that if they conscientiously could not live up to it, they should not consider themselves excluded from the Church. The encyclical was strongly criticised both inside and outside the Church because it failed to help in the control of population. Pope Paul was seen as indifferent to the pain of individual couples and unconcerned about the starving masses of people in the underdeveloped countries. While this was an unfair characterisation of him, it was one that stuck to him for the rest of his pontificate.

The significance of *Humanae vitae* was both pastoral and theological.

Tragically, *Humanae vitae* was the breaking point for many Catholics. They stopped practising. For some it was simply that the Church was no longer credible to them and the teaching on contraception was the last straw. Others of a more literal cast of mind could not keep the teaching, so they felt that they had placed themselves outside the Church, unable to keep its rules. Sometimes people were badly advised by clergy who applied the teaching of the encyclical literally without any pastoral sense. They told people: either stop using contraception or stop going to communion. There were fewer of these literalist clergy than people realised. Most priests were as confused as laypeople and their pastoral sense guided them toward a tolerant and merciful attitude.

The contraception issue brought many Catholics to moral maturity in one step. They assumed responsibility for their own moral behaviour. No longer could they ask the Church to decide everything for them. They learned to use and develop their own consciences. Certainly, many sought clerical support in this process. People quietly told each other who the 'pastoral' priests were! The well-informed kept away from those priests who held the strict line of the encyclical. For many it was a bit of a lottery as to which priest they might ask.

Some Catholics heroically followed *Humanae vitae*. Many of these used natural family planning. The method was developed largely by Doctor John Billings in Melbourne. The natural method is approved by the Church and, under favourable circumstances, can be very successful for couples. Unfortunately, there has been a division in the ranks of the natural family planners. The split began in the early 1970s. St Vincent's Hospital in Sydney favours a sympto-thermic method of determining ovulation, whereas in Melbourne Doctor Billings insists on his original method. Generally speaking, natural family planning is 80 to 85% successful overall, although many experienced and dedicated couples have had a much higher rate of success. Experienced doctors consider that natural methods are a way of regulating rather than preventing births. In the last five years many couples have been moving away from the use of artificial contraceptives and opting for natural methods. The more militant proponents of the natural methods tend to take a strong stand against Catholics who decide to use artificial contraceptives.

Unfortunately, one major result of *Humanae vitae* is that a large number of Catholics have come to view the Church as *in*credible in the area of sexuality. This is unfortunate for some real values are enshrined in the Church's teaching on sexuality. However, the Church has got so much out of touch with its own people that the incredulity of large numbers of Catholics is to be expected. Further, there is evidence that the Catholic community is moving away from seeing sexuality and personal morality as the central and most important moral issue. It is being replaced by an emphasis on social justice. Young people today are less concerned about the morality of their sexual activity than they are about integrity in their interaction with other persons.

Theologically, the whole *Humanae vitae* affair has confronted the Church squarely with the question of papal teaching power. What is the status of a non-infallible papal teaching that is largely ignored by the very people to whom it is directed? As both Cardinal Hume (Westminster) and Archbishop John Quinn (San Fancisco) told the Synod of Bishops on the topic of the family (1982), the Church cannot possibly maintain that all of the Catholics who use artificial contraception are in bad faith. Many of them are the best people in local parish communities. The Church today is confronted by a series of questions not about contraception, but about papal magisterium (teaching power). In all of this we can be certain of two things: John Paul II will not back away from a strict interpretation of *Humanae vitae*. He considers it binding on the Church. But we can be equally certain that laypeople have made their decision: that their fertility is their own affair.

In the minds of most people *Humanae vitae* is the most well known event of Paul VI's pontificate. But this is to underestimate a most significant period in the history of the Church. I want to touch on two other important issues of the years of Paul VI: his attempted reform of the Roman Curia and the rewriting of the *Code of Canon Law*.

We have already seen the widespread dissatisfaction at Vatican II with the Curia. Paul VI determined on a major reform of the Roman bureaucracy. This had also been attempted during the pontificate of Pius X (1903-1914). It had only succeeded in reinforcing the process of centralisation. The size of the Curia had been growing steadily as the table on page 120 shows.

The cost of running the central bureaucracy has significantly contributed to the inflation of the annual Vatican deficit. The great increase in staff occurred between 1961 and 1967. This was the direct result of Pope Paul's attempted reform. Instead of

Year	Curia Officials
1900	185
1932	205
1961	1322
1967	2866
1977	3146

demolishing the old system of Congregations and replacing them with a new, streamlined structure, the Pope grafted a 'new Curia' onto the old. The 'old Curia' remained pretty much as it was. A series of new secretariats and other bodies were set up during or after the Council:

• Secretariat for Promoting Christian Unity (1960)
• Secretariat for Non-Christians (1964)
• Secretariat for Non-Believers (1965)
• The Council on the Laity (1967)
• Papal Commission for Justice and Peace (1967)
• The Prefecture for the Economic Affairs of the Holy See (1967)
• The Administration of the Patrimony of the Holy See (1967)
• The Prefecture of the Papal Household (1967)
• General Statistics Office of the Church (1967)

To try to bring some order into the doings of the old Curia, the Secretariat of State (or Papal Secretariat) was made the central organising and supervising body for the whole Curia. All business now flows through this body – including business from the congregations and secretariats. It has become a curia within the Curia. The Secretariat of State has been separated from the Council for the Public Affairs of the Church, which deals with the Church's relationships with civil governments, including the supervision of the papal diplomatic service. In order to meet new demands, the Secretariat of State has increased its staff from 77 in 1970 to 114 in 1980. Giancarlo Zizola has pointed out that the Papal Secretariat which was intended to be a co-ordinating body for the Curia has become a duplicate Curia that surrounds and protects the Pope. It is a centralised personal papal bureaucracy. Assertions have been made about an increasing number of Polish clerics surrounding the present Pope, but a check of the *Annuario Pontificio* (the Vatican Year Book) does not bear this out. Most of them, however, are probably on the Pope's personal staff and are therefore not listed. Guiseppe Alberigo sums up the attempted reform of Paul VI this way:

After ten years the overall characteristics of the Pauline reform can be assessed. The abandonment of a re-structuring, let alone a re-thinking of the Curia in terms of collegiate government of the Church has taken the impetus and vigor away from the whole exercise, leading to results on a smaller scale than those envisaged by Paul VI himself. On the other hand, problems that he did not wish to bring about have assumed even greater importance, such as the ever-expanding size of the workforce and a new centralisation of authority in areas that a few years ago were immune from curial interference, such as lay organisations. (G. Alberigo in P. Huizing and K. Walf: *The Roman Curia and the Communion of Churches*, 1979, pp 24-25)

It should be noted, however, that the new Curia has achieved much, especially the Secretariat for Christian Unity. In 1985 the Congregation for the Doctrine of the Faith (the old Holy Office) tried to eviscerate the Secretariat for Christian Unity by absorbing it into itself. This move was defeated.

The most common question that people ask me when they hear that I am interested in the contemporary Vatican is 'Do you think that Pope John Paul I was murdered?' They have either read or heard of David Yallop's book *In God's Name* (1984). My answer is that there is no evidence that he was murdered. What Yallop has done, however, is to show up the shoddy underbelly of the Vatican and there is enough accurate material in his book to show that sections of the papal administration have been directly linked to known and convicted swindlers and criminals. There is nothing new about Yallop's evidence. Yet, at the same time, it is hard, if not impossible to get to the bottom of the whole sorry mess of Vatican finances. Longtime Vatican expert, Father F.X. Murphy, admits that he is at his wits end to sort out what has gone on. At best, the Vatican has been thoroughly naive. At worst, it has engaged in illegal and criminal activities, utterly unworthy of the Church.

Until very recently Vatican finances were a terrible mess. Popes since Leo XIII (1878-1903) had been trying to get order into them. It was Paul VI who achieved a major reform of the financial system in 1967 as part of his overall reform of the Curia. The Prefecture for the Economic Affairs of the Holy See was set up 'to co-ordinate all the administrative bodies handling the property of the Holy See and to exercise a supervisory function over them.' Thus the Prefecture controls all administrative bodies responsible for the property of the Vatican. The main administrative body responsible to the Prefecture is the Administration for the Patrimony of the Holy See. This body pays Vatican employees, administers and maintains buildings and pays the expenses of the College of Cardinals, the Synod of Bishops and the Lateran University. It also administers the liquid assets of the Holy See (equity stock, bonds, bank deposits). Most of this money comes from investments resulting from the indemnity paid by the State of Italy at the Lateran Treaty (1929). Many people have the impression that this amounts to vast sums. The real figure was probably close to US$400 million in 1975.

The Vatican claims that it is running at a loss – a deficit of US$56 million is expected for 1986. Most of the losses occur in the area of wages, maintenance and administration. The Vatican has been hard hit by wage increases. Also the increase in the size of the staff of the Curia has been a major factor in escalating costs. Late in 1985 a number of Cardinals suggested closing down the Vatican Radio as a way of saving money.

Other administrative bodies coming under the control of the Prefecture of Economic Affairs are the Government of the Vatican City State, the Council of the Fabric of St Peter's and the Congregation for the Evangelisation of Peoples. The Government of the Vatican City pays lay employees working in the Vatican City itself, runs the post office, the Vatican museums and Vatican Radio.

The Vatican Bank or the *Instituto per le Opere di Religione* (IOR) – the Institute for Religious Works – is separate from and not responsible to the Prefecture for Economic Affairs. The IOR is the main source of the financial scandals of the Vatican. It was founded on 29 June 1942. It is responsible for ' . . . seeing to the custody and administration of monies (in bonds and cash) and properties transferred or entrusted to the institute itself by fiscal or legal persons for the purposes of religious works and the works of Christian piety.' It all sounds very righteous, but the IOR has consorted with persons of very doubtful piety. It operates as an ordinary bank and is headed by Archbishop Paul Casimir Marcinkus. Marcinkus, born in 1920, is of Lithuanian extraction from the Cicero area of Chicago. Al Capone was active in the same area! Marcinkus came to Rome in 1950. He first gained fame as an organiser of papal tours abroad and as an unofficial papal bodyguard. Since 1970 he has been administrative head of the IOR. Despite the scandals surrounding Marcinkus, he is still close to John Paul II – they are both Slavs. He was made Governor of the Vatican City State in 1980. Experienced bankers consider that Marcinkus is no financier and it is probably his innocence that led him into trouble.

The IOR operates as a bank. It is thought to have several thousand investors and US$2 billion in deposits and inter-bank accounts. Profits of the bank go directly to the Pope. Thus the bank is not responsible even to the Vatican. Marcinkus reports either to the Pope or to the Secretary of State. It is precisely this independence that Vatican insiders resent. When questioned about the propriety of the Catholic Church running a bank, Marcinkus replied: 'You can't run the Church on Hail Marys!'

In his early days at the bank Marcinkus looked for friends to guide him in the world of finance. He found one in Michele Sindona, a Sicilian, then resident in Milan. Sindona had close Mafia ties, both in Italy and the United States. In the late 1960s the Vatican began to diversify its investments. They wanted to move money out of Italy, largely to avoid Italian dividend tax. Sindona helped the Vatican shed one third of its investment in the Società Generale Immobiliare (an Italian property company that had interests in buildings as diverse as the Rome Hilton and the Watergate building in Washington, DC). He guided the Vatican to tax havens in Luxembourg, Liechtenstein, Panama and Switzerland. In the early 1970s the Vatican participated in a number of business dealings with Sindona, who had meanwhile built a financial empire in Italy and overseas.

By 1974 cracks were beginning to appear in the Sindona edifice. He had used the IOR to launder his own and Mafia money out of Italy – thus avoiding Italian currency laws. He set up a tangle of front companies abroad using the good name of the Vatican. In 1972 he moved his operations to New York where he bought the ailing Franklin National Bank. That bank was forced to close in 1974 with losses on foreign exchange dealings exceeding US$40 million. Sindona's Italian operations also crashed. He vanished from Italy in 1978. He had been sentenced to three-and-a-half years jail for violation of Italian currency laws. In 1980 he was found guilty in the United States for his part in the crash of Franklin National. He was sentenced to 25 years imprisonment. Early in 1986 he was extradited to Italy and within three weeks he was poisoned in jail. It is uncertain if it was murder or suicide.

Back in 1971 Sindona had introduced Marcinkus to Roberto Calvi, born in Milan in 1920. Like Sindona, he was declared by the Vatican to be *uomo di fiducia*, a man of trust. As Sindona's star wained, Calvi's waxed. He was the chairman of *Banco Ambrosiano*, a conservative Catholic-run bank in Milan. Marcinkus' relationship with Calvi was even more disastrous than that with Sindona. The IOR was useful to Calvi as a funnel for moving money out of Italy. He was a member of the infamous Masonic Lodge, *Propaganda Due* (P2). Continental Masonic Lodges are far different to the English or Australian variety – which are really businessmen's clubs with the spice of some ritual thrown in. In Italy the Lodges were anti-clerical and were condemned by the Church. No Catholic could or can join. It was Licio Gelli who organised P2 as a right-wing anti-communist lodge. By fair means or foul, Gelli persuaded many power-brokers to join. The size and influence of P2 is impossible to assess. There are even accusations that members of the Vatican hierarchy belong to it. Certainly Gelli and members of the Italian secret service (SID) helped Sindona to escape from Italy in 1978. P2 maintains close links with a number of right-wing military regimes.

Calvi was able to break Italian law because he used the IOR as a shelter for his illegal dealings. He set up companies abroad and ran up debts in the name of the Vatican. Even as late as August 1981, when Calvi was a proven criminal, the IOR gave him letters of patronage which helped him to survive in business. Calvi's Banco Ambrosiano and the Vatican Bank were interlocked. Some of the Calvi front companies were actually owned by the Vatican. One of the best-known was the United Trading Corporation of Panama.

Eventually Calvi's empire collapsed. He was found hanged under London's Blackfriars Bridge. He was almost certainly murdered. A few days after his death his Banco Ambrosiano crashed. US$1.5 billion was missing. Because of the close ties between the Ambrosiano and the IOR, creditors began to seek repayment from the Vatican. Eventually Rome agreed to hand over US$250 million to the Bank of Italy as a goodwill offer. The reason for this seems to have been that the Vatican was anxious for a settlement of the negotiations for a new Concordat with Italy.

What are we to make of all of this? Enough facts have emerged from this tangle of criminal activities to say that Archbishop Marcinkus and the IOR have consorted with a ragbag of fascists, international swindlers, convicted thieves and murderers. Yet nothing has been done to explain it to the Church. Because of the absolutist and centralised system of the Vatican, final responsibility for all this must be laid on the Pope. Yet he seems unwilling to clean up the mess and tell the truth to the community of the Church. The fundamental issue is that he and his curial staff do not admit any responsibility to the Church for their exercise of authority. They feel that they own the Church like a personal fief. They see themselves as responsible only to God, and God can be remarkably distant when you are doctoring the books. Yet ordinary Catholics cannot let this pass without protest. The People of God have as much right to exercise fraternal correction as the leaders of the Church. The sin of the hierarchy is more infectious than that of the ordinary Catholic. Catholics have a right to demand that this scandal be cleared up by the honest admission of the truth.

The period after the Council also saw the revision of the Code of Canon Law. A Code of Canon Law is a very recent invention in the Catholic Church. The old code was first promulgated in 1917. This is not to say, however, that the Church had no law before that. In fact there was a vast confusion of laws and the code is precisely what it says it is. The original Code was drawn up by a Commission headed by Cardinal Pietro Gasparri and it played a major role in the centralisation of the Church under the papacy and Curia at the beginning of this century. Pope Benedict XV (1914-1922) said that he would establish a group to update it regularly, but this never materialised. As happens with code law, canon law was out of date by the time of the pontificate of John XXIII. At the same time as he announced the Council (25 January 1959), he also announced the creation of a pontifical commission to revise the Code. This began work in November 1965. In 1966 Cardinal Pericle Felici, former Secretary General of Vatican II, was appointed President of the Commission, a position he held until his death in 1982.

Felici was one of the leading conservatives at Vatican II and under him the renewal of the code became increasingly more canonical and less pastoral. The terms of reference laid down for the renewal were that the new Code was to be faithful to Vatican II. It was meant to implement the decisions of the Council and it was to reflect the Council in the way it was applied. It was to move away from a vision of the Church where there were superiors and subjects to one where the Church was seen as a communion of persons working together in faith to serve the wider world. The Code was to express the common dignity and responsibility of all Christians in virtue of their baptism. The law must reflect the new pastoral climate in the Church.

At best the new *Code of Canon Law* (promulgated by Pope John Paul II on 25 January 1983) only partially lives up to these expectations. John Paul II himself and a coterie of close advisers went through the final draft in 1982-1983 and eliminated a number of reforms that would have made the Code more acceptable to people of the common law tradition. For instance, administrative procedures were eliminated by John Paul's fiat. An administrative procedure was a kind of appeals tribunal with power to hear and recommend on cases of alleged abuses of rights; the tribunals would not have power to enforce their decisions, but they would have been able to exercise some check on arbitrary decisions by bishops and ecclesiastical bureaucrats. Their elimination reflects the fear of some hierarchs of any check on their power or review of their performance. For the Anglo-American mind a court of review is absolutely necessary for justice to be done and to be seen to be done.

The Anglo-American legal system is very different from the code system. It is important for those of us who come from a common law tradition to understand the way canon law works. We take law literally. For us it expresses the absolute minimum to which all must conform. If we come to a red light or stop sign – we stop, regardless of whether any traffic is coming in the opposite direction. If we don't stop, we pay the fine – if we get caught! For an Italian a red light is more an advisory sign, especially if there is not much traffic about. The ideal would be to stop, but most people slow down and proceed with (more or less) caution. If a law is impractical or unreal, people simply do not keep it. This is called 'reception' in canon law. A law becomes firm when it is accepted. If it is not accepted, it lapses. American canonist Father James Coriden calls this 'creative extinction'! This is a very useful principle to remember: practices contrary to the law can, after a period of time, supersede the law. Also, in the canon law system dispensation is an important factor. For instance, the ideal is that a Catholic marry a Catholic, but a dispensation can always be given if this does not work out. The dispensation system is open to abuse and it presupposes that people do not have intrinsic rights and thus they require permission to do things. This again is foreign to the common law tradition. Finally, the new Code must always be interpreted in the light and spirit of Vatican II. And the Council aimed to open up the Church, not to close it tight.

I will conclude this discussion by a brief comparison of the two different approaches to law.

ANGLO-AMERICAN/ COMMON LAW SYSTEM	CHURCH CODE LAW SYSTEM
This system derives from the common law and from case law. It states the minimum requirements that must be observed by all.	This is modelled on the European code system. It expresses the ideal for which all must strive.
Common law is based on concrete cases. From an accumulation of cases principles of jurisprudence are evolved.	Code law is based on values, principles, ideals, preaching. Concrete practical law is deduced from principles.
Characterised by: • being more concrete • being more pragmatic • more open to change • expressing minimums • has no system of dispensation	Characterised by: • expressing ideals • being more abstract • more normative • system of dispensations • *epeikeia* = a liberty in interpretation
Interpretation lies with the court system. Final arbiter = the highest court. The judicial system interprets and applies the law. The law giver is parliament. It is subject to its own laws.	Interpretation comes from the law giver. In practice this comes down to being: • Pope • council • canonical traditions • expert canonists • Roman Rota • custom – this can be established after 30 years
Changed by new legislation.	Not easily changed – tends to ossify.

Before looking at the Church in particular countries and specific areas, I want to look at Catholicism as a world Church. How big is it and how big will it be in 2000? What trends can be observed through a consideration of world-wide Catholic statistics? Fortunately, the international research centre *Pro Mundi Vita* in

Brussels provides this information in its Bulletin (no. 82) *The Institutional Church in the Future* (1980). It was compiled by the French demographer, Gabriel Marc.

Let us begin with overall figures for 1980:

World population 4,371,266,000
Catholic population 784,660,000
Thus Catholics are 17.9% of the world population.

Marc estimates that the world population in 2000 will be 6200 million. In his view the Catholic increase will not keep pace with the world increase and that Catholics will number about 950 million in 2000. Marc breaks up the figures by continent. By an examination of the following table one can easily see where the priority for evangelisation lies:

DISTRIBUTION OF CATHOLICS BY CONTINENT

Continents	December 1977		Year 2000	
	Catholics	Population	Catholics	Population
Africa	53m	423m	94m	831m
Asia*	56m	2404m	96m	3689m
Oceania	5m	22m	9m	30m
S. America	204m	224m	279m	382m
C. America	97m	113m	130m	214m
N. America	58m	240m	85m	476m
Europe*	226m	669m	261m	733m
Total	737m	4095m	954m	6168m

(*These are estimates because statistics are not fully available for all countries.)

Thus there are more Catholics now in Latin America than in Europe and more outside the Western world (which still largely controls the Church) than in it. In percentage terms Catholics at present constitute:

18% of the world population
90% of the Latin American population
60% of the European population

26% of the Oceania population
24% of the North American population
12% of the African population
 4% of the Asian population

Marc's figures suggest that by 2000 Asia will have 60% of the world's population, but only 10% of the world's Catholics. Thus Asia is clearly a priority for evangelisation.

At present 36% of the world's population is under 16 years of age. Most of these are in Asia, Latin America and Africa. But the Church is still dominated by a Western gerontocracy of bishops and clergy and by countries with an ageing population (as we shall see the clergy especially are ageing rapidly). The Church tends to be conservative and has difficulty in hearing the young. If young people are to listen to the Church, much of the emphasis in evangelisation must shift to them. The non-Western world must become more normative if the Church is to hear the young. This realisation is slowly dawning as Third World Churches gain more influence in the world Church.

There is another way of looking at the statistics. Catholics still constitute a large percentage of the populations of the rich countries of the world:

42% of Catholics live in countries with a gross domestic product (GDP) of $3000 plus
33% of Catholics live in countries with a GDP of $1000 to $3000
25% of Catholics live in countries with a GDP of less than $1000

Twenty-five percent of the world's population live where GDP is below $200. Yet these countries contain only 4% of the world's Catholic population. Thus the poorest nations are the least evangelised. The question that confronts contemporary Catholics is the one put to them by Paul VI in *Populorum progressio*: what are Catholics doing to set up a new international economic order? Evangelisation and justice are co-relatives.

On all sides it is evident that on the whole Christianity and certainly Catholicism contradicts what it says – it is not the poorest nations that are the most evangelised. What is more, from the poor nation's point of view, it is the rich Christian world that appears not only as the origin of domination and world exploitation, but also as the biggest obstacle to the achievement of greater international justice and to the defense of rights already acquired . . . Those same countries are responsible for the mad arms race, and the shameful exportation of arms, the financing of which involves colossal sums of money which are sorely needed for the betterment of the planet . . . Such a situation touches the very core of evangelisation. (Gabriel Marc)

Marc then turns to the statistics for clergy. The simple fact is that the Catholic Church faces a major crisis in the numbers of clergy available for ministry – if the present model of Church is to continue as the norm. It is not such a great crisis if the Church is opened to other ministries. In fact it may be the only way that these new ministries will get off the ground. Let us view the statistics in the light of the present clerical model:

Diocescan priests on	
1 January 1971	274,794
plus ordinations	29,581
minus deaths	33,447
minus departures	12,625
plus various	1,662
Diocescan priests on	
1 January 1978	259,965

Of course there are considerable variations from area to area and from country to country. In Africa and to a lesser extent in Latin America, the Philippines and Asia, the clergy are young and rates of ordination high. For a number of religious orders the fastest growing provinces are in the Third World. But Marc notes a serious decline in numbers elsewhere:

Elsewhere there is a gradual but considerable decrease in the number of priests. The situation is frankly catastrophic in Europe, where two generations of priests as they die or leave are being replaced by one generation. The average age of the clergy is the highest in the world, as also is the proportion of old priests to young . . . . in Belgium, Switzerland, France and the Netherlands, the average age of the clergy is 55 or over.

But the problem is not confined to Europe. The United States faces a similar decline in numbers and ageing. According to a report issued in 1982 by the Archdiocese of Boston, by 2000 there will be a 50% drop in the number of diocescan priests in the archdiocese. Total numbers will decline from 1031 (in 1982) to 818 (in 2000). Those under 65 years of age will decline from 950 in 1982 to 470 in 2000. So the reality is that the Church will be forced to be declericalised – there simply will not be enough priests to go around. Either more laity will have to become involved in full-time ministry, or the Church will have to begin to ordain married men. Either way, great changes will have to occur in the clerical structure. The statistics for Australia are discussed in chapter 7.

Dioceses and parishes are under great stress. Both these structures have deep roots in Church history. Dioceses continue the social and political organisation of the late Roman Empire and parishes continue the social and agricultural units of the early middle ages. The diocese was originally geared to an urban conception of Church (it was based on small urban units), the parish was geared to a rural social structure. They have been superimposed on each other. The original intention of both was to touch the local community at the base level.

The size of today's dioceses (and parishes) renders any sense of local unit meaningless. The average number of Catholics per diocese varies from place to place, and often great variation can be found within a country. In Australia, Sydney, the largest diocese, has 940,000 Catholics, and the smallest, Broome, has 5,238 Catholics. Melbourne has 873,000. The average number of Catholics per diocese is:

Africa	130,000
Oceania	90,000
Asia (except Philippines)	65,000
Europe	390,000
North America	240,000

| Latin America | 420,000 |
| Central America | 600,000 |

Thirty-five per cent of the world's Catholic population live in 131 dioceses. While most are in Europe, the largest is Mexico City with in excess of 7.5 million Catholics.

Thus bishops are often heads of enormous territorial and structural circumscriptions. In urban areas especially, the bishop is cut off from both priests and people. Dioceses of this size spend their whole time maintaining themselves. Most of them act like large bureaucracies and there is no way that the ordinary Catholic, or even the ordinary priest, can influence them. It is physically impossible for the bishop of a large diocese to interview all the people who wish to see him. In this system the bishop becomes a more and more remote figure, protected by a phalanx of secretaries. The monolithic dioceses have to be broken up. Some have already successfully tried schemes of division: Westminster (the greater London area north of the Thames) and Paris already have working schemes. Sydney has just been broken up into three separate dioceses. The ideal diocese would be one bishop for 15,000 to 30,000 Catholics with 15 to 18 priests and a number of lay leaders. This would mean 10 to 20 times the number of dioceses than the Church has at present. It would involve an increase from 2500 dioceses to about 25,000 dioceses. This may be an inefficient way of operating, but it would be more humane and more Christian.

Hilaire Belloc used to say 'Europe is the Faith and the Faith is Europe.' This view of the Church sounds today like extraordinary Euro-centric chauvinism. The European masses are said to be abandoning the Church in droves, and many see Europe becoming a place for re-evangelisation.

Contemporary men and women live with the paradox of a strong emphasis on personal rights, co-existing with a mass culture dominated by the media and manipulative governments. So many people today treasure anonymity and personal space. In this scale of values commitment to the Church is one of the optional extras. Many, of course, pay a terrible price for their individualism: loneliness, instability in relationships, the loss of a joie de vivre. Individualism requires an inner toughness and a clarity of mind. Francis Chichester sailing alone around the world, or the long distance jogger are the symbols of an individualist culture. But having said all this about individualism and its supposed consequences for religious practice, I still question whether religious commitment and practice in Europe are any less today than they were in the 19th century. Human beings have a great ability to idealise the past in order to criticise the present.

Until Vatican II the Dutch Church was very observant with a high rate of practice. Despite the smallness of its population the Netherlands produced more overseas missionary priests and sisters per capita than any other Church except Ireland. With typical Dutch thoroughness, the Netherlands embraced Vatican II seriously and radically. The Dutch bishops gave priests and people free rein. The results (widespread lay participation in the Church, calls for optional celibacy, questioning of papal authority and a decline in the rate of practice among Catholics) worried the Vatican, and Rome tried to bring the Dutch Church to heel by the appointment of a string of conservative bishops. The final move in the Vatican scenario was the summoning of the Dutch bishops to a synod in Rome in 1980. Conservative bishops and priests have now taken over the Dutch institutional Church, but at the cost of the alienation of large numbers of people. The recent papal visit to the Netherlands (1985) was marked not so much by protest as by people ignoring a hierarchical Pope who had no relevance to them.

In 1984 the total population of Holland was 14.2 million. The Catholic population was 5.7 million – or about 40%. There are seven dioceses – an unusually small number for the Catholic population. England has 21 dioceses for a Catholic population of about 6 million. It is the smallness of the Dutch hierarchy that has allowed it to be so easily subverted by Rome. In 1980 there were 3500 diocesan priests, a proportion of 1630 Catholics per priest. There are just on 300 full-time lay pastoral workers. Religious orders of both men and women face a disastrous situation. There is hardly anyone joining and the vast majority of religious are over 65.

Nevertheless the rate of practice is still more than 25% of all Catholics every Sunday. This compares favourably with France where the practice rate is 19%, Belgium where it is 20% and is about the same as Western Germany where it is less than 30%. Dutch Catholics are not passive spectators in the Church. They are willing to sing and read at Mass, to take communion to the sick, teach catechetics, work on the pastoral council and participate in work for peace and disarmament. Those who leave the official Church tend to commit themselves to work for nuclear disarmament, protection of the environment or they join organisations like Amnesty International. Younger people believe in Christ, but they feel little attachment to the official Church.

France is different from the Netherlands in that it has been recognised as 'pagan' for many years. The French Church is supposed to have lost the working classes during the 19th century, although historians today seriously question if the urban masses were ever really Catholic. In the 19th and early 20th centuries French Catholicism was middle class, anti-republican and reactionary. It was the experience of the German occupation and the Vichy regime that moved the Church more to the centre of the political spectrum. The worker-priest movement and Vatican II committed the French Church to social reform.

France today is an example of a country with priestless parishes. In 1977 Sunday-Assembly-in-Absence-of-a-Priest was held in 1100 parishes in France. The number of participants varied from 15 to 100. In these assemblies the community is led by a layman. The readings for the day are proclaimed, the lay leader gives a sermon and then communion is distributed. France has been losing priests at a steady rate. In 1947 there were 1649 ordinations; in 1979 there were 99! The total number of clergy has also sharply declined:

In 1913 there were 59,000 priests
In 1965 there were 41,000 priests
In 1985 there were less than 29,000 priests
In 2000 there will be about 16,000 priests

A 1985 survey found the French clergy to be politically slightly to the right, but 83% of priests were in favour of the ordination of married men and 36% approved the ordination of women. Another survey at the beginning of 1986 (carried out by Sofres for *La Croix*) found that 81% of the French population said that it was Catholic. Of these they were:

19% went to Mass at least once a week (a little higher than six years previously when it was 16%)
17% went occasionally to Mass
64% never went to Mass except for baptisms, weddings and funerals

Sixteen per cent of the population said they had no religion. The survey showed more women than men at Mass. Also executives and professional people as well as older people are more likely to be committed to the Church than manual workers and young people. The Church is still strong in rural areas. The survey did not take into account regional differences, which are very marked in France.

The finding that such a high proportion of priests approved of the ordination of married men is significant. It confronts those who continue to demand that celibacy be a pre-requisite for ordination with the question: are they changing the essential nature of the Church by denying the eucharist to an increasing number of communities because there is no ordained minister to celebrate it, *in order to 'protect' celibacy*? Thus the question arises: in this situation who are the radical innovators? It would seem to me that the innovators are those who deny whole communities access to the eucharist.

About 30% of all European Catholics practise their faith. There are differences, however, from country to country. Gabriel Marc says that in 1980 'The lowest, as far as available figures go, is that of France (16%), though in reality the lowest rate is probably that of Portugal.' He suggests that available information tends to indicate that the decline in religious practice is linked to modern urbanisation. He says bluntly:

At the present time a greater number of European countries is witnessing a real collapse of Catholicism, and a still more wide-spread collapse of Christianity. This confirms the feeling . . . that the future of Catholicism, in the medium term, lies elsewhere.

It is this reality that leads Pope John Paul II to suggest the need for re-evangelisation in Western Europe. He seems to envisage the disciplined Catholicism of Eastern Europe as a model for a Western European return to the faith.

What are the real choices for European Catholicism? It seems to me that there are three. The first is to drift with the prevailing mood and to hope for a religious revival. In this way the Church is not alienated from its social matrix. The second is to retire to the ghetto, to see the Church as a faithful remnant among the unfaithful masses. This choice would involve the Church in making a decision to stand over and against the world which is construed as essentially evil and opposed to Catholicism. This attitude has strong roots in Catholic history. It is the 'fundamentalist' solution.

The third choice is to try to discover new ways of being the Church. This means accepting the reality of the modern world with its stress on liberation, but at the same time looking for new ways to form ministerial communities. People who take this view tend to be Christian humanists, citizens of both worlds – the religious and the secular. Such people, however, are not naive; they are critical of many aspects of modern culture with its extreme emphasis on self-realisation. Human beings are born to be with others and politics and the effort to change society are part of being Christian. Linked to this is the development of a new spirituality in which the struggle for justice is linked to a serious commitment to living the radical call of the gospel. This group is still small in Europe.

The British Catholic Church is an exception in Europe. Its history and experience are quite different from the Church of the Continent. For 270 years the Catholic Church was a persecuted minority in England. The official proscription of Catholicism only ceased in 1829 with Emancipation. By then Catholics were only a tiny minority in the United Kingdom, with the exception of Ireland. Nowadays, there are between 5.5 and 6.5 million

Catholics in England and Wales (population about 49 million) and probably more than 800,000 Catholics in Scotland (total population 5 million). This means that there are more Catholics in the United Kingdom than in the Republic of Ireland (3.1 million). The practice rate of Catholics in England is about 40%.

The English Catholic community is formed from four main groups. The first group are the recusants, the old Catholics, those who remained faithful to the Church during the centuries of persecution, plus those who became converts during the penal period. The second group are the post-Emancipation converts. Big numbers came over to Rome in the wake of Newman's conversion in the 1840s. Some of the most important names in English Catholicism come from this group. The largest group by far, however, are the Irish. They began arriving from the end of the 18th century. Their descendants have come to dominate English Catholicism. During and after the Second World War a fourth group of immigrants arrived: West Indians (although many of these people had been in England since the end of the 18th century), Poles, Asians and migrant workers (from Spain and Italy). Thus the English Catholic community has very diversified origins.

The Church is especially strong among the middle class. It manifests considerable homogeneity within the general British community in terms of social and sexual morality. Most British Catholics nowadays enter a mixed marriage (as high as two-thirds of Catholic marriages in the 1970s were mixed). British Catholics are generally perceived as conservative by observers. This is not necessarily true. English liturgy tends to be stilted and seemingly traditional, but this does not accurately reflect the English Church.

British Catholics have been slow to accept the deeper changes flowing from Vatican II, but recent years have seen a shift in this. Central to this change of attitude was the National Pastoral Congress held in Liverpool in May 1980. Also there has been a shift in the composition of the English hierarchy. A series of more pastoral, open bishops have been appointed. The Church in Britain has inherited the strong English emphasis on civil rights. Amnesty International, for instance, was founded by an English Catholic lawyer, Peter Benenson. Monsignor Bruce Kent has been a national leader in the Campaign for Nuclear Disarmament.

Certainly, there are problems: there is evidence of division in the Catholic community along the lines of progressive/conservative. The progressives are the educated middle class – the type who appear in David Lodge's novels; the conservatives come from the entrepreneurial and commercial classes. There is a vocal minority of traditionalist Catholic followers of Archbishop Lefebvre. English Catholicism faces the usual pastoral problems of developed countries: divorce and subsequent remarriage of Catholics, the contraception and control of fertility question and the decline in the number of clergy.

In turning to the United States the first thing that strikes the observer is its sheer size and complexity. It is like visiting five or six countries rolled into one. The Catholic Church reflects the country. Its origins are very diverse: Irish, French Canadian, Italian, German, Slavic, Polish, Hispanic. Beginning as a Catholicism of the national ghettos, the Church now permeates the mainstream of American life. In many ways it seems to resemble Australian Catholicism – especially at the parish level. But this is only partly true.

It is a large Church. The Catholic population in 1981 was 51.2 million (the total population was 226.9 million). Catholicism is growing at the rate of about 1.5% per year. The only religion growing faster than Catholicism is the Assemblies of God. The Church is well organised, and has slowly but seriously begun the task of genuine community participation at both the parish and diocesan level. Generally Catholics are well educated. There is a significant minority of theologically informed Catholics who form the core of the leadership of the emerging lay elite. There has always been a stress on tertiary religious education in the United States through the Catholic college and university system. The predominant group within the Church are middle class and upwardly mobile. Catholics are no longer found in the ethnic neighbourhoods, but in the suburbs. The Church, however, has retained a commitment to the poor. It has been and continues to be a powerful voice for social reform and for care of the marginalised. The United States has no tradition of democratic socialism. By Australian standards, even the Democratic Party is well to the right. Both now and in the past the Church has fulfilled the role of spokesperson for the voiceless. This is especially true today as more and more welfare programmes are cut by the Reagan administration. The religious orders of sisters have sought new avenues of ministry to the increasing numbers of people who have slipped below the poverty line.

Foreign visitors often miss one of the most important demographic changes in the United States – the Hispanic influx. By the year 2000 the US will probably be a bilingual society. This already profoundly affects US Catholicism. According to 1980 figures there are at least 14.6 million Catholics of Hispanic background living in the US. While they are concentrated in certain areas of the south – southern California and Texas especially – they are also to be found all over the US. Clergy in most areas now need to be bilingual. A number of Hispanic bishops have been appointed and Hispanic married deacons have helped to bridge the gap between the official Church and the people. The charismatic movement has also helped Hispanics adjust to the dry, abstract Catholicism favoured by the Anglos – the descendants of the Irish, French, Germans and Eastern Europeans. Unfortunately, fundamentalist sects have made inroads into the Hispanic Catholic community.

Most US Catholics stand in the middle of the theological spectrum, but ideological polarisation has become something of a problem for the Church. This is especially true of the ideological right. There are a number of small but organised and very well funded groups who have taken it upon themselves to save the Church from the 'liberals' – in this case the liberals include most of the bishops and the United States Catholic Conference (the central organising body of the US Catholic Church). These reactionaries of the far right have attained an influence with Rome far out of proportion to their numbers. They write constant letters of protest and the Curia is bombarded with their publications. The situation has become so bad recently that the US bishops have had to consider the possibility of appointing a kind of delegation residing permanently in Rome to counter the propaganda of the far right. One of the funnels for the right into the Roman Curia is Cardinal Silvio Oddi, former Prefect of the Congregation of the Clergy. The main newspapers of the far right are the *Wanderer* and the *National Catholic Register*. There are various groups, of which the most important is Catholics United for the Faith (they are known in the US as 'Cuffers'). They carry on a constant guerilla war against the renewal of the Church.

Working in United States parishes one has the impression that a significant minority of lay people are really involved in the Church. The preliminary report of a major study of US Catholic parishes being carried out by Notre Dame University bears this out. Forty per cent of those who attend Mass are involved in one or more parochial activity. The Catholic Church in the US faces the paradox of both growth and decline at the same time. A large growth in numbers continues to characterise US Catholicism, but there has been a drastic decline in the number of professional ministers – priests, sisters, brothers. Yet to replace this decline there has been an enormous growth in lay ministries. As the effects of the structural changes in US Catholicism begin to effect a growing group of people, there is an increasing development of parish councils and a wide variety of consultative bodies. The period since the Council has also seen the growth of team ministries with priests, religious and laity working together.

The picture is that of a Church in transition. Symptomatic of this change are the bishops. The days of the prince bishops – men like Spellman, Cushing and Cody – are over and gone. John Krol, Cardinal of Philadelphia, is the last survivor of this species. In the smaller dioceses one finds excellent pastoral bishops, many of them appointed when Archbishop Jean Jardot was Apostolic Delegate in Washington. Often the bishops are the meat in the sandwich between the expectations of the people and the demands of Rome. Many US bishops have been confronted with difficult pastoral situations. As a body they have not backed away from hard issues as the pastoral letter *The Challenge of Peace* has shown.

As early as 1919 they published a pastoral letter *Problems of*

Social Reconstruction which dealt with the situation of workers and the need for a living wage in the period after the First World War. Even then they were accused of being dupes of socialist unionists and anti-capitalist. A current pastoral on the economy is passing through the same process of consultation as the peace pastoral. The bishops are sincerely trying to consult the Church. The process is almost as important as the result.

The bishops know that mainstream Catholics are steadily climbing the socio-economic ladder. So they warn: ' . . . as many Catholics achieve greater economic prosperity' they will be tempted 'to forget the powerless and the stranger in our midst.' They insist that all members of the human family have an equal right to share the goods of the earth. The bishops speak of 'the sins of indifference and greed . . . embedded in certain economic and cultural presuppositions of our society.' But the proposed pastoral does not remain at the level of theory. Its policy applications call for full employment, the 'rejection of our punitive attitude toward the poor', the development of a more consultative and co-operative spirit, especially from the management of large corporations. It categorically rejects the policy of the US government which links US economic assistance to national security interests. The bishops are critical of Church institutions that have failed to introduce a just wages policy or who refuse to permit the formation of labour unions.

One of the central concerns of the US bishops has been the attitude of the Reagan administration to Central America. The Church has consistently called for a non-interventionist and non-military policy. The US Church has been constantly better informed on events in Latin America than the US government. It is the most important area of the world for the future of Catholicism. It is there that the majority of Catholics live.

At the present moment there is a massive struggle going on for the soul of Latin American Catholicism. It is a struggle that epitomises what is happening through Catholicism. It concerns what Catholicism in the contemporary world is all about.

Until the pontificate of Pius XII (1940-1958) Latin America was considered politically backward and unstable. Pius XII sent many foreign missionaries in the 1950s to lift it out of 'ignorance and superstition'. Even then it was realised how profoundly Catholic Latin America was. Over the last 20 years the sub-continent has passed through a profound revolution and Catholicism has been at the centre of it. Latin America is still politically unstable and economically exploited. Military juntas and 'the doctrine of national security' are in decline but are still powerful. The faith of the people has been and is being tested through upheaval and often physical persecution.

Three events are pivotal in the contemporary history of Latin American Catholicism: the formation of CELAM (the Latin American Bishops Conference) and CLAR (the Latin American Conference of Religious Orders); the Second Vatican Council; and the CELAM Conference at Medellin, Colombia, in 1968. These events have brought Latin American Catholicism from the backwaters of the world Church to the forefront.

Latin American Catholicism was founded in the wake of Spanish and Portuguese imperialism in the 16th and 17th centuries. The great native American (Indian) cultures were quickly conquered and either destroyed or driven underground. The culture of Latin America today is a Latino-Indian mix (only about 12% are pure native American). Traditionally there has been a strong link between the Church, the State and the wealthy power-brokers. Latin American countries are usually dominated by small land-owning oligarchies, supported by politicians and the military. In contemporary Latin America the military have emerged as more and more powerful. Also the influence of multinational corporations, mainly of US origin, is significant. Most countries in the region are hopelessly in debt to foreign banks. Countries like Brazil, Argentina and Mexico are unable to pay the interest on their loans. This places enormous pressure on governments and standards of living are dropped in order to repay loans to foreign lenders. Thus people already experiencing deprivation find their standards of living dropping even further.

Traditionally Catholicism was characterised by mass baptisms with little or no formation in faith. Religious expression centred around festivals and public displays – what religious sociologists call popular religion. There are strong non-Christian folk elements in this. The institutional Church was very clericalised and it strongly supported the authority of the wealthy oligarchies. The turning point in the Church's attitude was the Medellin Conference. The conference committed the Church to a 'global, daring, urgent and basically renewing change . . . a thirst for complete emancipation, liberation from every subjection . . . and social solidarity.' But in typical hierarchical fashion, the bishops saw themselves as the leaders of this process of liberation.

The Conference was attended by Pope Paul VI. The bishops at Medellin placed the blame for social and economic injustice squarely on the shoulders of the rich, those with ' . . . the greater share of wealth, culture and power', those who ' . . . jealously retain their privileges, thus provoking explosive revolutions of despair.' The Conference marked a profound change in the attitude of the ministerial elite of the Church, and placed them in direct confrontation with the wealthy power-brokers and their military henchmen. Behind the local autocrats stood the economic interests of the United States. The Church set out on a collision course with powerful vested interests.

Even before Medellin a process had already begun which was to take this call for liberation and apply it to practical life. The 1960s and 1970s saw most Latin American countries controlled by vicious military dictatorships. These governments claimed to be protecting their countries from communism. Using the doctrine of national security these neofascist regimes tried to destroy all intermediate structures between the State and individual – structures like trade unions, political parties and student organisations. Anyone who opposed the regime was a subversive, and when captured, was summarily dealt with. The lists of those who had 'disappeared' grew. The Church remained as one of the few mediating structures. Poor people began to form small clusters to try to protect themselves – small clusters of 15 to 20 neighbouring families. Neighbourhood ties are very strong in Latin America through god-parenting. A new educational method was evolved from the theories of the Brazilian educationalist, Paulo

Freire, which aimed at 'conscientising' people – that is making them aware of their oppression and of the strength they would have if they worked together. All of this happened under the aegis of the Church. Thus before Medellin the *communidad de base* (grassroots community) was already a reality.

After Medellin the base communities began to develop their own leadership. Their growth and vitality is amazing. Today there are probably more than 80,000 in Brazil alone with as many, if not more, spread throughout the rest of Latin America. It is from this matrix that liberation theology has emerged. It needs to be emphasised right from the beginning: liberation theology is the *product of the experiences of the base communities*. Peruvian theologian, Father Gustavo Gutierrez, explains liberation theology this way:

Its two basic themes . . . are poverty and the approach to theologising. The first element is the viewpoint of the poor; and for that we have to make a commitment to the poor, to identify with their life, their sufferings, their struggles, their hopes. Theology follows as a reflection that presupposes the earlier act of commitment. The distinction between these two acts is not simply methodological; it is the key idea in a life style, a spirituality. (*Concilium*, 96, 1974)

Father Leonardo Boff describes the new reality as something that comes from the heart of the people themselves guided by the power of God's Spirit.

What has emerged is a living Church based on local communities. Liberation theology – which is really a whole new way of doing theology – is based on the experience of the poor. The methodology works through a series of steps:
• People experience the reality of oppression.
• Through conscientisation, they become aware that they are being oppressed.
• This consciousness leads them to analyse their experience in interaction with small groups of other people.
• Because they are Catholics the analysis is reflected on in the light of scripture and their experience as a Christian community.
• In the light of this Christian discernment, the people decide on

community action. Often the action is designed to fulfill very practical human needs.

It is interesting to note that this methodology has much in common with Joseph Cardijn's Young Christian Worker process: see reality, judge it in the light of scripture and community discernment; act to make Christian service real in the world. The key words for liberation theology are liberation and participation. The word liberation refers to the biblical sense of physical and spiritual salvation, with strong emphasis on the theme of the Exodus from slavery in Egypt. Participation refers to people gaining control of their own lives and working in community to bring about change.

It is important to understand the process of liberation theology because once understood you realise how false the accusations of it being Marxist are. Remember that liberation theology is a way of doing theology, rather than a specific theological interpretation of revelation. Experience is its starting point. This is in contrast to the old way of doing theology which began with dogma or Church teaching. Liberation theology proceeds from experience to prayer, reflection and worship and from there to belief. Theology is reflection on that belief. In the old system belief flows straight from dogma. In both cases belief leads directly to ministry. As Saint Paul said, 'I believed, therefore I spoke' (II Corinthians 2:14).

There are two forces utterly opposed to liberation theology, base community and the whole renewal of the Latin American Church. The first is obvious: the powerful, the wealthy, the military, US interests and the multinationals all oppose either overtly or covertly the movement for renewal. Either by force or political pressure they have tried to destroy the struggle for liberation. Many base community members as well as priests, sisters and even bishops have paid with their lives for their commitment to the poor.

The power-brokers and the oppressors have ecclesiastical allies. Many Latin American bishops did not accept Medellin. The hierarchy of Colombia, for instance, was utterly opposed to the conference documents. As host hierarchy, that was rather ironical. By 1972 CELAM had been taken over by a reactionary Secretary General, Bishop (now Cardinal) Alfonso Lopez Trujillo. He is a hard-nosed business executive type who has taken over the machinery of the Bishops Conference. He has been assisted by the Belgian Jesuit, Father Roger Vekemans, a fanatical anti-communist. Vekemans has been bankrolled by right-wing foundations in the United States and Europe. Lopez Trujillo and Vekemans have focused their attack on the theology of liberation which they present as subversive of both Church and State. They suggest that the Church close ranks against the communist threat and avoid internal conflicts. They focus their attacks on clergy construed as left-wing or progressive and try to link them with the promotion of marxist ideology.

Lopez Trujillo, Vekemans and their allies have succeeded to a considerable extent. They have played on John Paul II's hatred of communism by linking progressive clergy with marxism. Obviously there are marxist overtones in liberation theology. No one involved in commenting on social structure can avoid using marxist concepts. John Paul II himself uses marxist ideas such as class conflict, alienated work, work as self-realisation in his encyclical *Laborem exercens (On Human Work)*. No one could call John Paul a marxist! So the use of this terminology cannot be avoided, especially when describing a situation of oppression, such as in Latin America.

Lopez Trujillo tried to subvert the CELAM Conference at Puebla, Mexico, in January 1979. John Paul II made his first overseas trip to attend this Conference. The liberals among the Latin American bishops, led largely by the Brazilian hierarchy, defeated moves to condemn liberation theology and the base community Church. It was at this Conference that John Paul seems to have changed his mind about liberation theology. He arrived intending to condemn it, but the bishops got to him and persuaded him that this would be a disastrous policy. Lopez Trujillo was not successful, but the Vatican learned a lesson on this trip. They now make sure that everything is well prepared in advance and that the Pope never has time to listen to the local people. The anti-liberation theology interests have succeeded in a number of countries in having conservative bishops appointed. Peru is an example. A series of progressive bishops (a couple of whom have died in strange 'accidents') have been replaced by members of the integralist and reactionary organisation Opus Dei, creating a real division in the Peruvian hierarchy.

The Peruvian theologian, Father Gustavo Gutierrez, has been denounced to Rome for 'reductionism' and 'horizontalism', that is of stripping away the 'vertical' dimensions of the gospel and reducing it to 'mere' interpersonal relationships. Gutierrez is said to have advocated a 'people's Church' in conflict with the hierarchical Church. Franciscan Father Leonardo Boff of Brazil has been in trouble for similar ideas. He has been dismissed from his teaching post and silenced by Rome after he had given the Congregation for the Doctrine of the Faith a satisfactory explanation of his views and had been defended by the Brazilian hierarchy. So much for Rome taking any notice of the views of the local bishops! Lopez Trujillo has a strong supporter in Cardinal Ratzinger of the Congregation for the Doctrine of the Faith.

This Congregation issued an *Instruction* about 'certain aspects' of liberation theology (6 August 1984). The *Instruction* admits that Latin America experiences 'shocking inequality', 'crushing poverty' and 'the seizure of the vast majority of wealth by an oligarchy of powers bereft of social consciousness.' But the *Instruction* still manages to accuse liberation theology of using 'concepts borrowed from various currents of marxist thought.' Boff was 'silenced' for a year after this instruction was issued. At present the issue is at a stalemate, but Rome seems determined to clip the wings of the liberation theologians. Marxism notwithstanding, the main reason for the Roman attack on liberation theology is the fear of the development of a base level Church which Rome does not directly control. As in so many other issues, the question is not one of orthodoxy but of power.

Latin America faces several other problems. Firstly, the clergy are still 50% foreign with no possibility of replacement. Fortunately, local seminaries are gaining students now, but serious questions are being asked about the institutional nature of the training and the intellectual and personal quality of the candidates. Thus there is still a terrible shortage of priests. Between 1969 and 1979 more than 200 priests per year left the ministry, and these were often the best educated and the most committed. Thus there is a radical lack of pastoring of the people and in many areas there are big losses to the fundamentalist sects. These are pouring money and personnel into Latin America, most of it coming from the United States. These sects, which are uncommitted to social reform, have become a serious problem in countries like Guatemala, where one of the recent military dictators was a born-again Christian. Catholic lay leaders have certainly emerged in Latin America, but they cannot be ordained because they are married. Here again is an example of large numbers of people deprived of the sacraments and leadership and left prey to fundamentalist missionaries in order to protect the law of celibacy.

But renewal in Latin America is not finished. Base communities and the theology of liberation are too deeply rooted for that. So many people have paid the ultimate price for justice and liberation – they have paid with their blood. 'The blood of martyrs is the seed of Christians.' Latin America will be the source of living Catholicism for a long time to come.

Africa, like Australia, is a very ancient continent. North Africa was a cradle of both civilisation and Christianity. All of north Africa was Christian from the late Roman Empire to the Arabic invasions of the 7th century. Nowadays only the Copts of Egypt and Ethiopia have managed to remain Christian. From the late 19th century onwards the Europeans pushed increasingly into sub-Saharan Africa. Christian missions followed in their wake. Africa had been superficially known to Europeans since the 16th century when over 30 million Africans were exported as slaves to North and South America.

The great period of growth for the African Church was from 1952 to 1972. This was also the major period of decolonisation. During that period Catholics increased in numbers from 12.5 million to 36 million. The number of local priests grew from 1400 to over 4200, and the local bishops from 2 to 147. It is estimated that by 2000 57% of sub-Saharan Africa will be Christian. The success of the local Church is due to schools and education, the deep religious predisposition of the African people and the fact that religion has penetrated the whole of social life.

While it is hard to generalise about the issues facing the African Church, certain problems seem common to most African countries. Tribalism and chronic political and economic instability are key issues. Another more specifically religious one is the integration of African culture in the liturgy, in morality, philosophy and theology and in marriage and religious customs. For instance, how much can the liturgy be 'Africanised'? How are Christian doctrines to be expressed in terms of African thought patterns and philosophy? Many other observers are concerned about the development of an African clericalism which develops from the feudal nature of African society. Another question concerns the role of women. Many women join religious orders to escape oppressive clan and tribal structures. An external threat comes from missionary Islam pushing down from north Africa. It is hard to assess this Islamic movement and what threat it poses to sub-Sahara Africa. Despite all these problems, the Church in Africa seems set for an optimistic future.

The statistics quoted earlier in this chapter have shown that Asia is the priority area for evangelisation. The Catholic population of 56 million constitutes only a small portion of the Asian population. If the Philippines, with 30 million Catholics, were excluded from this, Asian Catholicism would make up less than one per cent of the whole area's population. Yet Asia is very religious. Most of the great religions of the world find their origin there: Hinduism, Buddhism, Confucianism. The Church has been present in Asia for 400 years, but has never really penetrated the culture. There was a failure to follow the example of the great Jesuit pioneer missionaries Matteo Ricci and Roberto di Nobili, who claimed that Christianity must enter into the great cultures of Asia and express the Christian faith in terms of those cultures. They were asking for 'inculturation' the the 17th century. Due largely to the failure of subsequent missionaries to follow the example of these men, the Church has had little or no success in

Asia, except in the Philippines and later in southern India.

Where the Church does exist today it is still partly introverted, lacking in courage and dynamism. India, for instance, has a surplus of priests, but it does not use them as missionaries in India but exports them to other countries. Asian religiosity is still largely European and old-worldly. But some very good signs have been emerging over the last decade. Asia has a very active and creative Federation of Bishops Conferences. Turning to specific countries: the Church in South Korea is growing very fast and it is deeply socially committed. Opposition to the military government is based to a considerable extent in the Churches, which have made strong stands to support the poor, the exploited and the politically disenfranchised.

The Church in India is still small in numbers, but it is well known. India's population in 1985 was about 700 million. There are 14 million Catholics. In 2000 India may well have a population of 1000 million, so population control is a key issue. Here Church and State are in conflict. The Church is only a tiny drop in the ocean of Hindus, Muslims, Sikhs, Buddhists, Jains and Parsis. If the Church is really to take root in India, it has to become less Western and more Indian. Some Indian gestures have been incorporated into the liturgy, but these are relatively superficial. True inculturation will mean that the cultural and religious pattern of the nation be absorbed. In other words the Church will have to integrate Indian categories of thinking, symbolism, rites and social practices. It will have to do what the Jesuit pioneers suggested 400 years ago.

India, like other developing countries, presents the Church with a dilemma: is its task to convert and baptise, or is it to concentrate on development programmes and work for the liberation of the poor – in other words to develop an Indian liberation theology? Many Indian religious are becoming impatient with the traditional approach of setting up elite schools and colleges. It was precisely disquiet with this ministerial approach that led Mother Teresa to leave the Loreto order and to set up the Missionaries of Charity. In India the Church also faces hostility from militant Hindus who claim that Catholics and Muslims blatantly poach lower caste and tribal Hindus. Many critics think that the Church must emphasise its contemplative tradition in India, especially because they feel that the emphasis on education has failed.

The position of Catholicism in the People's Republic of China has been extremely difficult since the early 1950s. All foreign missionaries were expelled and a section of the Chinese Church was forced into schism by the fact that they ordained bishops without Rome's permission. Since the accession to power of Deng Xiaoping, the position of the Churches has improved and religious life has begun to return to normal in China. Churches are being reopened and the training of clergy has begun again. A number of Catholic bishops, including Archbishop Henry D'Souza, Secretary of the Federation of Asian Bishops Conferences, Bishop Wu of Hong Kong and Cardinal Jamie Sin of Manila have visited China. Contacts have been made with Patriotic Catholics – those forced into schism. Rome now seems willing to negotiate with the patriotic bishops. All the signs are that the Chinese government is prepared to allow Christians to participate in their programme of modernisation. The signs are hopeful that China will once again open its doors to Christianity. One can only hope that the Church does not repeat the mistakes of the past as it begins its ministry in China again.

Finally, just a few words about the Pacific. The area is vast, the population is small. The small Pacific nations are almost 100% Christian now. The Pacific is about 63% Protestant and 37% Catholic. From the early 19th century the Boston Missionary Society and the London Missionary Society were very active in the Pacific. Catholicism came in the 1830s with the French Marist Fathers. Most Pacific nations are very small (Nauru, for instance, has a population of 7200). Their economies are under-developed. The backbone of the Church is increasingly the lay catechists. The level of development is similar to that in Africa and the issues are much the same – except that the Pacific has so far been less exploited by the imperialist powers and the structure of traditional society and community is still largely in place.

At the end of this survey one can only conclude that the

Catholic Church is in reasonable health throughout the world. Slowly it is beginning to face up to the mammoth task ahead: the deeper development of the local Churches that really belong to the culture in which they exist. Here again Catholicism is called to real creativity.

6
THE POLISH POPE

For many Catholics the present Pope is a problematic leader. They are pleased with his charismatic style, his importance on the world stage, his articulation of moral principles in international relationships, his call for respect for the rights of the individual and his unhesitating proclamation of Jesus Christ as Lord and Saviour. Then confusion sets in: within the Church human rights and conscience are ignored and even abused. The theological and ecclesiological teaching of Vatican II seems forgotten or is interpreted in a narrow and legalistic sense. The influence on the Roman Curia of small minorities of right-wing conservatives from the Anglo-American and European world and the pervasive presence of the integralist organisation, Opus Dei (especially in the Latin world) cause real concern to many serious and committed Catholics. Further confusion is caused by John Paul's apparently personalist rhetoric which seems to overlay a rigid neo-scholastic ideology.

He is deeply influenced by his Polish background. While this may be admirable, it is quite out of touch with the experience of Catholics from the rest of the world. His clear determination to reshape the Church in the light of his own insights simply increases tensions latent in the post-Vatican II period. He may well bring these tensions to boiling point.

Since the late 19th century there has been a real but unspoken 'taboo' about assessing, let alone criticising, living Popes. Dead Popes are fair game, but living ones are untouchable. This was broken down to a certain extent under Pope Paul VI, and increasingly many serious and committed Catholics are being forced into a critical stance as the papacy of Pope John Paul II unfolds. Part of the problem has already been mentioned: Pope Wojtyla comes from an unusual background and one that is not well understood in the West. Thus, to an extent, we are to blame. Eastern Catholics have been too long neglected. But the reciprocal is also true. The Pope does not seem to understand the wider Church whose leadership he has assumed. He is no longer a Polish bishop dealing with the specifics of a Church under a form of seige. This may be the only model of Church that he has experienced, but its very peculiarity means that it is not universally applicable. Given the important position of the Pope in the Church, Western Catholics cannot ignore the background and views of John Paul II.

Poland is the exceptional country in Eastern Europe. As a Slavic nation its cultural roots have much in common with those of Russia, but it has always seen itself as more Western. Polish Christianity originated in the East with the Byzantine Saints Cyril and Methodius, but the Polish Church has remained Western and Roman, while most of the Slavs are Eastern and Orthodox. Through the Roman Church, Poland has forged strong cultural links with the West. Yet Poland is in the difficult position of being wedged between two powerful countries – Germany and Russia. Roman Catholicism has become part of the national identity as Poles try to define themselves in close proximity to two such powerful cultures. Membership of the Catholic Church gives Poland a reference point outside itself and its two dominant neighbours, and it helps Poles define themselves over and against the nation most likely to rule and absorb them – Russia. Thus Catholicism is a pivotal reality for Poland and it forms an integral element of the national consciousness. The Church played a similar role in Ireland. The Irish people, conscious of their cultural identity but deprived of political freedom, struggled to define themselves over and against the English. Catholicism was an integral part of the Irish national definition. The experience of oppression often leads a nation to a never-ending search for the essence of national identity.

Between 1772 and 1795 Poland, as a political entity, was divided between Russia, Prussia and Austria, placing almost half the country under the dominance of German culture. This political division lasted until the end of the First World War. During the period of romantic nationalism in the 19th century, Poles became profoundly aware of their identity. This was a time of revolt, especially against Russia. Because Poland did not exist as a political unit, Poles learned to distinguish between the nation as a cultural entity and as a political unit. Cultural identity became the important motif. Between 1918 and 1939 Poland existed as an independent republic with its own government. Since 1939 it has experienced the vicissitudes of another German occupation (1939-1945) and after 1945 the imposition of Soviet communism. Poles have had to learn to distinguish again between the nation and the political entity.

The homeland of John Paul II is in south central Poland. This part of the country was occupied by the Austro-Hungarian Empire until 1918 and Karol Wojtyla's father served as an officer in the army of Austria-Hungary. Thus 'Polishness' was overlaid by the paternalistic German culture of the Hapsburg Empire. The future Bishop of Rome was born in the small town of Wadowice in 1922. His Polishness is obvious to the most superficial observer; his features are archetypically Slavic. But the German element in his background is often missed. His mother, Emilia, was from Silesia and Wojtyla grew up speaking German as a second language. His second doctoral thesis was a study of the German phenomenologist philosopher, Max Scheler. There is good evidence that it was the Austrian cardinal, Franziskus Keonig of Vienna who rallied the non-Italian cardinals to the support of Wojtyla in the conclave of 1978. The German cardinal Josef Ratzinger has become increasingly important in John Paul's papacy.

Pope Wojtyla views himself today as a European and not just

as a Pole. He believes strongly that Slavs are Europeans. Since the division of Europe in 1945 into Eastern and Western blocs, the term Europe in Western minds has become co-terminous with western and south-western Europe. We may still use the term Eastern Europe, but the tacit assumption is that it is not really Europe. I have already stressed that Poland has remained strongly *Roman* Catholic, even when the papacy was willing to undercut and abandon Poland for political advantage. Poles see themselves as Europeans. They have even cast themselves in the role of saviours of Europe. This is a strong influence on John Paul; he is aggressively European. For centuries Rome has neglected and misunderstood Poland specifically and Eastern European Catholics generally. They have been largely ignored in the mainstream concerns of Western European Catholicism. Peter Hebblethwaite perceptively comments that ' . . . anyone who wishes to understand him [Wojtyla] must . . . understand the historical resentments which haunt him.'

This pan-European sense leads the Pope to a very different evaluation of politics from that of the Anglo-Saxon tradition. Wojtyla does not really believe in frontiers or states in the political or nationalistic sense, but in nations and peoples. Church, language and culture are the adhesive forces that hold a people together. This is why John Paul is much more interested in the people as a collective, than in rulers, politicians or conventional political processes. One might remark in passing that this is a rather Marxist view! In Anglo-American terms he is essentially a populist. This explains the importance of enormous crowds to the Pope. His aim is to become the leader of the common people, to speak to them, to reach them over the heads of the conventional political leadership. It is the people who are the permanent reality, not the politicians. While his message to them might be Christian, there is a dangerous element of demagoguery in this approach.

George H. Williams has distinguished several key cultural components in the psychological makeup of Pope Wojtyla. The first is the bond between Church and nation. Anglo-Americans have very clear ideas about the separation of Church and State. The disentangling of the two has been a long historical process for us. But in the action of separating Church and State a deeper dislocation has unconsciously occurred: the separation of Church and culture. Western Catholics do not see the Church in the role of guardian of culture or feel that it must maintain European cultural traditions. Because of its universality, the Catholic Church must be multicultural in the fullest sense. Wojtyla sees things differently: Church, nation and culture are inextricably interconnected, and it is from this matrix that human values arise. But the insularity of his culture and the importance of the European tradition for him unconsciously bring him to the conclusion that his cultural and human values are normative for all. While he plays at being an international and multicultural person, he is quintessentially Polish and European. His views are more medieval than modern. He identifies religion (with culture as an inseparable element) and nation as being the essence of national identity. For John Paul the State in a political sense is something quite separate, a reality that comes and goes and is not fundamentally important. In this view, day-to-day politics lose significance. The role of the Church is to preserve nation and culture. These realities transcend particular governmental forms. Church and culture are sacred entities which impregnate every aspect of life. Politics are merely the pragmatics of government and are therefore secular. This is the main reason why he insists that priests should stay out of politics for their vocation is to the realm of the sacred.

Another aspect of Polishness mentioned by Williams is what he calls 'Polish messianism'. Nineteenth century pan-Slavism was often expressed in visions of spiritual salvation emerging from the East to save the corrupt West. Polish poets have pictured Poland in terms of the suffering servant of Isaiah, the messiah whose victorious parousia will come. In this quasi-biblical vision Poland, after being tested by suffering will be, like Christ, the source of salvation for the West. This theme – which has a parallel in the Russian literature of the 19th century – is expressed by the romantic poets Adam Mickiewicz (1798-1855), Juliusz Slowacki (1809-1849) and Zygmunt Krasinski (1812-1859). This messianic trait identified the partition of Poland with the crucifixion of Christ. Wojtyla's favourite poet, Cyprian Norwid (1821-1883) stressed the redemptive value of suffering for others as part of Poland's role in history. Certainly, Wojtyla has strong messianic conceptions of the papacy and of himself in the papal role. Polish messianism even foreshadowed a 'Polish Pope':

Behold the Slavic Pope is coming,

A brother of the people.

Here the word 'brother' suggests ' . . . the brother of all the common people or the working class and the peasants' (Williams). Such a reference would not be lost on Eastern European workers oppressed by their own government and by the power of the Soviet Union.

Another component in Polishness is devotion to the Blessed Virgin Mary at the shrine of Czestochowa. The object of veneration is a Byzantine icon. Our Lady of Czestochowa is seen both as patroness and protector of Poland. While devotion to Mary is, of course, a characteristic of Catholicism, in Poland this has been integrated into the national myth and national consciousness. Perhaps for Wojtyla it fulfils as much a personal as a national need. His mother died when he was very young and there is a seeming lack of any strong feminine figure in his background. Like many celibate males he seems to have replaced the real earthly person with the projected motherhood of the Church and that of Our Lady. Some celibate men fail to pass through the process of separation from the mother. The symbol of Mary becomes a surrogate, for she is both mother and virgin. She replaces the lost human mother, and as virgin, she is inaccessible and pure. She is the woman who never confronts the celibate man's sexuality.

I will turn now to the contemporary Polish Church. There is a general impression throughout the West that Poland is a paragon of commitment to Christian values and to Catholic practice. This myth contains elements of truth, but like all such impressions it is an inaccurate oversimplification. The Church in Poland is insular both theologically and ministerially. Church life centres around the parish where the priest is a dominant paternalistic

figure. The laity play no part in the ministerial life of the Church.
Attendance at Sunday Mass seems to be little better than in Australia or the United States: it is 31.5% of all Catholics in urban
districts and 57% in rural districts (M. Pomian-Srzednicki: *Religious Change in Contemporary Poland: Secularisation and
Politics*, 1982, p 126). Western television usually only reports the
crowds at pilgrimages and at large celebrations. Very few people
receive communion at Sunday Mass and the liberty with which
Western Catholics approach the eucharist is regarded in Poland
as a scandalous loss of the sense of unworthiness and sin. The
widespread use of contraception in Poland keeps many people
from receiving the eucharist.

Statistics usually do not prove a great deal about commitment
to faith, but they do assist in forming an overall picture. The
United States Catholic Church is often compared unfavourably
to the Church of Poland in terms of vocations to priesthood and
religious life, but the statistics tell a different story:

	United States	*Poland*
Catholic population	51,207,000 (1983)	35,000,000 (1981)
Priests (diocesan and religious)	58,040 (1983) (i.e. 1/882 Caths)	20,234 (1981) (i.e. 1/1750 Caths)
Religious sisters and brothers	129,250 (1983)	26,745 (1980)
Deacons	5,886 (1982)	nil
Seminarians	11,600 (early 1980s)	6,285 (1980)

(Statistics for the US are based on D. Liptak: 'Emerging Trends and Statis-
tics Regarding the Present American and US Catholic Setting'. Research
Paper. CARA. Polish statistics are based on T. Beeson: *Discretion and
Valour*, 1982, pp 156-157.)

This type of comparison cannot, of course, be pushed too far,
but it does indicate the inaccuracy and superficiality of charac-
terising Poland as the archetypical Catholic country. Often the
Church in the West is doing better than it thinks!

The Polish Church tends to reflect a conservative and non-innovative approach to speculative theology. This is significant, for Pope John Paul II sees himself as an important theologian. Contemporary Polish poet Czeslaw Milosz comments: 'After Poland had disintegrated as a country and a wounded nationalism made its appearance, the notions of Pole and Catholic came to be equated . . . when the line between national and religious behaviour is erased, religion changes into a social power and becomes conservative and conformist.' The struggle for survival tends to obliterate individual differences and the importance of authority (in this case episcopal authority) is emphasised. Priests, for instance, do not engage in public contestation with bishops nor bishops with each other, for this means discord and division. Dissent is a danger in the life and death struggle with the State. Uniformity is imposed.

Yet the laity have achieved a certain deviance of their own and not all toe the line, especially in moral matters. There are about one million abortions performed annually and contraception is widespread. Divorce and alcoholism are other major problems yet there are few pastoral solutions offered. Just under the surface there is a strong anti-clericalism. Despite the patronage of the Pope, the trade union Solidarity is as much a threat to the power of the Church as it is a threat to the State. It is an independent organisation of laypersons and lower clergy and it has emerged as a potential third force in Polish politics. It is as much to the advantage of the Church to limit the power of Solidarity as it is to the State.

Wadowice, where Karol Wojtyla was born, is only 30 kilometres from Auschwitz (Oswięcim in Polish) and 100 kilometres from Czestochowa. Here geography creates profound formative influences. No one could grow up so close to Auschwitz and not be touched by this 'Golgotha of the modern world' (John Paul II). In the context of this monstrosity there are no answers for Wojtyla but spiritual ones. It was here that Saint Maximilian Kolbe died giving his life to save that of a married man with a family. In Auschwitz the evil was gigantic, cosmic. Only spirituality can set it in perspective and transform it. Wojtyla has come to see existence as a cosmic struggle and in the light of this 'the liberal agenda [for the Church] pales into insignificance' (Peter Hebblethwaite). This, of course, conjures up Slav apocalypticism. Yet without trivialising the evil, there is another way of seeing this reality and it is suggested in Thomas Keneally's fine book *Schindler's Ark* (1982). Oskar Schindler was no saint, but it was due to his courage and shrewd, passionate determination that the lives of several thousand Jews were saved in and around Krakow at the very time when Wojtyla was studying in the underground seminary of the city. It is not just a matter of contemplating evil in its cosmic proportions, but of doing something about it as Oskar Schindler did.

Karol Wojtyla's father was a retired Austrian army lieutenant who lived on a small pension. Karol's mother Emilia died in childbirth when Karol was nine. His brother Edmund died as a medical student when Karol was thirteen. He was educated in the State primary and high schools in Wadowice. He was a good sport and an accomplished actor. In fact acting was to be an important part of his formative years and he seems to have contemplated entering the theatre professionally. The Polish romantic poets influenced him as a young man and he delighted in reciting them, especially Adam Mickiewicz' *Pan Tadeusz: The Last Foray in Lithuania.* He quoted *Pan Tadeusz* in his inaugural speech after his election to the papacy:

O Holy Maid, who Czestochowa's shrine
Dost guard and on the pointed gateway shine . . .
As thou didst heal me by a miracle . . .
So by a miracle thou'lt bring us home.

The relationship between father and son was very close although the father was a disciplinarian. In 1938 they moved to Krakow. Here they lived poorly. In this same year Wojtyla entered the historical Jagiellonian University to study Polish language and literature. He joined the Polish language society and the theatrical confraternity.

On 1 September 1939 Nazi Germany invaded Poland and a vicious and brutal occupation began. The persecution of the Jews is well known. Less well known is the treatment of the Polish people themselves. A third of the population died between 1939 and 1945. Nazi terror was directed especially against intellectuals and clergy, the aim being to eliminate any form of Polish leadership elite. With the closing of the universities and high schools, underground networks of students began to operate. Wojtyla continued his studies in secret in Polish philology and wrote poetry. Studio 39, an underground rhapsodic theatre was formed and Wojtyla participated in a number of plays. He became deeply influenced by the poetry of Cyprian Norwid who stressed the themes of both death and resurrection.

For some time the future Pope worked as a labourer in the quarry of the Solway chemical plant. His father, the last remaining family member, died in 1941. Wojtyla was 21. Earlier that year he had been knocked down by a tram and had suffered a fractured skull. During the war years he came increasingly under the influence of Jan Tyranowski, a lay mystic, who introduced him to the study of Saint John of the Cross, the great 16th century Spanish mystic. In late 1941 he joined the underground seminary in the residence of the Archbishop of Krakow, Archbishop (later Cardinal) Adam Sapieha. He never seems to have looked back in his commitment to the priesthood. With the reopening of the university in 1945 he returned and took final examinations in theology in August 1946. He was ordained by Cardinal Sapieha on 1 November 1946. A very successful ecclesiastical career began.

Sapieha sent him to Rome to do a two-year doctorate at the Angelicum University. His mentor was the French Dominican, Reginald Garrigou-Lagrange whose theology was deeply rooted in the neo-scholastic tradition of the 19th century (even in the 1940s Garrigou-Lagrange was nicknamed 'Reginald the rigid'). Under his direction Wojtyla completed a thesis entitled *Doctrina de fide apud S. Joannem de Cruce (The Doctrine of Faith of St John of the Cross)*. The degree was awarded on 19 June 1948. While in Rome he lived at the Belgian College. He seems to have come under the influence of the *Jeunesse Oeuvrière Chrétienne (Young Christian Workers – YCW)* founded in 1925 by Joseph

Cardijn. After completing his degree he returned to Poland.

After a brief curacy in a small rural parish (1948) he moved to a much larger urban parish in Krakow (1949-1951). Some of his poems were published. He returned to the Jagiellonian University in 1951 and began a study of the German phenomenologist, Max Scheler (1874-1928). The title of his second thesis was *The Possibilities of Building A System of Christian Ethics on the Basis of Max Scheler* (1953). As these two theses give clues to his thinking I will return to them. In October 1953 he began lecturing in theological ethics at Krakow Theological Seminary. In 1957 he was given the chair of ethics at the Catholic University of Lublin and he commuted the 200 kilometres between the two cities each week. He was soon head of the Institute of Ethics at Lublin. His first philosophical work *The Acting Person* was not published in Polish until 1969.

On 4 July 1958 he was made Auxiliary Bishop of Krakow. His book on sexuality, *Love and Responsibility*, was published in Polish in 1960. It was first given as a series of lectures to the students at Lublin. As a bishop he attended the whole of the Second Vatican Council. There he was identified with the liberal majority. In 1964 he became Archbishop of Krakow and was created cardinal by Pope Paul VI in May 1967. As Archbishop he held a diocesan synod, was mildly reformist, was pastoral, close to the people and very popular.

In his diocese he always showed great interest in the intellectuals and this interest has continued as Pope. The term 'intellectual' is very European and sounds foreign to us. It is a term used to refer to *savants* – men (very few are women) of learning: philosophers, scientists, theoreticians of one sort or another. Such people generally take themselves very seriously. Coming from the Anglo-American tradition, we tend to be very suspicious of intellectuals largely because of the strong empirical tradition within our philosophy and culture. English-speaking people have a genuine distrust of ideology of any sort as a solution for human problems. We are more pragmatic – prepared to adopt what works and to jettison what does not. Many European intellectuals take a more metaphysical and doctrinaire approach. The mind of Pope Wojtyla is in tune with the European intellectual tradition.

In questions of Church-State relations in Poland, Wojtyla always maintained a secondary status to Cardinal Stefan Wyszynski, the Polish Primate, who was the clearly recognised leader of the bishops. But the cardinal from Krakow was increasingly active in Rome through membership of several curial congregations. He did a considerable amount of travelling, visiting the United States, Canada, Australia, New Zealand, the Philippines and Papua-New Guinea. He usually stayed with Polish communities in each of these countries – which meant that his experience of the wider Church was limited. But he did have many visitors in Krakow from all over the world and no doubt many of his views on the wider Church were formed before he was elected Pope. In 1976 he gave the Lenten retreat to Pope Paul VI and the Roman Curia. This was later published as *A Sign of Contradition* (published in Italian in 1977).

Pope John Paul II is the first non-Western European Pope for over 1000 years and the first non-Italian since the death of Adrian VI in 1522. But the contrast with his predecessors is deeper than this. There is one sense in which his background is conventionally Catholic: he is the product of the clerical and priestly system. His training at the Dominican Angelicum University in Rome prepared him for a successful ecclesiastical career as priest, professor, bishop, cardinal, Pope. But there is a sense in which he has never been a 'normal' clerical priest. His training for the priesthood was not carried out in a conventional seminary, but in hiding in the Archbishop's palace during the dark days of the Nazi occupation. His entire ecclesiastical career has been lived out in the unique situation of the successful struggle by the Polish Church against an avowedly atheistic State. He is a man of strong personality, tough physique and with a determination to realise on the world stage his vision of the meaning of human life and of the role of the Church.

He has certainly brought a new vigor to the papacy and enhanced its standing in the world. His constant travelling has made the papacy present to the wider Church in a way it never was.

The most obvious thing about John Paul is his image. He is a media superstar. Enormous crowds seem to be his life-blood. He is much more interested in the people than in the leaders of nations, who come and go. But there is a danger built into the populist style. It so easily becomes a personality cult, a form of manipulative demagoguery. It seems to be precisely for this reason that Jesus was so careful of avoiding it. While Jesus was surrounded by crowds he was constantly on his guard against the cult of personality. He refused to allow the crowd to project on to him any political role. He avoided using the term 'messiah' because of its political overtones. He always pointed beyond himself to the God who had sent him. Jesus had no institutional power; he had no established church to support him. His influence flowed from the power of the Spirit of God within him, from the strength of his personal conviction, from the gentleness of his humanity and from his intimacy with God. He was never a demagogue.

While Pope John Paul cannot undo the history of the papacy, there seems a strange incongruity in his actions. He is clearly determined to be a powerful leader in the institutional Church, as well as an actor on the world-wide stage. But he claims to represent Christ, 'the man who had nowhere to lay his head', the man who constantly guarded against the cult of personality. It is the actor in him that needs the crowds and very few actors have ever had such a powerful institutional base from which to operate.

John Paul is a deeply religious man. His religiosity is very simple. It centres around prayer, daily Mass, spiritual reading, the stations of the cross and devotion to Mary. He lives poorly. When Cardinal Koenig of Vienna first met him he noted Wojtyla's shabby clothes. Marian devotion is a central focus of his spirituality. He often emphasises the importance of Mary, especially in the lives of priests. In his Holy Thursday *Letter to Priests* (1979) he said: 'I entrust all of you to the mother of Christ who in a special way is our mother, the mother of priests.' Pope John Paul is also interested in prayer. As a young student he read and studied the Spanish Carmelite mystics Saints John of the Cross and Teresa of Avila. There is an element of the contemplative in Pope Wojtyla and this stands in contrast to the man of action on the world stage. But one wonders if this element in his personality has had a real chance to develop. A time in the wilderness is required for the gift of contemplation to take root and to grow: time in the wilderness of rejection, doubt, uncertainty and questioning.

Wojtyla's career shows no evidence of an institutional wilderness; he has risen steadily up the ladder of ecclesiastical promotion from priest to Pope. Dark nights of the spirit, of course, come to different people under different guises. But one can discern the effects of genuine contemplative experience in a personality. There is a tolerant gentleness, a willingness to live and let live, an appreciation of the complex beauty of reality. One experiences a spirit, an élan, that suffuses everything that is said and done by the person who has passed beyond the religion of moralism, law and obligation. In order to be able to begin to experience the depths of living faith, the person must drop their guard and in a sense step beyond the institutional Church, abandon the limits set by their own unconscious fear of experience. The person who has entered with living faith into the life of God is transparent. One somehow discerns in them something intangible, something transcendant. It is, of course, a manifestation of the face of God shining in the face of the person who has encountered God in a living way. Such people are gentle and forgiving towards other people for they have experienced their own fragility and humanity.

John Paul is also an intellectual, but of a quite specific type. He is basically a philosopher specialising in ethics. He is neither theologian, scripture scholar nor historian. The ethicist focuses on the human person and specifically on human action. Pope Wojtyla is a profoundly personalist philosopher; that is, the human person is the centre of his thought. His speculation begins not with God but with human beings and with the unique personality of each. But here the English-speaking reader needs to make an important distinction. He is a personalist philosopher in the abstract European mode. He is not interested in psychology or personality theory. His personalism is not intrapsychic in the sense of Freud or Jung, nor is it geared to counselling, psychiatry or guidance. For John Paul the human person is the central focus of human endeavour and the starting point for philosophical speculation. He asserts that persons and their relationships are at the core of reality. They are more important than abstract ideas or things. Reality has no meaning except in relationship to persons. As I will indicate later, it is precisely here that I think that personalism is flawed.

The influence of Max Scheler (1874-1928) on Pope Wojtyla is very marked. Scheler was a German phenomenonologist and social philosopher. He was, for a brief time in the early 1920s, a convert to Catholicism. Scheler focuses on the human person's search for God. Each of us is a *Gottsucher* (a God-searcher). There is a strong note of this in Pope John Paul. At the core of Wojtyla's own spirituality is God, the ultimate goal of the human person. We long to discover the meaning of our lives and it is God who alone can fulfil that longing. Thus Wojtyla (and Scheler) are very Augustinian; Augustine's great saying 'You have made us for yourself, O Lord, and our hearts are restless until they rest in you' seems a good summary of the Pope's spirituality. This is a very absolutist philosophy and it calls for radical commitment.

It is at this point that the reason emerges for the Pope's harsh treatment of priests who leave the active ministry. He sees them as men who made a commitment and then turned away, thus betraying 'the search for the Absolute'. Those who leave are to do so in silence (as they do in Poland). The new *Norms for Laicization* (27 October 1980) condemn the departed priest to disgrace and failure; he is meant to be a pariah in the Church. It is precisely here that a genuine mysticism (and a consistent personalism) would be more understanding and gentle, more tolerant of differences, more accepting of the reality of the human condition. But this is where Wojtyla's personalist ethic clashes with his neo-scholasticism. Neo-scholasticism was an attempted revival of the philosophy of Saint Thomas Aquinas in the late 19th century. One of its key exponents was Father Reginald Garrigou-Lagrange, Wojtyla's theological mentor in Rome. Neo-scholasticism is essentialist, that is it seeks the essence of things – and it is of the essence of the priesthood to be permanent. Here we have an illustration of the two philosophical strands which influence him clashing with each other; it is significant that neo-scholasticism wins out!

The absolutist strain fits in well with Slav apocalypticism. But it is also very dangerous, especially if it is viewed as the only path for the followers of Jesus to take. To absolutise is to exclude all other possibilities. That seems to be the way of Pope John Paul.

One would expect that his personalism would soften the absolutist tendency. He says that the love of God and of others is the deepest dignity of the human person. Christ is the perfect person; thus the more we are like him, the more we are truly human. Human dignity is of immense importance to Wojtyla. But again the English-speaking reader needs to be warned: he is not speaking about human dignity in the sense of liberal democracy. The supreme freedom for John Paul is religious freedom, the freedom to reach full human personhood in union with God. (This is Wojtyla the personalist speaking). But God has already pre-ordained the nature and essence of full human personhood; it is only achieved through a life lived in accordance with his law. (This is Wojtyla the neo-scholastic speaking.) Political freedom is not an end in itself (as it is in the Anglo-American tradition), but is only a means to achieve a deeper human fulfilment through a life in keeping with God's law.

At the core of his ideas on human dignity is the person of Jesus. Jesus is united to us by becoming one with us in the incarnation. In our inmost being Christ has re-created us, reconciled us with God, with ourselves and with our brothers and sisters. The incarnation gives every human life enormous worth. Every person is sacred. It follows from this that any form of exploitation of persons is intrinsically evil. Pope John Paul has consistently and unequivocally condemned all forms of exploitation – economic, political, social and personal. He has been very consistent on this. He attacks communism in all its forms, especially Soviet and Polish communism. But he has been just as scathing on capitalism and what he calls 'consumerism'. Any form of exploitation of persons must be decried.

He has also tried to break out of the body-soul dualism that so deeply impregnates the Christian tradition. He keeps saying that the body is good. Sex is one of the primal expressions of bodily existence. Thus John Paul often talks about sex. He has scandalised pious pilgrims in Rome with his frank and open talk on the subject at public audiences. In fact he gave a long series of talks on the subject to pilgrims at the Wednesday audiences during 1981 and 1982. It was during these talks that he made the much quoted (out of context) remark about the sin of the husband who looks at his wife with lust! Actually, when you examine the comment in the context of the Pope's views, it makes much more sense.

Wojtyla's views on sexuality were first developed in his book *Love and Responsibility* (Polish edition 1960. English trans. 1981.) Here he argues that sexual intercourse is only truly human within the context of marriage. He bases this on what he calls the 'personalistic norm': that is true love and commitment is only possible within the context of a permanent relationship – marriage. In all other contexts intercourse is using another person, for the only true love is permanent love. To use another person is to act according to what he calls a 'utilitarian' and not a 'personalist' ethic. Utilitarianism is an English philosophical system (it originated with Jeremy Bentham (1748-1832)); it is a quintessential expression of Anglo-Saxon pragmatism. Wojtyla seems to consider that Anglo-American morality has been too influenced by pragmatism and utilitarianism, and that English-speaking Catholic moralists have largely surrendered to 'situational morality'. Situational morality involves the abandonment of Christian moral principles as the norm of behaviour, and the replacement of these principles by a stance which says that the morality of an act is determined by the needs of the persons involved and their circumstances. Conservative French Catholics, with typical Gallic superciliousness, have coined a term for situational morality: they refer to it as 'Anglo-Saxon morality'. John Paul's view of the Catholic Church in the United States seems to be influenced by this type of thinking. In papal terminology the word 'utilitarian' is paralleled by the word 'consumerism'. To consume means to eat up, to destroy. Consumerism is a perjorative term for Wojtyla. Thus he speaks of sex outside of marriage as 'consumerism', for it is a use of the other person without commitment. This is an unusual use of the word for English speakers.

John Paul also uses the personalist norm to exclude all forms of artificial contraception. For conception is the natural result of intercourse – even if it does not always occur. To introduce anything artificial (such as the contraceptive pill) that impedes that (possible) result prevents the persons involved acting according to their full personhood. He also argues that artificial contraception vitiates the essential nature of marriage.

Hence, when a man and woman capable of procreation have intercourse their union must be accompanied by awareness and willing acceptance of the possibility that 'I may become a father' or 'I may become a mother'. Without this the marital relationship will not be 'internally' justified – quite the contrary. Mutual betrothed love demands a union of persons. But the union of persons is not the same as sexual union. This latter is raised to the level of the person only when it is accompanied in the mind and the will by acceptance of the possibility of parenthood . . . Sexual (marital) relations have the character of true union of persons as long as a general disposition towards parenthood is not excluded from them. This implies a constant attitude: to master the sexual urge means just this to accept its purpose in marital relations . . . *Nature cannot be conquered by violating its laws.* [author's emphasis] (K. Wojtyla: *Love and Responsibility*, 1981, pp 228-229)

The final statement is interesting for it reveals the strong neo-scholastic trait in Wojtyla. This leads him to emphasise the 'natural law'.

This is very well illustrated in his views on women. In *Love and Responsibility* he sees in intercourse a paradigm for the role of women: 'It is in the very nature of the act that the man plays the active role and takes the initiative, while the woman is a comparatively passive partner, whose function it is to accept and experience' (p 271). The woman is biologically bound by her maternal role, for being a mother is much more tangibly binding than being a father. Pope John Paul also gives expression to the romantic German notion of the woman as 'mystery' because new life comes out of her. The mystery of womanhood finds its culmination in Mary, the mother of Jesus, from whom comes the source of life itself. Thus John Paul believes that biology, psychology and theology determine woman's actual destiny as mother and wife or as virgin. Thus he is opposed to women in the workplace (their *natural* place is the home), and he utterly opposes those who say that it is sociology and formation rather than nature itself that determines a woman's destiny.

I want to conclude this treatment of Wojtyla's philosophical ideas by making a brief critical comment on his personalism. We have already seen how it conflicts with his rigid and traditional neo-scholasticism. Thus his personalism is not always consistent. While personalism seems an attractive and existential philosophy, there are serious limits to its application. Certainly, the human person is the summit of creation and the central focus of ethical speculation. But creation is not exhausted by human beings. We human beings are only the most conscious part of the cosmos. Reality and life are interlocking and interdependent. It is myopic to subordinate all life to human life. The cosmos does not exist simply for the use and exploitation of human beings. To make men and women the be all and end all of existence is to forget the first five days of creation. Thus uncompromising and unnuanced personalism is a limiting view of reality and of life. I have tried to develop a more positive approach to this issue in the last chapter.

What then are we to make of this pontificate? It is still very difficult to answer. There can be no doubt that the brakes have been applied to the post-Vatican II Church. But Pope John Paul II does not want to drag the Church back to some romantic restoration of the pre-conciliar institution. Pope Wojtyla will cause as much discomfort to Archbishop Lefebvre and his conservative followers as did Pope Paul VI. It would be simple and straightforward if John Paul were a die-hard reactionary. But he is not. His vision for the Church is much more subtle, personal and idiosyncratic.

There are die-hards in the Curia and elsewhere in important positions who advocate a restoration of pre-conciliar Catholicism. Often enough their agendas intersect with that of John Paul and they happily work together to rein in the Church. The attack on liberation theology is one example of this. On this issue the reactionaries and John Paul are at one. But I suspect that the Pope has a much more personal agenda that fits into neither the reactionary nor the liberal categories.

Hans Küng is right when he compares John Paul II to Pius IX (1846-1878). Pius IX loved crowds and the adulation that was projected onto him. It was he who evolved the idea of papal audiences in the modern sense; it was he who encouraged the development pilgrimages to Rome. And it was he who aimed at the constant enhancement of the power of the papacy in the Church, which he achieved through the definitions of papal primacy and infallibility. But Pius IX had to depend on people coming to Rome to see him. John Paul has the vast resources of the modern media at his disposal. Küng speaks unkindly but accurately of John Paul II:

With his charismatic radiance and his acting ability, he finally gave the Vatican what the White House was soon to have and what the Kremlin, at least until recently, lacked. He was the media-wise 'great communicator', the man who, with charm and flair, with athleticism and symbolic gestures could present the most conservative doctrine or practice as acceptable. (H. Küng,: 'Speaking Out After Silence' in *The Tablet*, 239, 1985, p 1110)

Pope John Paul's aim, it seems to me, is to re-fashion the Church according to his own insights. A basic element of his vision is a strong emphasis on a high public profile. Paradoxically he does not insist on the traditional paraphernalia of the institutional Church. He leaves that to the Curia, especially to people like Cardinal Ratzinger. It is the Curia that deals with the suspect theologians such as Küng, Schillebeeckx and the proponents of liberation theology.

John Paul meanwhile travels the world. The problem with this is the danger that the papal travels will undercut the development of the local Church. His presence can easily lessen the influence of the bishops and the local leadership elites. Pope John Paul – and modern communications – have created a situation without parallel in the history of the Church – an omnipresent papacy. This is hardly a fertile ground for the development of local initiative and creativity. Unfortunately, the Pope has shown no willingness to listen to those who have had the courage to speak publicly to him of the real issues that trouble the local Churches. When people like Mercy Sister Theresa Kane in Washington, D.C. and laywoman Barbara Engl in Munich publicly articulate the real questions that confront Catholics, the Pope simply hides his head in his hands. He seems neither interested nor able to articulate an answer to the questions addressed to him by faithful Catholics. He makes it absolutely clear that it is his agenda that is normative. He is obviously not interested in the questions that haunt so many Catholics on their journey to God. In my view, this is a disastrous policy. Each age has its own questions, and it is to these questions that the Word of God must be addressed. To fail to answer these questions is to ignore the people who ask them.

John Paul II has something else in common with Pius IX. The 19th century Pope conceived of the Church as a beleaguered fortress or as a ship tossed in a stormy sea. The attacking forces were liberalism, socialism, democracy, equality – all of the modern 'evils' condemned in the Syllabus of Errors (1864). Pope Wojtyla conceives of the Church in much the same way. Like Christ, it is a 'sign of contradiction'. Struggle against the forces of evil is the task of the Church. The forces of evil manifest themselves today through atheism, secularism and marxism:

Perhaps we are experiencing (today) the highest level of tension between the Word and the anti-Word in the whole of human history. Alienation . . . implies not only the denial of the God of the covenant but also the very idea of God: denial of his existence and at the same time the postulate – and in a sense the imperative – of liberation from the very idea of God to bolster man. (*Sign of Contradiction*, pp 34-35)

Abstracting from the fact that the prophets of doom have said that every age was the time of the anti-Christ (in John Paul's term the 'anti-Word'), one cannot avoid the pessimistic Augustinian theology which underlies this view. It conceives of reality in terms of a mighty cosmic battle between the forces of good and evil.

The problem with this type of dualistic religiosity is that it can be self-fulfilling. By conceiving of reality in these terms one develops a siege mentality. There is already considerable evidence of this developing again in the Roman Curia and among some Catholics. It is paradoxical that the Pope with such skill in media and communication should be the one who tries to lead the Church back to the ghetto.

Linked to this is what can be called the remnant mentality. There is good evidence that Pope John Paul II has opted for a remnant Church. The idea comes from the Old Testament. The prophets spoke of a 'faithful remnant', a small core group of people who strictly adhered to the Mosaic law. 'Israel, your people may be like the sand on the seashore, but only a remnant will return. A destruction has been decreed that will bring inexhaustable integrity' (*Isaiah 10:22*). It is the remnant who will be the heirs of God's promises. The majority are lost to the chosen people because of their infidelity. They are seen by the remnant as apostates. American theologian, Elizabeth Keating, comments perceptively on this attitude:

If a remnant philosophy, or theology, is really seen as an option by Rome, it will not matter how many Catholics leave the Church over issues like contraception, divorce and re-marriage, priestly celibacy or denial of lay rights. It will not matter how many women no longer attend their parish churches because they cannot in conscience support an institution which denegrates and alienates them by keeping the feminine out of the picture in symbol, ministry, language and system. According to a remnant, separatist mindset, such departures are healthful purges. One gets rid of the bad eggs. ('Women and the Church: A Look Back and a Look Ahead in Justice', private paper, 12 March 1983)

This is an extraordinarily dangerous attitude for the universal Church, but there is evidence that it is the mindset that is developing in Rome and elsewhere. It obviously grows out of the idea that the Polish Church is the paradigm for the Catholic Church. One can only comment that such a view is both presumptuous and myopic.

Thus I am forced to conclude that Pope John Paul II is a very mixed blessing for the Church. The danger is that he could push the inevitable tensions of the contemporary Church to breaking point. Or, even worse: he may well push more and more sincere people to seek the God of life and meaning outside the Church. Either way, he bears a terrible responsibility.

PART THREE

AUSTRALIA AND THE FUTURE

7

RESPONSES DOWN UNDER

In this chapter I want to express some personal observations on Australian Catholicism. I stress that I speak as an insider, as one committed to the Church and to its ministerial task. Obviously my treatment will not be exhaustive and it will reflect all of the limitations built into one person's point of view. I am conscious that Australians do not take too kindly to criticism. We are generally a self-satisfied crowd. We are also a non-reflective people, still involved in the task of evolving a sense of national identity. Australian Catholicism is often more Australian than Catholic, sharing something of the paradoxical self-confident uncertainty that is an integral part of the Australian cultural ethos.

Australian Catholicism seems to keep backing away from some hard decisions about itself and its role in this culture. These decisions are being forced on the Catholic community not only by the results of the Second Vatican Council, but also by the enormous changes that have occurred in Australian society over the last 30 years. Unlike Americans, Australians are wary of naming fundamental issues and articulating problems. Certainly, one can over-emphasise problems and become a carping critic. However, in Australia the risk is that we sweep our problems under the carpet, and the person who identifies a problem runs the risk of being blamed for creating it!

So it is with trepidation that I name some of the issues that face the Australian Catholic Church. A basic problem arises from the way that the Church in this country traditionally does things: most of the Church's responses are ad hoc, unplanned, a response to the latest and most insistent stimulus. There is a significant lack of reflection and serious planning. In the majority of important issues, many of them of intimate concern to the Church – such as policy toward migrant settlement – Catholics have uncritically followed government policy. There has been a significant failure to insist on participation in the formulation of that policy. Secondly, Australian Catholics tend to define 'Catholicism' very narrowly. Most, in practice, reduce their religion to a very narrow and circumscribed reality – their personal experience of the Church. Australian Catholics lack both a historical perspective and a vision of the world-wide Catholic Church. Their Catholicism is very *un*catholic. The Catholic Church today is one of the most dynamic agents of change in the world. A person could be forgiven for not knowing this, if his or her experience was limited to the Australian Catholic sample! This brings us back to where we started: the time has come to assert what is truly Catholic in Australian Catholicism.

Patrick O'Farrell expresses the paradox of Australian Catholicism precisely: 'In all their social relations, Catholics' attitudes to public affairs and political activity have been divided between the desire for independence and the wish to conform' (*The Catholic Church and Community in Australia*, (1977), p 395). Over the last 30 years Catholics have socially 'arrived' in Australia – that is they have become socially accepted and part of the mainstream. This means that the tendency to conform is much stronger than the tendency to differ. Thus the Church offers little in the line of a coherent critique of Australian society.

What is the typical Australian Catholic like? Some of my friends look at me rather oddly when they catch me reading the 'Letters to the Editor' columns of Sydney's *Catholic Weekly*, Melbourne's *Advocate* and Brisbane's *Catholic Leader*. Self-respecting 'liberal'

Catholics just do not read such things! And as I read I sometimes wonder if I am not being a bit masochistic? Yet these letter columns are one of the few places where the religious underbelly of Australian Catholicism is revealed. It is here that one can read what *some* Australian Catholics think and feel. It is one entrance into part of the Australian Catholic psyche.

The majority of the letters manifest a quite specific stance on the nature of the Church. They reflect a static and authoritarian image of Catholicism. A number of writers are obviously trying to give expression to a deeply felt piety, but the symbols and rhetoric are from the Church of the 1940s and 1950s. This is especially true when the letters are about devotion to the Blessed Virgin Mary. Many writers see themselves as members of the little flock of Mary's faithful followers who have hung on to the 'true devotion'. They tend to define themselves in opposition to ordinary Catholics whom they view as soft on secularism, communism and modernism! They see other Catholics as having surrendered to the 'great apostasy'. The letters also unconsciously convey the need within the Catholic community for a popular religiosity and piety and for accessible symbols. The modern liturgical movement has unwittingly driven this human and religious need to the periphery.

The majority of letter writers are clearly 'right-wingers'. This is demonstrated by their religious, social and political stances. Such people often express their views in strong and passionate language that reflects deeply felt anger. A minority of letters reflect moderate views from the mainstream of Catholicism, and only a small percentage could be construed as 'left-wing'. The bias to the right could reflect editorial policy, or more likely the readership of the Catholic press. Some letters are obviously part of campaigns that target specific persons, organisations and issues. These campaigns are generally orchestrated by small right-wing pressure groups. What these letters do show is that the right wing is only a minority, but it is articulate and well organised. The journal of right-wing opinion loosely associated with Catholicism is *News Weekly*. This reflects the views of the National Civic Council and Mr B.A. Santamaria.

The Catholic left in Australia has little voice. Perhaps the revival of the *Catholic Worker* in Melbourne may provide some vehicle for views from that perspective. Of course, I should be wary of using the term 'left-wing' to describe any Australian Catholic. By world standards, the Catholic left wing here is both moderate and tame. Many Catholics who are seen as liberal or radical are actually moderates trying to make some sense of their faith in the context of contemporary Australian society and experience.

My reason for outlining the spectrum of Australian Catholicism is to help the reader situate the 'ordinary Catholic' somewhere in the middle. But it is important to remember that the extremes belong to Catholicism also. Saint Paul says that he had become 'all things to all people' that he might save some (*I Corinthians 9:22*). *Omnia omnibus* (all things to all) was the episcopal motto of Archbishop Daniel Mannix, Archbishop of Melbourne from 1919 to 1963, the most famous of all Australia's prelates. The consequence of Saint Paul's teaching is that Catholicism must be able to contain persons from right across the political, social and religious spectrum. Unity does not mean uniformity. There are, however, very few facts available about the ordinary Catholic in the pew. Father Cyril Hally states the problem clearly:

The Catholic laity has not been studied in detail. We need much more information on matters such as class, occupational and status differentiation among Anglo-Celtic Australian Catholics and the ethnic and cultural diversity which has resulted from post-war immigration programmes. ('Growth Patterns in the Catholic Church' in D. Harris, D. Hynd and D. Millikan (eds): *The Shape of Belief. Christianity in Australia Today*, 1982, p 79)

What can we establish about Australian Catholics? Statistics provide basic raw material. The *Official Directory of the Catholic Church in Australia. 1985-1986* states that there are 3,786,505 Catholics in Australia. This is 26% of the total population. Don Edgar states that in 1976 Catholics constituted 28% of the population. So Catholics constitute about 27% or about 4 million people out of just over 15 million. The Catholic population is growing at a marginally faster rate than the general population, it is much younger, has more women than men, is centred in south-eastern Australia and in the capital cities and has a larger number of migrants from non-English-speaking backgrounds. The largest proportion of Catholics per capita are to be found in the Australian Capital Territory, the smallest proportion in Tasmania. The following table is based on the 1981 census:

	Total Population	Catholic Population	Percentage
ACT	221,609	67,591	30.5
New South Wales	5,126,217	1,424,499	27.8
Northern Territory	123,324	25,177	20.4
Queensland	2,295,123	554,912	24.2
South Australia	1,285,033	255,322	19.9
Tasmania	418,957	78,143	18.7
Victoria	3,832,443	1,064,518	27.8
Western Australia	1,273,624	316,337	24.8
Total	14,576,330	3,786,505	26.0

Source: Official Directory of the Catholic Church of Australia 1985-1986.

Cyril Hally estimates that between 30% and 40% of Catholics are either migrants or the children of migrants of non-English-speaking background. Many parish schools in both Sydney and Melbourne have children from as many as 25 or more different language backgrounds, and in Sydney's inner western suburbs as many as 37% of parish school children do not speak English at home. Spanish, Arabic, Italian and Maltese are the most common languages. The urban concentration of Catholicism is vividly illustrated in the fact that almost half of all Australia's Catholics live in the two archdioceses of Sydney and Melbourne. Sydney archdiocese has a Catholic population of 941,000 (total population 3,311,000) and Melbourne Archdiocese has 837,000 Catholics (greater Melbourne has a population of just on 3,100,000).

The serious practical Catholic – the type one might see at downtown churches such as St Francis's in Melbourne or at a typical middle-class urban or rural parish – probably occupies a position on the socio-economic ladder between the lower middle class and the middle class. If the person is a migrant, he or she will probably be working class, although the worker's economic status is probably only marginally different from those who consider themselves middle class. Being Catholic no longer isolates or divides the person from the mainstream of Australian life. The so-called Catholic ghetto has largely ceased to exist. Although the majority of Catholics still vote Labor (there is still a much higher proportion of Catholics in the Labor Party than in the Liberal Party), Catholic social attitudes are conservative. There is very little evidence of radicalism in thought or practice. The opposite is probably true: there is evidence of right-wing and reactionary responses on social and theological issues. Although Catholics are relatively well educated, their continuing religious and theological development is stunted through lack of opportunity for on-going education. Adult religious formation might help to bring Australian Catholics into the mainstream of world Catholicism and place their conservatism in a broader perspective.

In terms of religious convictions and practice, it is even more difficult to be specific. I can only draw on my reasonably wide experience of Catholics in a number of states. Adult Australian Catholics still place considerable importance on attendance at Sunday Mass as a symbol of commitment. Many are still passive participants in the renewed liturgy. There is considerable disquiet with the generally low level of preaching. Australian religious practice is normally non-demonstrative. Many people, however, manifest a desire for 'something more', 'something deeper'. They find that most clergy are unable to help them articulate this need, let alone to answer it. Prayer and the use of the scriptures have emerged as important issues for Australian Catholics. But there is no contemplative tradition here and scriptural education is still at a rudimentary stage. The Church is significantly lacking in imaginative and creative solutions to the religious needs of its adults.

Thus Australian Catholics tend to appear conventional, middle-of-the-road, non-descript. This may not reflect the inner questioning, the spiritual uncertainty of many. The conventionality is more a symptom of inadequate rhetoric, of an inability to articulate the questions that lurk in the religious unconscious, than an innate spiritual dullness. Despite the sour diagnosis of the state of Australian 'soul' by critics such as Ronald Conway (*The End of Stupor?*, 1984), Australians seem to me no more nor less religious than people of equivalently developed countries such as the United States or Canada. In fact I suspect that there is a lot less difference between serious practical Catholics in Australia and in the United States than critics have allowed.

Australian Catholic women are probably in better shape than their male counterparts. They are more spiritually mature and less rigid in their moral stances. A high percentage of Catholics practise artificial contraception or believe that it is morally permissible. In the absence of empirical evidence it is difficult to express this in precise terms. My own guess would be that more than 85% of practising Catholics under 45 years practise artificial contraception. It is not that they are anti children; most already have two or more. Many have been through acute personal pain on this issue and some still experience it as a moral dilemma.

The papal condemnation of artificial contraception (1968) was a watershed for many Catholics. Suddenly the Church of 'absolute' moral imperatives found itself in the midst of a serious dispute about a papal decision. The area of dispute was significant: it was something that concerned Catholics in a practical and intimate sense. It was not something that could be quietly put aside – like papal teachings on social justice. For the first time this century Catholicism experienced genuine dissent and everyone was unprepared to handle it. I do not think that the significance of the contraception issue can be underestimated. For many Catholics it was a turning point. For a considerable number it was the beginning of a process which led them to abandon the practice of their faith. Many felt cut off through exclusion from communion. Eventually, they abandoned any practical commitment to the Church.

For the majority of Catholics, contraception was the turning point that led them to take the first major personal moral decision of their lives. Either with or without priestly advice, couples decided that their sexuality was their own business. They resolved to use artificial contraception and to remain practising Catholics.

They often did this after pain and terrible soul-searching, but it did lead them to the point of assuming responsibility for their own moral lives. Thus they have come to feel that while the Church is their home, they are free to examine the moral teachings of the hierarchy, especially on questions of sexual ethics, very critically.

The tragedy of Pope Paul VI's encyclical was that it was so badly presented by official Church spokesmen. I still remember one eminent Australian Archbishop saying on television that the encyclical 'was not infallible, but almost infallible!'

Here it should be noted that most Catholics still consider that decisions about fertility are moral decisions and this issue still continues to exercise their consciences. But the parameters wherein they make their moral decisions have widened to include inter-personal values, the changing role of women, economic reality, social responsibility and the question of population.

A major issue for Catholic married couples is the education of their children. Increasingly, they have to assume responsibility for religious formation, especially as more parish and family-based catechesis is introduced. Catholic schools are less willing to accept exclusive responsibility for all religious formation. Many parents are uncertain of themselves as religious educators. They are afraid that they will foist many of their own doubts onto their children.

Doubt is very much part of the spirituality of Catholics today. Most live more with the questions than with the answers. A major part of the problem with preaching in the Catholic Church is that many Australian priests seem unable to articulate the questions which lurk in the recesses of the spiritual lives of their congregations. The effective preacher can voice the questions that arise from life and experience and relate them to the scripture. These questions centre around the meaning of human existence and the relationship between the human community and God. Many priests seem tied up in conflicts about their own role, or seem preoccupied with their own agendas. They are unable to hear and articulate the questions of the Catholic people. It is so often the question that is important, not the answer.

Australian Catholics have had their traumas, but there is still a deep reservoir of ministerial energy in the Catholic community waiting to be tapped. But there are still very few structures that are able to channel this energy. Lay ministry is very threatening to those clergy who are uncertain of their own role. Some priests deny the existence of this lay energy, for they do not allow themselves to experience it. This is because of their own defensiveness. The Church is just beginning to develop structures to channel and support lay people devoted to ministry. The Catholic school system is now largely run by laity. An increasing number of professional and committed lay religious educators are starting to permeate the schools. The Saint Vincent de Paul Society continues a low-key but very effective ministry to the marginalised and especially to the homeless. Beyond these established structures there are very few ministerial possibilities for laypeople.

Australian Catholics have always been enormously generous. This generosity has been matched by the Australian clergy. Most priests are hard-working and gain little in terms of personal reward. The priesthood has been a vocation and not a career in Australia. But the hard work of Australian priests has left them little time for reflection. Also isolation cuts Australia off from the centres of Catholic intellectual life overseas. Australian Catholicism presents a bland image which oddly belies many of the interesting individuals who are to be found within the Catholic community.

Part of the problem is that the divisive passions raised by the Labor split of the 1950s have frightened Catholics away from the discussion of issues that could cause division. The only exception to this is the Catholic Commission for Justice and Peace which has been willing to confront tough but important issues facing Australia such as youth unemployment, Aborigines and the attitude of Australia to the US alliance and questions of nuclear war and peace. The Commission has been attacked for confusing moral and political issues. For instance, its recent statement *Work for a Just Peace* (1985) has been criticised for confusing strategic questions such as the US spy bases in Australia with moral questions of peace and war. Some of its critics have argued that it is doing exactly what Santamaria and the Movement did in the past: equating a particular political stance (in Santamaria's case anti-communism) with the official teaching of the Church. This is not a view that I accept as I will indicate later in the chapter.

Part of the dullness of Australian Catholicism is lack of leadership. Archbishop Mannix of Melbourne never avoided a tough issue. From the conscription campaign of the First World War to the Labor split of the 1950s-1960s, Mannix had a position and he stated it unequivocally. Another Australian bishop who for many years was a leader in his state was Archbishop Guilford Young. While he was prepared to take on tough public issues such as the famous Orr case, he was above all a leader in the postconciliar renewal of Catholicism. Young seems to have seen himself in the Mannix mould, and his flamboyant oratory and style certainly disturbed stuffy clerics both in his own diocese and in the Australian episcopate. Young has become more conservative over the years and no other bishop has emerged with either the style or the willingness to confront tough public issues.

Of course, the question has to be asked if Catholics want or need bishops like Mannix? The years of the Labor split were very divisive. The main challenge before bishops since Vatican II has been to give corporate leadership to the local Church. On the national level in Australia, the bishops have been slow to take the initiative on many issues, especially issues of public policy or pastoral renewal. (Here, of course, abortion is an exception.) The Australian bishops seem to have difficulty reaching consensus. I will never forget the extraordinary 'pastoral guide' on contraception which they published almost eight years after *Humanae vitae* (1968). It was as though two diametrically opposed documents had been pasted together. On the one hand it said that people had the right to make conscientious moral decisions and on the other they were bound to obey the papal magisterium! It was hardly a solution to the moral dilemma of the majority of Catholic people. And why did it take so long to arrive at this conclusion? Recently, the bishops issued a statement on divorce, a difficult social issue for Catholics. It is entitled *When Dreams Die*. It is a sensitive and to an extent a practical document. It tries to offer ways of dealing with the reality of divorce and, of course, suggests recourse to the Church marriage tribunal if there is a possibility of an annulment. Naturally it says nothing about pastoral solutions to this difficult problem. The statement is, however, a step in the direction of real pastoral leadership. The Australian Church needs more positive steps like this from the bishops.

However, they still seem to lack the initiative of the United States Bishops Conference. They have been prepared to confront really difficult questions of real national importance – such as war and peace and the moral implications of the US capitalist economy. Some of the Canadian bishops have also been able to achieve a consensus about tough public issues. A group of them in 1984 put out a document highly critical of the economic policies of the then Trudeau Liberal government. The consensus did not include all of the bishops, for Cardinal Carter of Toronto felt free to criticise strongly the views of the predominantly French-speaking bishops. In October 1985 the English and Welsh bishops were able to put together and publish an excellent document in preparation for the Extraordinary Synod (November, 1985). The English hierarchy is almost exactly the same size as the Australian. In the last few years the English bishops have begun to show real initiative in their own Church. Obviously there is good leadership within the episcopal conference itself – probably from Cardinal Basil Hume (Westminster). Also a pastoral type of priest is now being made bishop.

In contrast to the Americans and the English, the Australian bishops still seem a hesitant, unadventurous group, unable to master much creative leadership. They still fail to provide stimulus to Catholics and seem suspicious of anyone who does.

The bi-annual Bishops Conference meets at Saint Paul's National Seminary in Sydney. One gets the impression that the whole exercise distances the Conference from the ministerial and social reality of Australia. The group is made up of 26 residential bishops, 11 auxiliary bishops, two Eastern rite bishops and one military vicar. Many of the bishops individually have shown pastoral leadership in their own dioceses, although the group pressure from other bishops has prevented some from being as creative as they would have liked. Here again the problem is probably partly historical. The divisive legacy of powerful individual leaders like Mannix has probably frightened most into conformism. Also those who have made creative decisions in their own dioceses (like Young in Hobart in the period after the Council and especially during the *Humanae vitae* crisis and more recently Bishop Francis Carroll in Wagga – Carroll is now Archbishop of Canberra) were attacked by small cliques of their own clergy and people.

In a paradoxical way bishops are more enslaved to the institutional Church than anyone else. They can become trapped by the structures which they technically control. (The same is true for a parish priest – especially if the parish is a large one.) The early Church image of a bishop being married to a diocese is accurate. Church administrators become trapped by role expectations, the projections of others and by a sense of responsibility to maintain the structure. Australian bishops also seem hamstrung by their membership of the episcopal club, by the unspoken control exercised by the most conservative members of the hierarchy. Bishops become trapped in ad hoc decision making; they can lose the ability to rise above the ruck to see the larger picture. There are bishops and priests who are open to a new model of the Church and to the concept of a truly pastoral leadership. But they are captured by the structure in which they work. Catholic leadership today requires a toughness of mind and clarity of vision that will not be syphoned off by the demands of ecclesiastical administration. If bishops and priests are primarily pastoral leaders, their fundamental responsibility is to the ministry, not to the maintenance of institutions.

Andrew Greeley speaks of the need ' . . . for leaders who incarnate the goals, values and élan of an organisation.' Such leaders work from consensus. The Church is neither a democracy nor a monarchy. It is a group of people called together by the Spirit who attempt to discern the way in which God is leading them. The leader must be able to discover within the community the promptings of the Spirit. Thus Church and bishops must abandon the exercise of power in a worldly or political sense.

The failure of the bishops to give leadership on a national level has led to a crisis of authority. For an increasing number of priests and laity the bishops are becoming sadly irrelevant. What they say and do has little relationship to the lives of ordinary Catholics. In some ways this is good: the laity will have to assume responsibility for their local Church. But the danger is that no one is giving a sense of unity to the Church, no one is drawing the whole thing together. The gifts of individual members and of communities in the Church need to be encouraged and co-ordinated. It is hard to know if no leadership is better than bad leadership.

Yet the paradox is that the bishops still have most of the institutional power in the Church. They make the major decisions, control the tangible resources and are seen by outsiders as official spokesmen. Power is a reality in the Catholic Church and it is a question of who has it and how it is used. Bishops are not accountable to the Church that they govern. The Church does not elect its bishops, has no power to remove them and has no say in setting the agenda and the priorities of the Episcopal Conference. Priests have no real influence on the Episcopal Conference either. The National Council of Priests is simply 'acknowledged' by the Episcopal Conference. The major superiors of religious orders have only very limited access to the Conference.

The Church needs to hear the views of a cross-section of committed Catholics. From this type of consultation a set of national priorities can be evolved. An Australia-wide conference of Catholics is one way of achieving this. Yet the bishops seem to be afraid of any type of national gathering on the pastoral ministry of the Church. The renewal of the English Catholic Church can be partly dated from the Liverpool National Pastoral Congress (1980) which brought together a wide cross-section of the Church to debate priorities for the future. The Australian bishops seem to be afraid that they will lose control and that emphases and priorities might emerge with which some of them would disagree.

While the bishops provide overall cohesion, leadership at the local level still depends to a considerable extent on priests. There is still a large fund of goodwill towards priests in the Catholic community. Unfortunately, some priests seem to be throwing this good will away, for they fail to provide any adequate inspiration as ministerial leaders and they are harsh and impersonal in their attitudes. Catholic priests, like Protestant clergy, are experiencing an identity crisis. Much of their role has been taken over by other professionals, such as social workers.

For the Catholic clergy the roots of the crisis lie basically in the idea of priesthood inherited from the post-Reformation period. Father Walter Burghardt has shown that the Catholic priest has been many things in the history of the Church. He distinguishes five basic models of priesthood. These can help us understand the changing role of the contemporary priest. The five models are:

• *The jurisdictional model*: in this the priest shares in the fullness of authority to rule the Church invested in the Pope and bishops. Through sharing in this jurisdiction priests can impose binding decisions on the faithful.

• *The cultic model*: in this the priest is the central figure in the Church as a worshipping community. The priest is the performer of the sacred mysteries - the hierophant.

• *The prophetic model*: in this the role of the priest is to proclaim the confronting Word of God, 'both in season and out of season'. In this model the priest is often called to a prophetic social radicalism. This model has never been popular anywhere, least of all in Australia.

• *The pastoral model*: in this the priest is the leader of the community. He gives the community a sense of unity and facilitates and supports the gifts of the other members of the community.

• *The monastic model*: in this the priest acts as guru, as spiritual leader and teacher. In this model the religious priest, especially the monk, becomes the norm.

Most older Australian priests were trained in the jurisdictional and cultic models. They were trained to see their task as providing clear, authoritative and binding leadership for the faithful. They did this through the confessional and the pulpit. Priests were sacred persons, the intermediaries between God and the worshipping community. A whole ethos was built up around this model. Its origins lie primarily in the reform of priestly life in France in the 17th century. The major elements of clericalism developed in their modern form in this period.

In the historical perspective of the 17th century the reforms made sense. In the contemporary Australian Church they are a stultifying and dead weight. Clericalism is the tendency to separate the priest from the people through a specific lifestyle, a uniform (cassock and collar) and through an unfruitful celibacy. Most Australian priests are neither stuffy nor status-seeking, but some have difficulty dealing with ambiguity, are emotionally under-developed and occasionally rigid and authoritarian. A sense of separation from ordinary people was encouraged in the old seminary training. This has led to the development of an insulated priestly sub-culture.

The Australian Church needs priests who work out of the pastoral leadership model. This will be difficult but not impossible to achieve. Many Catholics still cast the priest in the role of cleric and are shocked if he steps out of it. But the biggest difficulties facing priests are structural. They are often hamstrung by the sheer size of parishes and by their ever-increasing work load. Most Catholic parishes are numerically at least ten times the size of equivalent Anglican and Protestant parishes. Many priests are bogged down meeting the ad hoc needs on their doorsteps.

The second structural problem is the increasing number of Catholics and the decreasing number of priests. At first sight there does not seem to be a real problem for the absolute number of priests has not decreased (in this I am referring *only* to diocesan priests). The following list shows numbers of priests:

Year	Diocesan Priests
1966	1975
1971	2025
1976	2050
1986	2370

(The 1986 figure is taken from the *Official Directory of the Catholic Church* and I have no doubt that the figure is inflated by the inclusion of retired priests and those no longer in active ministry. The real figure is probably closer to 2050 or even less.)

The first problem arising from these statistics is that the average age has increased significantly. In 1966 the typical priest was in his early 30s. In 1986 he is in his early 50s. The second problem is that in the period 1961 to 1981 the Catholic population has increased by 1.1 million, but the number of diocesan priests has remained constant. Hans Mol (*The Faith of Australia*, 1985, p 6) gives the 1961 Catholic population as 2.6 million and the 1981 Catholic population as 3.8 million. This can be illustrated by examining ratios of priests to people in several archdioceses:

	1966	1986
Sydney	1750	2670
Melbourne	1700	2240
Brisbane	750	2100
Perth	1275	2500

(I have adapted the figures in the *Official Directory of the Catholic Church* by subtracting the priests listed on the 'Supplementary List' and others not in full-time ministry.)

Paul Hewitt has emphasised that not all these priests are involved in direct parish ministry. A number of them (up to 14%) are involved in special ministries as the Church tries to find other ways of meeting the needs confronting it. There has also been a sharp drop in the number of seminarians for the diocesan priesthood: from 479 in 1976 to 288 in 1986. There is no doubt that on present figures the Catholic diocesan clergy in Australia are a dying race – it is just that the process is a little slower here than in other Western countries!

Priests have great expectations projected on to them by the community, but the majority of them are very ordinary men. Most priests tend to be fairly accepting, they are pragmatic and support whatever works. There is not a great deal of sympathy with theoretical solutions, the unconventional or the radical. The prophetic model of priesthood has never been accepted in Australia. Otherwise there is tolerance. Australian priests seem afraid of speaking about the deeper faith questions that trouble their congregations. They often seem inarticulate and afraid of expressing genuine spirituality.

Despite the goodwill of many priests, they are often caught within structures that cut across their good intentions. They are going to have to break out of a pattern whereby the priest is seen as the Church factotum, expected to cover all aspects of ecclesiastical life. This will only break down when the Church allows and encourages a diversity of ministries with full lay participation. Pastoral leadership does not mean doing everything yourself.

To conclude my discussion of the clergy I want to comment on the present system of formation of students for the priesthood in Australia. Most now go to the seminary after a period in the workforce or from some form of professional training. In the seminary they find themselves in circumstances which teach them to think and act institutionally. There is no doubt that the people in the business of priestly and religious formation have made great efforts to develop the ability of candidates and that care is taken in their formation. But despite this the very fact of the seminary inculcates an institutional attitude.

A number of serious problems have emerged in the formation process. Firstly, there has been a significant fall in intellectual standards. Certainly seminaries have tried to lift their performance through association with the universities. This has been achieved through participation in the Melbourne and Sydney Colleges of Divinity. But not all students sit for the College's university standard examinations. Further, a serious and coherent study of philosophy has been largely abandoned in most seminaries. This means that students are not trained to think critically and abstractly and thus are incapable of attempting serious theology. Seminaries generally have very well qualified staffs but the problem of standards arises because staff have to tailor courses to the abilities of the students.

Secondly, there is growing comment in the Catholic community about some of the students being attracted to the seminary. Some candidates openly declare that they are joining the priesthood to put the Church right after the 'excesses' of Vatican II. Not all students are conservative, of course, but some of them may be quite unsuitable for the role of community leadership. Psychosexual immaturity also seems to be a problem for some of them.

Ronald Conway puts the problem succinctly: 'While the religious life undoubtedly needs a "feminine" nurturant quality in its male aspirants, the uncritical social sentimentality and mushy messianic fantasies one finds harboured by some young men who lately want to enter our seminaries or religious congregations can be disquieting.' Shortage of clergy is stampeding some dioceses and religious orders into accepting unsuitable candidates. The so-called vocation shortage is a myth: there are well trained and committed sisters and articulate and willing laity ready to assist. The problem is that Church authorities do not want to have to adapt structures to include these people in ministry.

I do not want to over-emphasise the problem of unsuitable candidates, but the difficulty is that once a priest is ordained it is impossible to sack him. Priests become fixtures. And while they continue to be problem persons, it is the people in the parishes who have to live with them. Thus seminaries and religious orders bear a big responsibility to the people, who have no say in the ordination or appointment of the clergy with whom they have to deal. Certainly, because the Church is human, mistakes were made in the past and will continue to be made. But great care needs to be taken that a pattern is not set up whereby unsuitable candidates become the norm.

I said that religious sisters would be able to step into the breach left by the shortage of clergy. To an extent this is true; sisters can become a bridge between a clerico-centric Church and a Church where most of the ministry is carried by the laity. Sisters are laypersons, yet at the same time they are religious personnel. My own view is that their fundamental task at present is to build a bridge between the clerical and lay Church, by being prepared to train and work alongside laity as they prepare to take over both professional and volunteer ministerial tasks.

The sisters themselves are going through a crisis of numbers – one that has great importance for Australian Catholicism and its ministerial task. Catholic education in Australia was built almost entirely on the backs of religious sisters and brothers. It was the sisters who ran hospitals and carried most of the social welfare of the Church. The debt of the Australian Church to them is enormous.

In the last 20 years there has been a rapid decline in the number of sisters and of priests and brothers who belong to religious orders. Reactionary Catholics immediately blame this on Vatican II tampering with the structures of religious life by granting too much freedom. But the fact is that the Church had come to expect too much from religious. Their numbers had increased enormously since the late 19th century, and the Church had become lazy expecting them to meet every ministerial need. Since 1966, however, there has been a sharp decline in numbers and a great increase in average age:

	1966	1971	1976	1986
Sisters	14,622	13,869	12,469	10,575
Brothers	2,163	2,221	2,089	1,584
Religious priests	2,172	2,113	1,956	1,483

The average age of sisters is now 58; that of religious priests is 50. The decline in the number of sisters is especially significant in view of the fact that they constitute 65% of the Church's religious personnel. This has had an extraordinary effect on Catholic schools which have been virtually taken over in the last 15 years by lay teachers.

This radical realignment of personnel will mean that the Church will become a very different institution in the next 15 years. It will simply be forced to involve more laity in both full-time and part-time ministry. This highlights again the serious need for the theological and ministerial training of laity. You cannot just walk into ministry with goodwill, no training and a vacuous mind. Both formation and information are needed. The Catholic Church tried to involve laity in the days of the Movement. The consequences of that attempt are worth studying. Perhaps it is those years of painful division that make the official Church ambivalent about the involvement of lay persons in ministry and in the official structures of the Church.

Even today you cannot go far in Australian Catholicism without encountering the effects of the Labor split of the 50s and the sharp divisions between the archdioceses of Sydney and Melbourne in the early 1960s over whether it was a sin to vote for the Labor Party. The eminence grise behind it all was (and still is) Bartholomew Augustine ('Bob') Santamaria. In my view, Santamaria is both one of the most interesting and divisive influences in the history of Australian Catholicism. The tragedy is that the split caused by Santamaria and the Movement in the 1950s and 1960s seems to have frightened the Catholic Church away from analysis and comment on public issues in Australia (except, of course, those concerned with reproduction and personal morality). With the exception of the Catholic Commission for Justice and Peace, the leaders of the Catholic Church in Australia have made no significant contribution to the discussion of matters of national interest since the 1960s. The bishops are either unable to agree on issues or are frightened of making a strong stand in case it might be too divisive. The former archbishop of one large metropolitan diocese constantly asked his aides 'to keep him out of trouble'. By this he meant that he wanted to keep away from all contentious public issues.

The people who started the Movement were an interesting group. (The full title of the Movement was the Catholic Social Studies Movement, later the Catholic Social Movement; the National Civic Council (NCC) is Santamaria's present organisation.) Their interest lies in the fact that they were prepared to break the normal Australian pattern: they would neither conform to Australian society nor opt out of it. The origin of the Movement was the Campion Society, begun in Melbourne in 1931. The Society was founded by a small group of Catholics at the University of Melbourne who were inspired by Archbishop Daniel Mannix and by overseas Catholic social thinking. The Campions were influenced by writers such as Hilaire Belloc and G.K. Chesterton in England, by Dorothy Day and the Catholic Worker Movement in the United States and by the social encyclicals of the Popes.

Although the Campion Society was always numerically small, it did generate intellectual passion and it was committed to enhancing the role of the laity. The Campions were originally anti-capitalist. They published the *Catholic Worker* which Santamaria says was largely his responsibility. They supported co-operatives of workers, the need for support for the family and emphasised a return to the land. Santamaria was later to be instrumental in forming the National Catholic Rural Movement (NCRM). The Spanish Civil War changed the direction of these young Catholic idealists. The main enemy became communism rather than capitalism.

The important point about the Campions was that they emphasised the need for the Church to participate in society. They were doctrinaire and ideological and were not content with a Catholicism that comfortably conformed to secular values. The Melbourne Campions were also influenced by Canon (later Cardinal) Joseph Cardijn's YCW (Young Christian Workers) movement. The YCW organised young Catholics to be bearers of Christ's message to the workplace. The YCW developed a unique spirituality based on a three-pronged approach:

SEE – what is going on in the workplace, neighbourhood and society.

JUDGE – reality in the light of the gospel and the discernment of the Christian community.

ACT – as a minister of Christ to change what is evil, destructive and exploitative.

This approach was to make the YCW much more socially radical and they were eventually to break with the Movement.

B.A. Santamaria emerged from this matrix. He was a man of energy and determination, and by the end of the Second World War it was becoming clear that he wished to reshape Australian society in terms of his own vision of Catholic social principles. In other words, Santamaria was, and remains, an ideologue. Hard-nosed ideology is very foreign to Australian society, which is pragmatic and empirical. Santamaria is more in the European tradition. He views everything in terms of a cosmic struggle, a clash of absolutes. As I mentioned, the Spanish Civil War was the turning point for many Campions. A communist victory in Spain would have meant persecution for the Church. Communism came to be seen as the ultimate expression of evil. Santamaria became increasingly concerned about the infiltration of the ALP and the unions by the communists.

Meanwhile, in 1937, the bishops had placed all Catholic Action under the control of the Australian National Secretariat of Catholic Action. Santamaria was appointed assistant director. But it was communist power that preoccupied him.

Santamaria had already begun organising in 1940. He had obtained the support of Archbishop Mannix to begin a movement of Catholics dedicated to dealing with communists in industry and the ALP. The first meeting of the Movement was held in Melbourne in August 1942. The Movement encouraged the establishment of industrial groups in the ALP. Most prominent 'Groupers' were Movement men.

Communist-inspired strikes in the late 1940s led to a reaction in the electorate and the Liberal-Country Party under Robert Menzies gained power in the 1949 elections. The Cold War and the Korean War were under way, and Menzies judged that he could finally break the Communist Party with the Communist Party Dissolution Bill (April 1950). This bill was subsequently declared unconstitutional by the High Court and defeated in a referendum.

With the death of Chifley, the ALP came under the leadership of H.V. Evatt. The left wing, frightened by the dangers to civil liberties in the anti-communist scare, tried to break the power of the right-wing Groupers. It was the Petrov affair on the eve of the 1954 elections which brought Labor disunity to a head. The doctrinaire aggressiveness of many members of the Movement, their self-righteousness and the threat posed to the power of established and experienced Catholic ALP politicians, turned moderate as well as left-wing ALP members against the Groupers. After the Petrov Royal Commission Evatt (who appeared before the Commission to defend members of his staff) was attacked as a 'pink' by the right wingers. The Groupers labelled anyone who disagreed with them as either pink or red. Evatt counter-attacked by denouncing the right wing of the ALP in Victoria, saying they were ' . . . disloyal to the Labor movement and to Labor leadership. It seems certain that the activities of this small group are directed from outside the Labor movement.'

This was a direct reference to Santamaria, the Movement, Mannix and ultimately to the Catholic Church. The sectarian infighting that followed led to the split of 1955 and the eventual formation of the Democratic Labor Party.

But this was not the end of the matter. The Movement was also to be instrumental in leading to the most public split in the ranks of the Australian bishops in the entire history of the Catholic Church in this country. It caused a most divisive and destructive division between Catholics, a division which still deeply affects the Church in Victoria. But at first the split was between Sydney and Melbourne.

In Sydney Catholic Action had always been kept firmly under episcopal control. A key figure in Sydney was Archbishop James Carroll who had close ties to the state Labor Party. Sydney Catholics became increasingly suspicious of the doctrinaire and confrontationalist policies emanating from Melbourne Catholic Action headquarters. When in May 1960, Bishop Arthur Fox (then Auxiliary of Archbishop Mannix, later Bishop of Sale) publicly said he would regard himself as 'having a bad conscience' if he voted for the ALP the assertion developed that 'it was a mortal sin to vote for the ALP'. Sacred Heart priest Doctor Leslie Rumble responded as official spokesman for the Sydney archdiocese that 'Catholic leaders in Victoria cannot instruct Catholics not to vote Labor'. A very public dispute followed between Rumble on the one hand, and Fox and Mannix on the other.

The results of this division still haunt the Catholic community. In the 1950s Santamaria and the Movement had generated hysteria among Catholics. Their manic preoccupation with communism was a product of their own dualistic conceptions of the world. They cast reality in terms of conflicting ideologies. Communist influence in Australia – especially in the unions – was a major problem. But the use of methods akin to those of the communists themselves by a movement officially sponsored by the Church, has to be seriously questioned. In terms of its attitude and ideology, the Movement was very similar to communism. It was the people in the middle who suffered.

Santamaria's activities continue. He never seems to have really accepted Vatican II. His own true métier was the absolutist Church of the 1940s and 1950s. He seems to be getting a new lease of life in the neo-conservatism of the late 1980s. He has also shifted his sights. His targets now are liberal and 'heretical' clerics, such as Hans Küng. In *News Weekly* (13 November 1985) he explains the situation of Christianity (and specifically the Anglican and Catholic Churches) in typically absolutist and apocalyptic terms:

The real question facing each denomination (the Anglican and Catholic Churches) is whether the great historical crisis through which Christianity is obviously passing is temporary or terminal. Such a statement is commonly dismissed as exaggerated or pessimistic. Facts, however, cannot be either optimistic or pessimistic. They are either true or false.

There is no use trying to tackle the specious logic of this statement. Santamaria goes on to argue that the only way to save the Church is to set the 'outer parameters of doctrinal orthodoxy'. He accuses both Anglican Bishop David Jenkins of Durham and Father Hans Küng of having strayed beyond those outer parameters. Küng is accused of not believing in the physical resurrection of Jesus, the divinity of Christ or in miracles. Santamaria seems to have forgotten Küng's views on infallibility! Then he admits that Küng's books do not *state* heresy but they clearly *imply* it. Thus Küng, the author of three major theological works in the last ten years, is dismissed by an untrained theologian in a 10 minute TV spot!

There is a sense in which Santamaria represents the old Catholic right in Australia. In the last five to seven years a new Catholic right has emerged, especially in Sydney and Melbourne. It is less directly concerned with communism, except in so far as it sees communist elements in liberation theology. The central focus of the new right is doctrinal deviancy. Groups of Catholics in Australia (and overseas – especially in the United States) aim to put the Church back on the track after what they consider to be the confusion and the misinterpretation of Vatican II. Their hero is increasingly Pope John Paul II.

One of the first organised groups was the Cardinal Newman Catechist Centre in Sydney. It was begun by Father James Tierney who, with a group of religious and lay people, organised a supply of 'orthodox' catechetical material. One can sympathise with the original aim. Some very poor educational material was put out in the years immediately following the Council. Much of it was without a great deal of theological content. But this was quickly corrected. The Cardinal Newman Centre now puts out material of a right-wing reactionary type that is, to an extent, in opposition to the publications of the official religious educational bodies of the archdiocese of Sydney.

Then there is the John XXIII Fellowship and the John XXIII Co-Op. The Fellowship is an association of lay people who are concerned with what they see as doctrinal deviance and confusion among the majority of Australian Catholics. The Fellowship has loosely organised groups in Melbourne, Sydney and Canberra. A number of members are university trained. They hold an annual national conference. The Co-Op is the active arm of the fellowship. It is a voluntary organisation run from Melbourne by a group of lay people and it imports and distributes books and material from overseas – mainly from the United States where Catholic ultra-conservatism is well established and well funded. The Co-Op also publishes an occasional newsletter entitled *Fidelity*.

It has, for instance, reprinted in Australia *The Ratzinger Report*. This book contains the now famous 1985 interview with Cardinal Josef Ratzinger, head of the Vatican Congregation for the Doctrine of the Faith. Ratzinger talks about the need for what he calls a Catholic restoration. His view is that the Church since Vatican II has abandoned the real spirit of the Council. He says: 'It must be clearly stated that a real reform of the Church presupposes an unequivocal turning away from the erroneous paths whose catastrophic consequences are already incontestable.'

I suspect that some of the people who participate in these right-wing organisations are older Catholics who feel disenfranchised since Vatican II. They have lost their simple faith and cannot deal with the complexity of the contemporary Church. Many of the others, however, are young people. They are probably the products of the catechetical confusion after Vatican II. Given nothing substantial in their youth, they have sought stability in hyper-orthodoxy. Many of them also reject the deep social commitment and concern of the contemporary Church. Some unconsciously seek a religion that contextualises their upwardly mobile lifestyle. For some people organisations like John XXIII Fellowship or the integralist organisation Opus Dei are very appealing. This hyper-orthodox line has been taken by a few journalists writing recently in Catholic newspapers. Gary Scarrabelotti, described in the *Catholic Weekly* as a Sydney journalist (presumably he is not on the staff of the *Weekly*) has written a number of articles on both theology and social issues. In 'Behind the Scenes in Nicaragua' (*Catholic Weekly*, 7 December 1983), he attacks the 'popular Church' in that country, and in February 1986 he mounted an attack on the Catholic Commission for Justice and Peace and their paper *Work for a Just Peace* (1985). Scarrabelotti's comments on the situation in Nicaragua are characterised by such generalisations as:

Nicaragua's basic Christian communities for more than a decade have provided the infrastructure, cadre and ideology of the People's Church. What has happened is that the so-called progressive clergy, led by figures like the Sandanista Minister for Culture, Ernesto Cardenal, have carved out a new sort of Catholicism with the help of liberation theology. According to this doctrine the chief end of Christianity is to bring about the Kingdom of God on earth by passing the judgement of revolution on the unjust and the oppressors. Nicaraguan liberation theology has turned the Catholic religion into a secular political movement.

No one who has read any serious liberation theology or who knows of the work of Father Ernesto Cardinal in the literacy campaign, in which 90% of the Nicaraguan people were taught to read and write, would recognise either of them in Scarrabelotti's caricature. To reduce basic Christian communities to a marxist front is an outrageous distortion. He clearly sets out to denigrate those sections of the Nicaraguan Church which do not agree with his political stance. His work is typical of the journalism of the new right, marred by vast and unsubstantiated generalisations and by a naive dualism that casts all reality in terms of good and evil, truth and error, God and Satan. Much of its rhetoric unconsciously betrays unresolved anger and resentment and a manic defence against life's complexity.

Anyone who writes about Australia and Australian Catholicism has to come to grips with Ronald Conway. He is a Melbourne clinical psychologist, the author of an impressive trilogy of books *The Great Australian Stupor* (1971), the *Land of the Long Weekend* (1978) and *The End of Stupor?* (1984). Conway has attempted an analysis of the Australian psyche and he has tried to tease out what constitutes a specifically Australian identity.

As is the case with most Catholic thinkers, people are more important to him than social issues or movements. He believes that the key formative factors for people are the modelling relationships formed in the family circle. Thus he harbours the usual Catholic suspicion of the influence of external structures on human life and development. This view seems to me to underestimate context and environment as formative factors on the human psyche and especially on human relationships. People do not exist in a vacuum. They are part of a societal structure which either enhances or debases their human dignity and human interactions. Human maturity is gradually achieved through personal and interpersonal development and through interaction with the structures within which one lives and moves. Certainly, as Conway suggests, the myopic focus on one trendy issue to the exclusion of all others is both dangerous and stupid. But issues do at least give people a focus for their energy. And the fact is that very few have the intelligence to develop a broad catholic attitude.

I think Conway's view of most Australians (especially men) as 'secular slobs' is too harsh. He contrasts Australia to the United States and implies that because Americans go to church, they are more religious than Australians. He has obviously never lived for any length of time in the United States, or perhaps has a more generous definition of religion than I. He seems to miss the fact that a lot of North American religion, especially of the fundamentalist type, is what he would call 'patrist-authoritarian' (in other words it is 'red necked', inhibited and sexually repressive, inclined to right-wing, militaristic violence, seeing money and status as signs of God's 'blessing'). Much North American religion is self-indulgent, superficial and geared to fulfilling the naive fantasies of its adherents. It is quite silly to confuse this with genuine Christianity. The Catholic Church in the United States has emerged as one of the few challenging and faithfully Christian bodies in that country. In Australia there are many people asking the precise questions that Conway considers important for a fully human and religious view of life. The very fact of Australian secularism forces intelligent and sensitive people to confront questions that centre around meaning and transcendence.

Mention of Australian secularism and its relationship to religion always triggers a reaction in this country. Australia has been generally presented as a truly 'secular' society. Even religious writers accept this view and refer to it as 'the first post-Christian society'. The assumption of most commentators is that the predominant national ethos is secular and this-worldly. The origins of this view of Australia are to be found in the *Bulletin* writers of the 1880s who presented Australia as a secular 'paradise' that would become increasingly free of religious dogmatism and cant. Secular education was seen as the vehicle of this process. The idea of Australia as an explicitly secular society has now attained the status of myth. Australian historian, Manning Clark, says that myth is always more important than fact. It is the myth that sustains us and gives meaning and structure to our lives. What we believe about ourselves and our past is always much more important than historical or sociological facts. We have come to believe that Australia is a secular society and always has been. Historians such as Russell Ward (*The Australian Legend* 1976) have developed the idea that religion was always a marginal influence in Australia and, in the bush at least, the main 'religion' was that of mateship. Subsequent writers have simply accepted the myth without question.

The myth insists that Australia has *always* been secular. It stresses that the country was founded in the wake of the deism and the anti-religion of the 18th century enlightenment. It is peppered with the story of the addition of Rev Richard Johnson as chaplain to the First Fleet as an afterthought. The fact is that the enlightenment was not all that anti-religious and that there was concern for religion in the colony, where the Anglican clergy played a most important role. After 1815 there was profound concern in the Colonial Office about morality and religion in the colony. Evangelical Protestantism and Irish Catholicism played an important role in the life and official structures of New South Wales and Van Diemen's Land. Colonial Office policy was profoundly influenced by James Stephen, Under Secretary of State for the Colonies from the mid-1820s onwards. He was a deeply pious evangelical. The Church Act of 1836 granted official status to the Churches, including the Catholic Church. To say that Australia was a 'secular society' before 1870 is nonsense. From the late 19th century onwards, the Churches continued to play a large part in the formation of the Australian ethos. Even that archetypical secular 'saint', Henry Lawson, spent much of his life struggling with questions of morality and religion.

A couple of variations have emerged on this theme of Australian secularism. Patrick O'Farrell has suggested that Catholicism has always acted as a deviant force, questioning the predominantly secularist ideology, while, of course, being only too happy to share in secularism's concomitant, materialism. Bruce Wilson (*Can God Survive in Australia?*, 1983) suggests that what was originally a 'Christian country' has now become a secular society. He quotes figures to show the sharp decline of Protestant (and to a lesser extent Catholic) practice in Australia since the 1960s.

In fact, Australia might well be more religious than a country like Britain. You have only to take off the blinkers imposed by the secularist myth and open your eyes to discover a large number of churches in the cities and the country towns. Not all of them are old. New churches are being built in the new suburbs. Canberra is an example. The Catholic Church cannot keep up with the new churches and schools required in the rapidly developing suburbs. And public servants are no more religious than the rest of the population! About one quarter of the population attend church with some degree of regularity. A high proportion of those who practise are Catholics. (By practise I mean attend a religious service at least once a week – for Catholics this will be Sunday Mass.) While the rate of Catholic practice has dropped from the extraordinarily high figure of around 58% to 60% in the 1950s, it is now steady around 35% to 38%. This is a higher level of practice than in many so-called 'Catholic' countries. A significant minority of Australians are obviously committed to a religious view of life.

It is, of course, the mainline Protestant Churches that have lost most adherents. In order to make themselves relevant and in order to communicate with the de-churched masses, they have tried to sanctify the superficial symbols of secularised Australia. Bishop Bruce Wilson, for instance, wants the Churches to see in 'ockerism' a set of values that can be embraced in the process of evangelisation. He defines ockerism in terms of egalitarianism, the celebration of life and the idea of the little battler who has to struggle to make a go of it. David Millikan has developed similar ideas in his essay 'Christianity and Australian Identity'. He sees Norman Gunston and Paul Hogan as archetypical Australian figures. To Wilson's list of ocker characteristics, Millikan adds anti-wowserism, anti-intellectualism, mateship and humour. Precisely what the Church is supposed to do with these characteristics is not clear. They strike me as being essentially male and fundamentally sexist. Presumably they propose to take these values and express the Church's message in terms of them. It is the type of relevance that Ronald Conway condemns.

An attempt has already been made to express key elements of the New Testament in ocker English. These ocker characteristics are supposed to be ways of approaching Australians who vaguely believe in God but who are not committed to the Church. Gordon Dicker, theologian at the United Theological College, takes up the same theme on a more serious theological level in his essay 'Keregyma and Australian Culture: The Case of the Aussie Battler'. The treatment still remains unconvincing, not because the theology is bad, but because the supposed cultural images are superficial and unreal.

On the other hand the Catholic Church in Australia is insufficiently interested in evangelisation. It tends to be self-satisfied and to rest on its laurels. What is needed for conversion is a quiet, steady and persistent approach to the deeper questions which trouble people. The problem of evangelisation is not one of advertising or of relating to stereotype images individuals might have of themselves. It is much more an ability to articulate the questions that people are asking themselves but have not yet brought fully to consciousness. The Church should be addressing the mature persons who are seeking meaning. It is no use answering questions that people have not asked, articulating needs that people do not experience. Being part of the culture does not mean being ocker; it means being so much in touch with people that one can discern the issues that stir individuals and the community at a deep level. It is not the task of genuine faith to address mythical sterotypes, but to be concerned with profound cultural and human questions.

While maintaining contact with children and youth, the Catholic Church in Australia needs increasingly to address the mature and experienced person. During the last decade there was much talk about the midlife crisis. This so-called crisis was simply the articulation of a range of important religious and life issues that face mature adults. The conversion of the masses is an illusion. In terms of numbers, Jesus himself was not roaringly successful. He finally ended up with a small band of followers who stayed with him until the crucifixion. To attempt mass conversion is a form of triumphalism. Charismatics seem particularly guilty of this. Profound and truly tested faith is the product of deep perception and profound questions.

The most up-to-date statistical survey of religion in Australia is the recent book by Hans Mol, *The Faith of Australians* (1985). This shows that the decline of religion in Australia is not as dramatic as has been made out. Mol argues that the contemporary role of the Church in the lives of Australians is to provide a sheet anchor, a point of stability. Alan Gill, in a series of articles in the *Sydney Morning Herald* (13, 14, 15 January 1986) also emphasises the steady and continuing influence of religion in Australia. The *Herald* survey seems to fit in with Mol's findings:

On any ordinary Sunday, the Catholic Church is far bigger than any other denomination . . . Catholics make up almost half of Australia's regular Church goers, and census data showing that Catholics have a younger age profile than any other denomination suggests that their numerical advance will increase. (*Sydney Morning Herald*, 13 January 1986, p 2)

It seems to me that one can argue from Mol's work that the Churches face two choices: either to retire to a ghetto and become sects, or to face out into the world by participating in it while retaining commitment to the person and gospel of Jesus. The first choice is the easiest.

The exclusive charismatic and fundamentalist Churches are growing fast. They offer safe separation from a complex and diversified culture through specific commitment and moral clarity. Hans Mol comments: 'The fact that they seem to have the fastest growth as well as the highest church-going rate may fore-shadow a twenty first century culture in which islands of strong ideological commitment mop up the increasing number of refugees from a society in which complexity, tolerance and moral vagueness . . .' are key components.

But the sectarian solution can never be a choice for Catholicism. What is happening in Australian religion is that a significant realignment is occurring. Ecumenism and common theological and scriptural study has broken down the old divisions of Catholic and Protestant. New groupings are emerging: one group comprises liberal and mainline Catholics and Protestants who are committed to social justice and to an inclusive understanding of the Church; the other group comprises conservative Catholics and evangelical Protestants committed to personal piety, fundamentalist theology and to an exclusive conception of the Church.

Since 1947 the two fastest growing groups in the religious affiliation section of the Australian census have been the No Religion and Catholic categories. The Catholic proportion of the population was:

1947	20.7%
1971	27.0%

1976	25.7%
1981	26.0%
1986	estimated at 27% or more

The No Religion category is also growing fast:

1947	0.4%
1976	8.3%
1981	10.8% (more than 1.5 million people)

If this is added to the no reply to religious affiliation category (10.9% in 1981), this means that 21.7% of the population (or 3.2 million people) have either no religious commitment or this commitment is not known. These are probably our secularists in the strict sense. It is significant that they are still not as numerous as Catholics, let alone all Christians together. So much for Australia as a secular, post-Christian society!

The main reason for Catholic growth has been immigration, for Catholic fertility is only marginally higher than that of the general population. Since the beginning of post-war immigration in 1947, the institutions of the Catholic Church have been put under enormous pressure. As usual, the Church's response to this pressure has been ad hoc, without a great deal of planning or thought. Some readers may remember a novel that was popular in the late 1950s called *They're A Weird Mob* (1957) by Nino Culotta, the pseudonym used by Australian writer John O'Grady. It purported to be the story of an Italian immigrant who arrived in Sydney in the 1950s. It described his initiation as a 'dinkum New Australian'. That was the aim of government (with the Church in unprotesting tow) until the late 1960s – assimilation. The task was to teach 'New Australians' English, to help them to adapt to Anglo-Australian mores and thus to conform, make money and be secure. As Pastor of a large Catholic parish in Sydney's eastern suburbs in the late 70s, I often went to naturalisation ceremonies at the local town hall. The speeches at these ceremonies normally reflected the theme: 'You are lucky to be here, so make the most of it! Australia has so much to offer you'. There was no inkling that the cultures from which the migrants had come (all of them much more ancient than Anglo-Australian culture) might have anything to offer our young nation.

Professor Jean Martin has explained the basis of this assimilationist ideology. It asserts that Australians are open, free of class prejudice and individualist. Migrants are lucky to be here. With some help and education, Australia can incorporate them within its own cultural structures. Ethnic national groups were seen as a potential threat to assimilation. Assimilation depended on the goodwill of individuals, not on structural change. Certainly, many migrants were 'assimilated', but the policy created a sub-culture of deprived migrants while Anglo-Australians maintained their power and privilege.

In the late 1960s and the early 1970s it was finally seen what was really happening to migrants in Australia. The high rate of return to the homeland and the material and cultural poverty in which many migrants lived became apparent. Father John Heaps (now Bishop), formerly director of the Catholic Immigration Office in Sydney says:

. . . because of mistakes and neglect hundreds of thousands of migrants have left Australia disillusioned and disappointed . . . In the five-year period of 1968 to 1972 the returning settlers averaged twenty-four per cent of the arrivals. These people made a deliberate decision to come to Australia and a deliberate decision to leave again. The unhappiness between these decisions will never be known . . . The fact that there is need for specific Christian caring is evidenced by these figures. ('Some Problems Involved in Immigrating')

In 1973 a change in the ideology of immigration occurred. Jean Martin cites A.J. Grassby's paper *A Multicultural Society for the Future* as the turning point. Grassby stressed the need for pluralism based on ethnicity. The implications of this are far-reaching, for it implies a shift in the direction of power-sharing in Australian society.

The official Catholic Church (through the Federal Catholic Immigration Committee) reflected the assimilationist line, but it has not shown a great deal of enthusiasm for multiculturalism. One would expect that an international Church would be the first to realise the religious values embedded in many of the migrants' cultures. But, as in so many other ways, the Australian Catholic Church has been more Australian than Catholic.

Yet the impact of immigration on Catholicism has been tremendous. Around 45% of all Catholics in this country are either born overseas themselves or are children with at least one parent born overseas. Most Catholic migrants are from a non-English-speaking background. Many of them are of rural or peasant origin, and so have been especially vulnerable in the process of adapting to urban Australian conditions.

The Catholic Church has done little to respond to this massive demographic change. The bishops made one early decision, not to allow the development of 'national parishes'. They were trying to avoid the experience of the United States' Church where the care of migrants was handed over to parishes devoted exclusively to one national group. This led to the development of the Church along ethnic lines and occasionally to minor schisms.

Chaplains were brought to Australia to care largely for the first generation of new arrivals. Their task was to offer Mass, the sacraments and counsel in the traditional language. Many of these priests were given very little personal or ministerial support by the Australian clergy. A number of religious orders also came to care for specific migrant groups: the Scalabrinian Fathers care for Italian migrants, the Society of Christ for Poles and the Paulist Fathers for Maltese. Some of these religious orders have been given parishes that have become de facto national parishes, but generally migrant chaplains have had to depend on parish priests for access to churches. Father Humphry O'Leary suggested in 1971 that migrant chaplains be granted 'the powers of a pastor' for the people of their own ethnic groups. Thus chaplains would have a kind of personal parish. But this idea has not been taken up by the Australian bishops.

The most extensive study of the relationship of migrants and the Australian Catholic Church is by Australian National University sociologist Frank Lewins (*The Myth of the Universal Church*, 1978). Lewins says bluntly: 'The migrant's experience of the Australian Catholic Church is generally characterised by neglect and antagonism' (p 92). While the book is highly critical of the Catholic response to migrants, there are serious problems with the over-simplified model of the Church adopted by Lewins. As Cyril Hally has pointed out, the Church is far more decentralised and complex in its inter-relationships than Lewins suggests.

Nevertheless, Lewins' criticisms should be taken seriously. The first is the failure of Catholicism to accept the different religious attitudes of various immigrant groups. Many migrants have difficulty adjusting to the Australian Catholic milieu, and the local Church has failed to be enriched from the experiences of much older Catholic cultures. To illustrate this it is worth looking at some of the practical situations which have developed in Australia. Italians, for instance, have a much more demonstrative faith, a consciousness that religion and participation in the life of the community are intimately connected, and a sense of the continuity of life after death. They find the Australian liturgy lifeless and uninvolving, and the tendency of Australian Catholics to rush off immediately after Mass socially abrasive. Lewins quotes an Italian migrant chaplain as saying: 'In Italy the Mass lasts 45 minutes, then the social life starts in the marketplace; whereas in Australia, after Mass the Australian goes to his car . . . leaving the Italian standing on the church steps wondering' (p 94). On the continuity of family and clan ties after death: Italians offer a stipend for Mass to be celebrated for a deceased relative and they want the name mentioned publicly. It is part of their sense of continuity of life after death. Many Australian priests brush this aside. Either they refuse to accept the proffered stipend, or they take it but do not publish the name or let the relatives know when the Mass will be said. In either case, many Italians are puzzled and hurt by this.

Catholics from Eastern bloc countries – such as Poles, Ukrainians and Croats – usually manifest a strong interrelationship between Catholicism, nationalism and anti-communism. The links between Catholicsm and nationalism are, at times, especially hard for Australian-born Catholics to comprehend. Strong anti-communism is also a characteristic of some Vietnamese Catholics. Anti-communism can sometimes lead to anti-socialist and anti-

ALP attitudes. Anyone familiar with both Croatian and Polish Catholics will immediately perceive the deep consciousness of homeland politics and the way in which the communities are haunted by historical resentments. While they may not approve of them, Australian Catholics have got to come to understand these realities.

Ukrainian and Lebanese Catholics are in a special category for they are Eastern rite and have their own bishops. They have tended to insist that their people be married (and even sometimes buried) only in the Eastern rite liturgy – even if the couple involved in the marriage do not want to celebrate their union with a liturgy that is sometimes foreign to them. This has led to some very difficult pastoral situations for Australian priests.

In summary, the Australian Church does not seem to have a researched or thought-through policy with regard to the pastoral care of new arrivals.

Father Cyril Hally has written a significant research paper entitled 'Migrants and the Australian Catholic Church' (National Catholic Research Council, 1979). He suggests the setting up of a research and policy development unit to 'collate the material necessary for working out and putting into practice as pastoral strategy' for the care of migrants in Australia. To my knowledge the bishops have done nothing about this to date.

The Church has assumed, and to a large extent in practice continues to assume, an assimilationist stance. Despite the change of government policy, the emphasis on multiculturalism has not changed the attitude of many priests and laypersons. In most parishes the demand is that migrants conform to the prevailing Anglo-Australian religious ethos. Multiculturalism has a close affinity to the concept of the Catholicity of the Church. In fact, government policy sometimes accidentally reflects the contemporary model of Church : a unity enriched by a genuine catholicity of cultural forms. But, as far as the Church is concerned, this will remain in the realm of pious theory if structural reform does not enshrine it in reality. The Church must move in the direction of giving a canonical basis to the ministry of the migrant chaplains, who need to be screened and specifically trained for their work.

Continuing human and material support should be given to migrants, especially to the most vulnerable groups and individuals. This will mean shifting resources from current priorities. The Australian clergy and laity need to be made more aware of the wide-ranging changes that are occurring. Any manifestation of racism – as Geoffrey Blainey has shown, this is a strong undercurrent in Australian society – needs to be confronted and dealt with through education and conscientisation, especially when it occurs within the context of the life of the Church.

I want to turn now to the Catholic education system. It is seen by many as one of the great achievements of Australian Catholicism. There is no doubt that it has been built on the continuing generosity and sacrifice of generations of Catholic laity and religious men and women. The granting of government aid to Catholic schools, however, has brought about a fundamental change in the position of the Catholic system, but few seem to have commented on it. While Government money has not come with obvious strings attached, such aid has a subtle way of subsuming Catholic education to its own ends. The Catholic system rests on the assumption that it provides an alternative to the education offered by the State. This implies that Church education offers something different. But it is precisely this which is open to question.

Certainly, there is a great danger in granting the State a monopoly of education. The unimaginative aridity of so much modern education reflects the superficial secularism which underpins it. Also State education is far too controlled by an all-pervasive bureaucracy.

But the danger of total State control does not alone justify the existence of the Catholic system. It needs a coherent philosophy of its own and it should be effective as a ministerial instrument of the Church.

Hans Mol (*The Faith of Australians*, 1985) devotes a chapter to denominational schools. He comes up with the following conclusions based on his sociological data. (The following is my summary):

1. Those attending Catholic schools are consistently more religious (in an external sense) than those who do not. In other words they practise their faith and pray regularly. However, Catholics from State schools still scored higher on religious practice than Protestants. This seems to indicate that the home is an important factor in influencing practice.

2. Catholics from Catholic schools are more ambitious – they want to get ahead (indicating, perhaps, a more competitive atmosphere?); but they think that the most important thing for a child to learn is obedience rather than independence.

3. Catholics from Catholic schools tend to be stricter in sexual mores than Catholics from State schools or Protestants.

4. The local parish is important for Catholics from Catholic schools for the majority find their closest friends there.

5. The Catholic school does not seem to have inculcated a great deal of personal piety in those under 40, but it has emphasised public religious practice, such as Mass.

If Catholic schools are to be genuinely alternative they must be different in a substantial sense from other schools, they must reflect in themselves and form in their students a coherent Catholic Christian understanding of the nature of human existence and they must espouse the values that underpin that understanding. If they were to do this, they would certainly be different, especially from the State schools which are underpinned by a secularist philosophy. It is my opinion that Catholic secondary schools – especially the more elite ones – have failed to offer a truly alternative Catholic education. Subtly, they have absorbed an ethos which is pragmatic, competitive, consumerist and materialist. They may well offer their students a verbal deviance, a critique of Australian standards, but the values that permeate the school, the ethos that subliminally expresses to the students what the school is really all about, is more often materialist than Catholic. Part of the problem is that the Catholic school system has a momentum of its own and it is hard to stop. A large number of people have a vested interest in maintaining it. It is going to be very difficult to change in any substantial way.

Catholic schools must be judged in the light of the nature of the Church and its mission. The Church does not exist for its own sake, but only to carry out the task entrusted to it by Jesus Christ. Therefore, I will attempt to set out the three basic ministerial tasks facing the Church today:

• To proclaim the person and teaching of Jesus Christ. The primary mission of the Church is that people may know him. This is *evangelisation*.

• To be the presence of Christ in the world today. The Church is his body, is animated by his Spirit, and it exists to lead people back to God, and to the fullness that he alone can give. This is *sanctification*.

• To serve the world, to be part of a particular culture, to promote the truly human values of that culture – which must always be judged in the light of the gospel – and to offer a legitimate protest against dehumanising values. Basic to this is the promotion of social justice. This is *humanisation*.

Catholic schools are, by definition, ministerial instruments that the Church uses to fulfil its mission in the world. Were they established for this purpose? Answers given by historians as to why the Church set up a school system are really variations on a theme and are closely interconnected.

T.L. Suttor contends that the issue was essentially one of secularism versus Catholicism. He contends that Australian democracy right from the start was hitched to ' . . . the bandwaggon of all-conquering ideas like liberty and progress', (*Hierarchy and Democracy in Australia*, 1965, p 244). Suttor says that the framers of the Education Acts of the 1860s and 1870s were secular liberals, men who ' . . . attacked the very idea of Christianity by attacking the concept of God the Creator, of religion . . . the supernatural, and so of revelation and dogma' (pp 246-247). The Catholic bishops discerned the secularist motivation of the Acts, and they determined to set up an independent school system. In this they succeeded because they acted in concert. Suttor sees the whole affair as the conflict of two principles. There are certain limitations to his view, for he tends to see everything in terms of ideas – an unusual tendency in an Australian academic! Probably the ideological issue was more important for Catholics than it was for the secularists.

Patrick O'Farrell (*The Catholic Church and Community in Australia*, 1977) sees the issue in terms of the Church's constant rejection of those values which have been predominant in Australian society. He considers that the rejection of the 'free, secular and compulsory' Acts was based on the refusal to admit the principle that was behind them. The bishops' pastoral letter of 1879 clearly indicates that principle: ' . . . education without Christianity is impossible'. O'Farrell maintains that Catholicism ' . . . has continually refused to adopt fully and in some areas has directly contradicted, the prevailingly accepted structure, attitudes and values of Australian society.' Establishment of the Catholic education system is an expression of this critical role.

Brother Ronald Fogerty (*Catholic Education in Australia*, vol. I, 1966) and Professor Manning Clark (*A Short History of Australia*, 1963) tend to see the Education Acts and the consequent setting up of the Catholic school system in terms of the philosophical themes of Australian history. The secular liberals were joined by the anti-Catholic Protestants ' . . . to drive religion out of subsidised state education'. Clark stresses also the importance of sectarian strife: 'Part of the price for the folly and madness of such sectarian strife was the introduction of the secular clauses in the new Education Acts.'

A.G. Austin (*Australian Education 1788-1900*, 1961) argues that the fundamental belief of the colonial legislators who passed the Education Acts was that the State had a responsibility to provide education. He admits that there was a strain of hostility to the Churches, but he maintains that there was little doubt in the liberal mind that it was the State and not the Church which should assume responsibility for education.

There is a real consensus in the views of these historians. The bishops simply refused to compromise on fundamentals. For them the basic principle was that Catholic Christianity must permeate all education. Certainly their motives were not totally religious or disinterested. Some of them were spoiling for a fight! But their action does have a prophetic ring. They contended that an explicitly Catholic ethos must pervade the whole of education. They realised that this could not be divorced from the Church's doctrinal teaching. Religion could not be tacked on as an added extra. It had to create an atmosphere that pervaded the whole school and all that the school stood for. The bishop's world view made spiritual and religious values the pivotal point of education. They saw the Catholic Church as offering an alternative view of society, one that would not totally accept the prevailing culture and ethos.

Catholic schools today face the same issue. They have to discover what it means to offer an alternative vision of education and society in the modern world. Here it needs to be emphasised that alternative does not mean ghetto or sub-culture or any form of opting out of society. It refers to the development of a critical sense among Catholics of the prevailing standards of the society to which they belong, a demand that a religious and spiritual world-view be recognised and respected, and that the Christian values of justice, integrity and a care for the marginalised be recognised as the duty of society. It will demand that peace education be an integral part of any syllabus and that Catholic children be taught to build the structures of reconciliation, not the instruments of war. Ultimately, the Catholic school must recognise the centrality of the person and message of Jesus.

Here the views of Ivan Illich (*Deschooling Society*, 1973) are helpful. Illich maintains that schools and similar institutions (such as seminaries) are means by which a society maintains conformity to prevailing values. The school is the institution where the sustaining myths of the culture are inculcated. It is precisely the myths of secular Australia that need to be questioned. Catholic schools need to confront the competitive, consumerist and materialist values that form the ethos of Australian culture. One would have to question whether Catholic schools are 'better' than State schools if all they do is prepare their pupils only to be better performers in the competitive rat-race. The inherent materialism of the culture needs to be confronted by the transcendant values embedded in the Catholic tradition. But the temptation to form a sectarian sub-culture must be resisted. The tradition of Catholicism is to participate in society, not to stand outside it. The task of the Church is not to reshape society from without, but to offer a coherent criticism from within.

I want to turn now to one body that has tried to offer a coherent critique of Australian society – the Catholic Commission for Justice and Peace (CCJP). The Catholic Church in Australia has been frequently criticised for favouring the well-to-do middle class in its allotment of resources and services. Groups such as Aborigines, Catholic students in State schools, migrants and those economically and socially deprived, have been badly neglected. Middle class Catholics have been good at getting justice for themselves. They have been very unwilling to stand up for the rights of the marginalised and the voiceless. But it is not just a matter of prophecy and strident denunciation. It also involves information. Because the Church has neglected the social sciences it often lacks the information necessary to make an informed statement. The National Catholic Research Council has been set up and has already produced good research work. But it is principally CCJP that has been prepared to face the tough issues in an informed way. This has been shown by a series of documents that they have issued over recent years: *A New Australia: Some Reflections on the Impact of Migration on Australian Society* (1977), *Aborigines: A Statement of Concern* (1978), *Beyond Unemployment: A Statement on Human Labour* (1979) and *Work for A Just Peace: Reflection on Peacemaking in An Armed World* (1985). The last of these statements has been attacked because it questions the morality of having US military facilities such as Pine Gap, the North West Cape and Nurrungar in Australia. It has also been argued that the statement enters into political and strategic areas of decision-making and that bishops and CCJP have no expertise in these areas. Leading the attack on CCJP are B.A. Santamaria, Father Terence Purcell and Sydney journalist Gary Scarrabelotti. CCJP's document on peace has also been criticised by Bishop Geoffrey Mayne (Bishop of the Military Vicariate).

By Australian standards CCJP takes a left-wing line. But, as I have already indicated, this places it in about the middle of the world Catholic spectrum. *Work for A Just Peace* is hardly radical by world Catholic standards. The first 30 pages simply outline the accepted Catholic position on war and peace, drawing on the Popes, Vatican II and bishops conferences, including the US bishops' statement, *The Challenge of Peace*. Critics of the document, including some in the US Embassy in Canberra, have focused on the section entitled 'Building Peace' (pp 30-38) and especially on the discussion of 'US-Australia Joint Defence Facilities' (pp 35-38). The three bases – Nurrungar, Pine Gap and the North West Cape – are judged in the statement by the clear Catholic teaching on deterrence: that it is intrinsically immoral to make threats to use or to actually use nuclear weapons. The United States bishops are quite clear that the doctrine of deterrence can only be tolerated if it is part of a transitional strategy linked to a resolute determination to pursue arms control and disarmament.

This is exactly what *Work for a Just Peace* says. It allows that Pine Gap and Nurrungar can be tolerated if 'clear steps' toward disarmament are taken.

Disarmament must be gradual, mutual, balanced and verifiable. As a means to such disarmament, deterrence is conditionally acceptable. Within this framework there is a need for independent initiatives toward effective bi-lateral disarmament. (*Work for A Just Peace*, p 38)

You could not get more squarely within the Catholic tradition of war and peace.

There is no doubt that some of the attack on CCJP is politically motivated. Certainly people may well differ about the specific application of Catholic moral teaching on war. But morality is not a purely abstract business; someone has to run the risk of applying it to concrete situations. It is absurd to say that agencies such as CCJP should confine themselves to pious generalisations. When it suits them, the right never hesitate to play politics. One has only to review Mr Santamaria's long career to see an example of this. Anyone with a knowledge of the Church's teaching on nuclear war can see that it is those who attack CCJP who are out of touch with the views of world-wide Catholicism, and they provide another example of a Church that is more Australian than Catholic.

The history of the encounter between black and white in this country has been a terrible one. White settlement has taken a disastrous toll on Aboriginal people through land dispossession, violence, massacre and exposure to European vices and diseases. The Church has been part of this dispossession. Certainly some churchmen such as Archbishop Polding and Reverend Reginald Threlkeld tried to protect the people, but their activities often led to an active collusion with white depredation of Aboriginal land. If the black people were on mission stations, they would not trouble white settlers who had taken their land.

There have been three phases in the history of the relationship between black and white. The first phase was that of the expropriation of land by white settlement and the dispossession of the Aborigines. This was often accompanied by violence and by the massacre of any Aborigines who dared to protest. Those who were not killed were exposed to white vices and diseases. European settlement was characterised by blatant racism. In frontier areas this first period lasted well into the early 20th century. The Churches were generally passive spectators of these appalling events. At most they provided physical shelter from white violence.

The second phase was that of the assimilation of the remnants of the Aboriginal people. They were herded onto mission stations and into camps. They were taught the basics of white 'civilisation'. Those who could were supposed to make it into white culture, but it was expected that the majority would eventually die out. The third phase was reached in the late 1950s and the early 1960s. It began with the land rights movement, and the gradual dawning on the consciousness of white Australians of the appalling conditions of Aboriginal people. They had become 'fringe dwellers' in their own country, subsisting in appalling poverty on the edge of rural towns and in ghettos such as Redfern in Sydney. Violence, crime and alcoholism compounded their problems of loss of dignity and the disintegration of their social fabric.

The Churches have been in contact with Aboriginal people from the beginning of white settlement. While the missions have contributed to the physical survival of the people and, to an extent, have protected them from the worst white excesses, they have also been a major factor in the destruction of the fabric of traditional Aboriginal society. The missions aimed to civilise and to convert the 'workshy nomads' – as Bishop Salvardo called them.

The Catholic Church has probably had more contact with Aborigines than any other Church. But the vast majority of Church workers were equipped for their ministry with no more than goodwill. With a few notable exceptions (like Father E.A. Worms in north Western Australia), the Church has not been interested in Aboriginal language, culture, or religion. The most useful studies of Aboriginal religion are by the anthropologists W.E.H. Stanner, T.G.H. Strehlow and R.M. Berndt. In the Northern Territory it was not until 1978 that a research-resource centre was set up, the Nelen Yubu Institute, to assist the Church in understanding Aboriginal people. Yet the Catholic missions have been in the Northern Territory since before the turn of the century. For many years the missions have been characterised by ignorance of the people and by paternalism.

Attitudes are beginning to change and in recent years the Catholic Church particularly has begun to adopt a more enlightened (and Christian) attitude. Those dioceses that have a significant number of Aboriginal people have been willing to invest some resources in this ministry. One of the first Church communities to honestly confront the problem of local Aborigines was the Catholic parish of Redfern in Sydney. Here the parish priest, Father Ted Kennedy and the Aboriginal people themselves, inspired by the work of Mrs Shirley Smith ('Mum Shirl') have set up a community that both cares for people in need and is also willing to confront the systems of white oppression and exploitation. A number of religious sisters, brothers and priests work with Aboriginal people in this ministry. With the emergence of Aboriginal leadership and the investment of large sums of government money, many whites feel that the 'Aborigines problem' is solved. This is a form of white self-deception. This nation will probably never recover from the violence perpetrated on the Aboriginal people and both black and white will have to continue to live with the legacy of Australia's guilty past. The role of the Church will be to stand with Aboriginal people, above all in the struggle for land rights. For a people as closely tied to the land as the Aborigines, this is the central issue. Finally, white Australians need to learn from the Aboriginal people a care and deep respect for the land that we share together.

Let me now try to put some final shape into this personal portrait of the Catholic Church in this country. It is a parochial Church and it has developed largely in isolation from world Catholicism. Irish-Australianism has dominated its ethos and moulded its attitudes. It has neglected the distinctive religious and cultural contributions of the migrants who have come since 1947. It is a Church that continues to expand. Much of its psychic energy is taken up in building a material structure to underpin its numerical increase. It is wealthy but it is also generous. Project Compassion, the Lenten programme of self-denial, for instance, raises more money for development projects from 3.5 million Catholics than the equivalent appeal in the United States from 50 million Catholics.

But the speed of development has meant that the Australian Church has never had a chance to pause and reflect. This leads to impatience with those who suggest the need for planning about where the Church is going and what its priorities are. The self-satisfaction typical of Australian Catholicism also tends to make it self-enclosed and uninterested in evangelisation and ecumenism. Catholic schools have unconsciously reinforced the religious isolationism typical of the community. Interestingly, in contrast to the Church's performance at home, Australian priests and religious have been sensible, well-adjusted missionaries in many other countries.

The spirituality of the Australian Church is characterised by externality. There has never been a strong contemplative tradition here. Attendance at Mass and the sacraments, material generosity and a badly celebrated and often lifeless liturgy are the hallmarks. Among Catholics there is a whole spectrum of expectations of what they want from the Church. Some want social change, others demand the reinforcement of traditional values. Some want more freedom, some want more discipline. And the majority of people are in the middle, between the two ends of the spectrum. These needs are not incompatible. The

Church needs both the radical and the traditionalist. For a more truly *Catholic* Church to emerge, Australian churchgoers are going to have to learn to live and let live. The effects of the great mutation of Catholic Christianity initiated by Vatican II have begun to affect Australia. But this small, backwater Church still has a long way to go to stay abreast of the Church Catholic.

8

THE REAL QUESTIONS

Does the Catholic Church have a future? I am sure that it does. In my view it is one of the most creative realities in the world today. But its future will be different from its immediate past. It has entered into the process of rediscovering itself. What will its future be like? It is very difficult to answer this question precisely, but we need to try. Hope for the future depends to a large extent on the human ability to imagine the future. But, as any historian will tell you, prophecy is a most inexact science. It is difficult enough to discern what is happening in the world or the Church now; predicting the future is more complex. Human events are so subject to a range of influences and to an incredible variety of individual decisions determined by freedom. It is dangerous to speak of 'irreversible trends' which seem so important today but which are forgotten tomorrow. History manifests an unpredictableness, a serendipity which is incomprehensible and uncontrollable.

As Catholicism confronts the future it must develop a new approach to the world and to spiritual living. The French Jesuit, Pierre Teilhard de Chardin has developed an integrated vision of the future which sees God's creativity and purpose working through the evolution of the cosmos. Teilhard sees humankind as participants in the process of the world's development. Thus we are called to build and to nurture the earth, not to destroy it. Teilhard's vision is called *spiritual futurism*.

Spiritual futurism is diametrically opposed to the secularist world view, which sees the world as profane and functional. The cosmos and nature are material realities which can be measured and used. Science shows us how reality came to be and technology shows us how nature can be exploited. For the secularist the world does not point beyond itself; it is self-contained. As Adrian Van Kaam says:

Contemporary man lives experientially more and more in a secularised world, a rather prosaic storehouse of measurable power. Nature is not . . . an open mystery in which (we are) vitally involved, but a supply of useful ingredients, a vast resource of physical energy, to be used cleverly for the maintenance of the 'organism' and for the execution of technical blueprints. (A. Van Kaam: *A Psychology of Falling Away From the Faith*, 1966, p 26)

This attitude has rid the world of much superstition, but it has also deprived us of a sense of the mystery of the cosmos. State education has opted for a secularist attitude and has become one of the most potent forces for the exclusion of a spiritual and religious world view. It has also helped to create a consciousness that a land like Australia is here simply to be exploited through short-term use with no regard for the fragility of the environment.

The secularist view still dominates governments. This is vividly illustrated by the willingness of the Australian government to grant export licences to wood-chippers who would destroy Australia's remaining forests (we have already lost 70% of rainforest since 1788) to supply Japan's short-term needs. They have no concern for the part forests play in the ecosystem, or for the unique species of fauna that are destroyed as a result of wood chipping activities. These products of secularist education are 'technical barbarians'. The Catholic Church unfortunately has not yet begun to realise that environmental destruction involves complex moral questions linked to the theology of creation. It is silent in the face of this major moral issue.

The Church could easily develop an 'environmental morality'. The theological bases are already laid in the strong scriptural emphasis on creation. Catholics will have to overcome an obstacle in their own tradition to a more positive evaluation of the cosmos: the profoundly influential Neo-Platonist/Augustinian theology which sees creation as the place of entrapment and sin for the soul. The prime cause of sin, in this theology, is the material body which roots the person in the world of evil. This Augustinian view will have to be jettisoned in favour of the integrated biblical understanding of creation and the body.

In the Old Testament the created natural world was good (*Psalm 104*) for it was a manifestation of God bringing order out of chaos (*Genesis 1:1-2*). Psalm 104 stresses that God's creativity is a continuing process, that it occurs every day. This is also shown by the God-given fertility of the Earth (*Deuteronomy 11:13-15*). God continues to create the world by protecting it from chaos. Without God's intervention, the world would revert to disintegration.

Most frequently God appears in nature as the saviour of the people. God will intervene as saviour to bring about a 'new heaven and earth'. The emphasis in Hebrew thought is on God's identity with nature. The cosmos is a manifestation of God who acts in and through it. Nature is not profane, a reality to be exploited. It is sacred, and at the deepest level it is a manifestation of the Transcendent.

The vision of Teilhard de Chardin has much in common with the biblical vision. Teilhard sees the process of the evolution of nature in terms of an increasing consciousness which will eventually find its consummation in the total consciousness of Christ. A similar vision is to be found in the work of the French Catholic writer, Robert Muller (*New Genesis. Shaping a Global Spirituality*, 1982). Muller believes that a new world can be built free of nuclear weapons and technological barbarism. He considers that this new world will be shaped by religious belief and not by secularist visions of technological Nirvanas. Belief must be underpinned by profound spirituality and a deep conviction that God is active to save the world.

Closely related are the ideas of US Dominican Matthew Fox.

He is probably one of the most original minds working in American theology at the present moment. In his latest book *Original Blessing* (1984) he points out that the Bible says nothing about 'original sin' and that Jesus had never heard the term. The Christian preoccupation with sin is Augustinian in origin. Augustinianism has deeply impregnated the Western Christian tradition and created a dualistic approach to the world, whereby creation is seen as fundamentally evil. Fox argues that this is not the biblical view. In the Bible creation is blessed. Its goodness should be embraced. Jesus, St Paul, St Thomas Aquinas, St Francis of Assisi, medieval mystics like Hildegarde of Bingen and the Dominican Master Eckhart, the Celtic saints and the much maligned Pelagius, viewed creation as a blessing and embraced it in their spirituality. Fox has consistently argued that modern science, which helps us understand creation, must be integrated with theology. Because the Augustinian tradition sees the world as the place of sin and evil, it has ignored and even persecuted scientists, such as Galileo.

This practical divorce of science from a theological view of the cosmos has allowed the development of a blatantly technocratic mentality. Sin is no longer part of the technocratic world view largely because moral theologians and preachers have trivialised sin. Sin is seen in terms of personal relationships but not in terms of the relationship of the individual to the community and to the world itself. Our culture allows a third of the world's forests to be cut down in 15 years and permits the dumping of an enormous volume of toxic waste on the earth, but it never thinks to ask if this is immoral or sinful. Fox argues that we must regain contact with the beauty, law and justice of the universe if we are to survive.

This brings us face to face with one of the key issues for the future of the Church: its willingness to commit itself to a spirituality and morality that is 'worldly'. Catholicism must rediscover a radical commitment to God's creation.

Linked to the environmental question is the problem of overpopulation. The facts of overpopulation and the destruction of the environment are well known. Developed countries have reached the point of zero population growth and there is little prospect that their birthrate will increase. This is not the case for the under-developed world, where increasing birthrates and economic and social exploitation keep the majority of people in grinding poverty. The figures speak for themselves:

Country	Fertility Rate*	1975 Total Population	Year 2000 Projected Population	Year 2025 Projected Population
Egypt	4.8%	37.5 m	53.5 m	64.5 m
Ghana	6.4%	10.0 m	15.6 m	20.0 m
Tanzania	6.4%	15.5 m	23.8 m	30.4 m
Bangladesh	6.0%	73.5 m	110.0 m	138.0 m
India	4.9%	615.0 m	880.0 m	1070.0 m
Indonesia	5.7%	139.0 m	202.0 m	251.0 m
Pakistan	6.8%	69.5 m	103.0 m	129.0 m
Philippines	5.9%	43.4 m	60.0 m	84.0 m
Mexico	6.4%	59.0 m	96.0 m	123.0 m
Thailand	5.4%	42.2 m	64.0 m	79.5 m

* This percentage figure represents the total number of children that each female will have during her child-bearing years.

The projected population of the world in the year 2000 (only 14 years away) is about 6 billion. It is instructive to place this figure of 6 billion within an historical context. It is then that the enormous increase in world population over the last 200 years becomes obvious. Again the figures speak for themselves. It look 1830 years for the world population to reach 1 billion (in 1830). But it has grown from 1 billion to 6 billion in 170 years (in the year 2000).

WORLD POPULATION INCREASE

Date	Total World Population
1 AD	200 to 300 million
1500	500 million
1750	700 million
1800	900 million
1830	1 billion
1925	2 billion
1962	3 billion
1975	4 billion
1980	4.5 billion
2000	6 to 6.3 billion

(Collins based on Aurelio Peccei: *One hundred Pages for the Future*.)

Between 1900 and 1980 the world population trebled. Discussion of a possible 12 billion people by the middle of the next century is purely academic, for the explosion caused by overcrowding and the shortage of resources will have already happened. This explosion will result from the unwillingness of the ever increasing number of young people in the poorest countries to accept their position. They will revolt against hopeless poverty and the injustice perpetrated by the wealthier nations.

Some experts still assert that the world could support 10 to 12 billion people. What they mean is that the earth may be able to produce enough food to support that number of people. But this only makes sense if human beings are prepared to live like ants in a world denuded of trees and plants (other than those that provide food), with most other species of animals and birds wiped out. Implicit in such a view is a frightening form of human arrogance. It presupposes that everything on earth exists solely for the sake of human beings. In other words, nothing has value except in relationship to human life. Resources are fast running out:

> Living resources essential for human survival and sustainable development are increasingly being destroyed or depleted. At the same time the human demand for these resources is growing fast. If current rates of land degradation continue, close to one third of the world's arable land . . . will be destroyed in the next twenty years. Similarly by the end of the century (at present rates of clearance) the remaining area of unlogged tropical forest will be halved. During this period the world population is expected to increase by almost half. Thus, an ever-growing number of human beings are in need of resources which are becoming scarcer and scarcer. (*Report of the International Union for the Conservation of Nature and Natural Resources, the United Nations Environment Program, and the World Wildlife Fund*, Geneva, 1980)

The voracious appetite of the developed countries for resources depletes and destroys our fragile earth. The poor destroy resources simply to live from day to day.

Despite consistent Catholic insistence on the need for the radical redistribution of the world's goods, and despite Pope Paul's admission in *Populorum progressio* of the connection between population and development, there is still an unwillingness on the part of the Catholic Church to face the population question. There are two reasons for this: the inadequacy of the current Catholic theology of creation, and the traditional papal teaching on contraception and marriage. The prevailing view in Catholic thought is that creation exists *exclusively* for the sake of the human species. The consequence of this is that there is no recognition that creation might have a value in itself independent of human beings. This attitude was well illustrated recently in a letter to an Australian Catholic newspaper from a woman member of *Right to Life*. She attacked, with obvious annoyance, those who wasted time, resources and energy trying to save the whale when X number of babies were being aborted every year in Australia. I share her concern about abortion, but the letter caused me disquiet. She expressed a very narrow view of life. For her, human life alone was of value. The whales were quaint, but their survival as a species was not important. Catholics talk about the seamless garment of life, but the teaching refers only to human life.

This seems to me an excessively narrow and myopic view of life. The world is made up of the interconnected fabric of all life from the most primitive forms to the most highly developed form, the human person. Not only is life interconnected, it is interdependent. Conventional Catholic theology makes too great a distinction between human life and the rest of the living world. My lady letter-writer reflected the conventional Catholic disjunction; she did not realise that life is something we share with the whole cosmos and that a great impoverishment occurs every time a species of life is extinguished. It may be more important to save the whale, for the life of a whole species may transcend in value the individual lives of an unthreatened species. The human species is not under threat – except from militarism and from the failure to confront the population problem.

The other reason why the Catholic Church has never been able to face the population question seriously is that it would involve questioning traditional papal teaching about the nature and purpose of human sexuality. This would involve the Church in admitting that its presuppositions about sexuality are based on an inadequate anthropology.

This anthropology teaches that the act of human sexuality is only redeemed by being always 'open to the transmission of life'. Underlying this is the idea that sexuality is somehow vitiated and sinful and that it needs to be redeemed. Certainly both Vatican II and Pope John Paul II have emphasised that a sexually fulfilling relationship strengthens the commitment of the spouses and is an important component of human interaction. But the view that procreation is the basic purpose of sexuality still deeply pervades the Catholic tradition. Past Popes have vigorously condemned all forms of artificial contraception.

Another problem is that the Church's conscience is still underdeveloped on environmental issues. Catholics need to develop a cosmic conscience. By this I mean the ability to make moral discernments about the created world. A cosmic conscience would demand that I care for the world in which I live, that I have a sense of commonality of all life, that I know that as a living being I have a responsibility for the planet and especially for that part of the earth on which I live.

Thus a whole new approach could be taken to the question of moral decision-making. Several presuppositions will underlie this new approach: firstly, the earth has limited resources and this or no other generation has the right to use them all. Second: the theory of unlimited growth must be abandoned; there are limits to human needs. This will have to be applied rigorously to wealthy nations and individuals. Third: the problem of pollution will have to be tackled. The dumping of millions of tonnes of chemical and other non-biodegradable waste into water, earth and air is no longer morally tolerable. Fourth: many people will have to be 're-natured'. The child that grows up on the 14th floor of a concrete apartment block has lost contact with nature – with water, earth and wind. Cooped-up in a concrete jungle, it looses its sense of connection with other living species. Many urbanised people, especially poorer people, have lost their sense of oneness with nature.

The Canadian Catholic ethicist, André Beauchamp, has outlined a number of elements that would form the basis of an environmental ethic. It will be a cosmic ethic. It will start with a sense of the sacrality of nature, not with God or society or the human person. It will be founded on humankind's basic biological constitution. Secondly, it will be an ethic of respect for nature, not one that aims to control and use nature. It will be more contemplative than transformational. For example, it will view a rainforest in terms of its beauty and integrity and as a manifestation of the Transcendent, rather than in terms of its usable timber. Thirdly, environmental ethics will involve asceticism: this means that individuals and communities will have to cut back on their needs and expectations and be prepared to live more simply. This has a public aspect as well: development can no longer occur while ignoring environmental questions. The moral question will have to be asked: is this or that project commensurate with the ecological risk involved? A development project may bring more money, resources and prestige to a local area, but what are the environmental risks? It may be that a specific area will have to forego development in order to protect its environment. Progress is no longer an end in itself. Fourthly, environmental ethics will force us to ask more long-term questions. What will be the effect of my actions or the actions of my community on people 50 or 100 years hence? It may be fine for me to use scarce resources, but what will be the effect of this action? I do not have the right to demand my individual happiness and satisfaction now if my consumption jeopardises humanity's future. Finally, environmental ethics are international ethics: the whole world is one ecosystem. If rainforests are destroyed in Latin America and the Amazon basin is turned into a desert, the world's oxygen supply is seriously effected. Decisions made in one country affect another. It is the business of us all if someone interferes with the world ecosystem. No individual person or country has an absolute right to do what it likes in its own territory. The fabric of life is too closely interwoven for that.

The Church will also have to develop a population ethic. Its aim will be to help Catholics understand that moral decisions concerning fertility are not just personal choices between spouses, but involve responsibilities to both the community and world. A sense of corporate and cosmic responsibility will have to be exercised when considering the question of fertility. An important element in developing this sense of responsibility will be the position of women. There seems to be a close connection between high fertility and the oppression of women. Where women are ill-educated, confined to home and domestic tasks, forced into arranged marriages and generally treated as inferior to men, there is high fertility. This can be seen in Moslem countries where the inferior status of women leads to the highest fertility in the world. It can also be seen in some Catholic countries. In developed Western countries, where the position of women is changing radically and reliable contraception is readily available, the fertility of Catholics is the same as that of the general population. Thus in the Catholic countries in the Third World the Church must focus on women, offering them the chance to break out of the fertility cycle.

Papal teaching has been quick to condemn government interference in questions of fertility. Yet in countries where overpopulation is already a fact, such as China and India, it is hard to blame governments when they promote policies that limit fertility. In predominantly Catholic countries, such as the Philippines and Latin America, the Church does have influence over the lives of people. It is more in keeping with human dignity if they can be persuaded to limit their fertility by free and conscious decision than by government decree. The Church could play an important intermediary role by using its moral authority to help people form their conscience about responsible fertility.

Turning now to internal issues: a basic question for the Church will be the shift in focus from the centrality of the hierarchical Roman Church to an emphasis on the local community. I have described the corrosive problem of two mutually exclusive models of Church operating side by side. As we move toward 2000 and beyond, the Church will have to shift focus from hierarchy to community, from clergy to lay people. This seems to be contrary to the emphasis of Pope John Paul II who is encouraging a papocentric style of Church. In the future the laity will emerge as the primary focus of Church ministry. The sacrament of baptism rather than that of orders will be the initiation into active Christian life. The Church will no longer be viewed as an institution based on cultic and jurisdictional divisions, but as a communion. By communion I mean a community of people who, in differing ways share a common faith and experience of Christ, which they express through ministerial service to others. Thus community will form the local Church, and a 'communion of communities' will form the diocesan Church, gathered under the leadership of the bishop. The universal Church will be a communion of diocesan communities gathered under the leadership of the Bishop of Rome. This view of the Church constitutes a return to a very ancient and traditional model.

This will demand of Catholics a whole new way of thinking. The Church in the New Testament is an outstanding example of the type of Church which I think will develop in the future.

Several issues will be of basic importance in developing the local Church. Firstly, there will have to be increasing local autonomy and decentralisation. By that I mean that the local community will need to have a major say in the appointment of its own leadership; it will determine the priorities of its ministry, draw up its own budget and elect its own governing body. In the tradition of subsidiarity, decisions that can be made at the local level should be made there. Secondly, the ministry of the Church will be less dependent on territorial divisions (such as the parish); smaller groupings of people will develop. This has already begun. These groups will focus around people with similar interests or professions (such as university chaplaincies), others will be ad hoc groupings of people as in prayer groups and social and family organisations. Others will form through common interests or concerns such as peace or social action groups. Clearly, the parish will continue, but it will have to become more personalised, more in touch with the individuals who are members and structured in a way that can activate the gifts of the participants.

Thirdly, the laity will need training in ministry. Untrained people, no matter how great their goodwill, cannot just leap into delicate and sensitive situations (for example dealing with people in grief) without preparatory formation. Those involved in sacramental programmes (such as preparation for baptism or marriage), those teaching young Catholics or preparing the liturgy will require some theological and scriptural formation. Continuing adult education will be a high priority. This process is only beginning in Australia. In North America it is more highly developed. Increasingly, local leadership will emerge from this group of trained laity. It must, however, remain *lay* and not become too clericalised, as have many acolytes in Australia and deacons in the United States.

Leadership will continue to be a key issue. The statistics make it clear that we are witnessing the demise of the present clericalised priesthood. This will leave the way open for a more ministerial type of priestly leadership to emerge. Leadership will focus around the facilitation of the gifts of the members of the community. Obviously, during the lifetime of John Paul II priests will continue to be celibate. But the denial of the eucharist to so many communities because of the demand of celibacy for priestly ordination, will eventually force the ordination of married men. The eucharist is the quintessential expression of the Church and its celebration is much more important than the survival of an outdated clerical lifestyle.

The question of ministry for women, including the ministry of liturgical leadership, will have to be faced by the Church. This will have to happen despite the fact that John Paul II has made opposition to women's ordination a litmus test of loyalty. I have used the term 'ministry of liturgical leadership' rather than 'priesthood' not because I want to stay out of trouble, but because priesthood is so clearly tied to a male, clerical mode of operation. I would hope that women as liturgical leaders (including the liturgy of the eucharist) would begin to create new, less clerical models. Women have made some progress in the Church in the 20 years since Vatican II. Religious sisters have been released from cloister and the habit and many have committed themselves to new and creative ministries, especially in solidarity with the poor. Women have become lectors and extraordinary (note the word!) ministers of the eucharist. In a few brave and creative parishes girls have begun to serve at the altar. In the new *Code of Cannon Law* women can now become diocesan chancellors (comptrollers of finance) and hold the offices of assessor, auditor, defender of the bond, advocate, and even judge in diocesan marriage tribunals. They can also serve as members of diocesan and parish councils. But they cannot be ordained to the priesthood or deaconate or be installed as lectors or acolytes. They can only be allowed to perform these ministries when no 'suitable' males are available! Pope John Paul II has ordered the US bishops to withdraw all support from individuals or groups who promote the ordination of women. Interestingly, the US bishops have continued to talk with such groups despite the papal order – a sign perhaps that they are courageous enough to try to keep in touch with their people.

The Church faces a terrible danger as it confronts the question of the role of women. As younger women grow up experiencing equality with men, they will be increasingly alienated by a Church which continues to deny their rights and aspirations (except, of course, as mothers and homemakers) and excludes them from all ministries that involve the eucharist. This is still considered too 'sacred' an area for women. Yet the same Church is prepared to continue to ordain unsuitable male candidates to the priesthood, many of whom lack intellectual, spiritual and psycho-sexual maturity.

I am confident that women will increasingly invade the ministry. It may be what Jesus means when he speaks of entering the Kingdom 'violently' (*Matthew 11:12; Luke 16:16*). Women do have sound theological and even canonical grounds to enter the ministry. As baptised believers they are radically equal to men in the Church. St Paul's charter of equality breaks down all divisions in the Christian community: 'There is neither Jew nor Greek (divisions and inequalities based on race are eliminated), there is neither slave nor free (inequality can no longer be based on economic or social divisions), there is neither male nor female, for you are all one in Christ Jesus' (*Galatians 3:28*). St Paul continues that 'all are heirs according to the promise.' For Paul men and women are equal in Christ.

Membership in the People of God means that all share in the priesthood of Christ and the Church, all share in the role of teaching, prophesying, sanctifying and shepherding. Women have been and are teachers in the Church. In Australia they carry much of the burden of religious education. In the United States they are increasingly recognised as theologians, biblical scholars and canon lawyers. In the past women have instructed Popes (Saints Catherine of Siena and Bridget of Sweden), they have acted as spiritual leaders and have been radical religious innovators (Mary Ward, Saint Angela Merici) and have, at last, gained the status of 'doctor of the Church' (Saint Teresa of Avila). Women acted as prophets in the New Testament Church and continue to do so today by their words and their actions. Dorothy Day was a prophet of peace and justice in the Catholic Church for the whole of her adult life. It is only in the last few years that the United States bishops have caught up with her profoundly Christian vision. Popular religiosity and the media have also cast Mother Teresa of Calcutta in the role of prophet. It is religious sisters, however, in renewed religious orders who have pointed the way to new ministries. The demand of women for full participation in the life of the Church is itself prophetic.

The areas from which women are excluded are the sanctifying and shepherding roles – in other words the liturgy and leadership. Women can begin to break down the barriers of exclusion by joining those Christian communities that emphasise the fundamental equality of all believers and incorporate a theology from below – the grass roots theology that is typical of the New Testament Churches. This form of community already exists in Latin America (base communities). It can also be found in the Netherlands, the United States, Italy, Asia (especially the Philippines) and in incipient forms in Australia. Women's religious communities are often key elements in the development of creative ministerial work for women. They can provide a supportive and caring structure for those women who are working in difficult new ministries.

There is one group of men in the Church who have been treated like pariahs: priests who have left priestly ministry and married. These men, many of whom are still willing to serve in the ministry, are excluded in a most unchristian manner from any activity in the Church. They have been highly trained at considerable cost to themselves and to the Catholic community, but they have been excluded from any ministry because they decided to exercise their radical *natural* right to marry. Many have been treated with pettiness, even with viciousness. They were called Judases by Pope Paul VI. Pope John Paul II has decided that the only way in which they can become laicised (and thus marry in the Catholic Church) is for them to admit that they were so sexually and humanly immature that they were incapable of making any form of commitment at the time of their ordination. The implication is that this immaturity and lack of integration has continued throughout their priesthood. Yet the vast majority of these men have carried on successful and fruitful ministries for many years in the Church and they have been highly regarded by the people and communities they served. There is considerable evidence that in Australia some Church officials have decided to exclude them from any form of employment in the Church. In one situation a married priest was denied employment as a librarian in a Catholic primary school because of his status. The State equal opportunity board refused to intervene, ostensibly because of Church-State tangles, but the real reason was the fear of the political fall-out from tackling the Church.

The vindictive treatment of these men is an ugly aspect of the underbelly of the papacy and the hierarchy. They are denied in perpetuity their inherent baptismal rights to minister. The loss to the Church through their exclusion from ministry is great, especially in view of the shortage of clergy. The responsibility for such a loss must be laid squarely on the Vatican and specifically on John Paul II.

If the local Church is to develop, a fluid structure and polity will be needed. Codified canon law is an unsuitable instrument for an evolving Church. The nature of code law is that it tends to harden and fossilise. The growth of the local Church will place more emphasis on community discernment. That is, the local community will decide for itself, in the light of the gospel, the direction of God's Spirit. This will bring about a more untidy Church; but perhaps it will be more humane and Christian.

The development of local Church is, of course, a threat to those with vested interests in the present structure of the Church. They will – and are – fighting change vigorously. Local Church emerged as a major topic at the Extraordinary Synod of Bishops in Rome in November 1985. In my opinion the constant travelling of Pope John Paul is counter-productive to the development of local Church. His visits could be helpful if they were more low key (and less expensive), and if he came, listened and learned, and then reinforced the efforts of local Catholics to confront local issues.

There are, however, a number of signs that the local Church is beginning and will continue to emerge. There are the base communities that are to be found on several continents. There is the adaption of the liturgy to different cultures. For instance, in Zaire a highly Africanised Mass has developed complete with the priest wearing a headdress and dancing accompanying the principal actions. Africa has also begun to produce a local theology as Catholics struggle to express their faith in terms of their own culture. This indigenisation led to a dispute with the Vatican Congregation for Divine Worship when the Pope visited Zaire in 1980. The local bishops wanted the Pope to celebrate this Africanised Mass with them, but the Congregation for Divine Worship was opposed to this, as it would be seen as approving this type of liturgy. Cardinal Joseph Malula of Kinshasa publicly expressed disappointment that John Paul had not experienced an African liturgy. Despite the liturgical fiasco, John Paul did encourage the growth of the local Church in speeches in Congo-Brazzaville, Ghana, Kenya and Zaire.

Another manifestation of the growth of local Church is that so many laypeople – especially in the area of marital sexuality – have assumed responsibility for their own conscientious moral decisions. Connected with this is a great decline in the use of personal confession and the increasing use by many Catholics of communial reconciliation. Very few people go regularly to a priest for private confession now, but large numbers will attend a liturgy of reconciliation at Easter or Christmas. Catholics have not lost their sense of sin, but an increasing number find that a communial expression of repentence and sorrow is more appropriate than private confession. There is also a growing sense that sin is an interpersonal and communial reality that requires a community expression to symbolise God's forgiveness. What is significant about this phenomenon is that large numbers of Catholics have decided this for themselves. Quietly, the majority of Catholics have simply stopped going to confession. Coincidently, this has meant a great decline in the influence of the clergy. Priests had great power when they could advise people about the most intimate aspects of their lives. With the decline of attendance at confession they no longer have this power. This, I would argue, is an extremely significant change.

A further local initiative of importance is the persistent use of what are called pastoral solutions to intractable ministerial problems. For instance, many divorced Catholics who have remarried outside the Catholic Church and who are now in stable relationships, have been quietly advised to begin practising again as Catholics, even though their second marriage is technically invalid in the eyes of the Church. Until recently they had been denied access to the Church's sacramental ministry. Local clergy and churches are subtly assuming the responsibility to offer the healing grace of Christ to those Catholics who have already experienced so much pain through divorce.

Finally, a number of religious orders, especially those of women, have introduced more participative and collegial models of government. The attempt has been made to break down hierarchical structures in order to give each member a stronger sense of participation in the decision-making process of the order. Here 'models of conviviality' are lived out in action. These orders recognise individual differences. Yet, at the same time, they have evolved structures coherent enough to hold the group together and to give it a sense of direction. Religious orders often assume responsibility for new and creative forms of ministry.

An excellent example of the local Church in action can be seen in the process whereby the US bishops evolved their *Peace Pastoral.* It was important that they speak about nuclear war for they come from the country most responsible for it. They had the courage to initiate, develop through consultation and publish the pastoral. We have already seen the opposition that they encountered in the process. Their persistence with a consultative process did much to develop a sense that the US Church must continue to address those moral questions which confront their nation.

If the Church can develop the local community, there will not be too much need to worry about Rome. The task facing most Catholics will be to get the local act together. I want to emphasise here that I am not advocating the abandonment of any need for a centre of unity. Part of the historical reason for the growth of the power of Rome was the need to appeal somewhere from the tyranny of local bishops! Today, however, the need is to use the doctrine of collegiality and the principle of subsidiarity as widely as possible. Bishops need to assume more responsibility for the local national Church, and the people need to experience a sense of participation in the diocesan Church and in the local community. This can be achieved through national synods and through local and diocesan pastoral councils. Bishops and priests will have to learn the discipline of true Christian leadership. The process has already begun, but it will take time to develop. Contemporary Catholics are in for what Daniel Berrigan has called 'the asceticism of the long haul'.

Catholic universalism will still be a very important element in the Church. Local communities can easily become self-absorbed, chauvinistic and uncritical of themselves. They will need an outside reference point and a focus for the expression of their communion with other local Churches. The Bishop of Rome will continue to fulfil this function. Local Churches will also need a point of doctrinal reference – what the early Church called a 'touchstone of orthodoxy'. This will also be Rome's function. But the primacy of the Bishop of Rome can no longer be interpreted in terms of the total dominance of the whole Church, as it has in the recent past – especially since Vatican Council I (1870). If the Church is a 'communion of communions' there has to be a recognition of diversity. This will be cultural, linguistic, organisational, doctrinal and liturgical. The Church of the future will also have to integrate an ecumenical perspective as Roman Catholics begin to recognise that their Church does not alone constitute the 'universal Church', but that the Orthodox, Anglican and Protestant Churches are part of that reality.

My own view is that there will be two major Christian groups in the future. The Roman Catholic Church together with the Orthodox, Anglican and mainline Protestant Churches will constitute one large group of intercommuning communities. Each will retain its own liturgy, structure and polity, but all will be united through a common ministry and a sharing of the eucharist and the other sacraments. This group will inherit and develop the theological, liturgical and pastoral tradition of the Christian past. The other group of Christians will be the fundamentalists. They will insist on scriptural literalism, they will be authoritarian in the sense that the Bible will be their 'paper Pope', and they will have flexible structures. It will be the influence of powerful personalities and charismatic leaders that will hold the groups together. Personally, I see very little chance for union between the mainline Churches and the fundamentalists.

German theologian Karl Rahner has pointed out that the contemporary Catholic Church is undergoing a profound shift of focus from a community whose structures are rooted in the medieval past and whose vision is Euro-centric, to a Church that is world-wide and whose structures are slowly beginning to reflect something of that universality. Another German theologian, Johannes Metz, has emphasised that the shift of focus is also from a religion that is middle class and bourgeois in attitude to one that is poor, under-developed and whose experiences are rooted in the Third World. In confirmation of this, the majority of Catholics no longer live in Europe and North America, but in the Third World – Latin America, Asia, Africa and the Pacific. Walbert Buhlmann (*The Coming of the Third Church*, 1976 and *God's Chosen Peoples*, 1982), is another theologian to focus on the new Churches of the developing world.

The basic task facing these Third World Catholic communities is 'inculturation'. By this I mean that the Church must take on a truly local colour, that it must become part of the milieu and culture of each of the areas in which it is implanted. Faith must grow in and through the soil of the local culture.

One of the great mistakes of the missionary methods of the past was to link the Church with Western cultural forms and to demand that those who joined conform to these. Much of the history of 19th and early 20th century missionary activity involved a form of imperialism, more subtle than that of Western secular governments, but far more pervasive.

As an example of the difficulty of inculturation, take, for instance, the question of the training of priests in Papua New Guinea. Intelligent young men left home in early adolescence to enter the seminary. The model of priesthood put before them was the celibate Roman model. Their intellectual formation was largely in the European/North American theological tradition. Since ordination many have experienced alienation from their own culture as a result of their seminary formation. Father William R. Burrows (*New Ministries. The Global Context*, 1980) says that in Papua New Guinea celibacy has become a pivotal issue. Melanesian culture is geared to fertility and so there is great clan pressure on students and priests to marry. High on the agenda of the local seminary (this has been moderated recently) was an attempt to get students to accept a quasi-monastic lifestyle and a priestly camaraderie in order to support a celibate spirituality. As a result of this students and young priests were cut off from their culture and had great difficulty readjusting to it when they went to work in parishes. Many, of course, left the seminary or priesthood. Burrows says: 'There can be no true attempt at developing indigenous forms of ministry until celibacy is made optional' (p 121).

This problem can be seen through another example. Father Tissa Balasuriya is a Sri Lankan priest. In his book *Jesus Christ and Human Liberation* (1976), he describes the image of Jesus presented to 19th and 20th century Asian converts. Jesus was seen as one who saved fallen men and women from the effects of original and personal sin. He became man in obedience to the Father in order to make reparation through his death. Through his obedience he redeemed all humanity. Of course, the emphasis on obedience and the personal unworthiness of the convert was important. For this was precisely what the colonial power demanded in the civil sphere from the natives. There was no conscious collusion, of course, but both Church and State were working out of the same set of presuppositions. As Balasuriya points out, the gospels could have been used to present a very different image of Jesus: one who cared for the poor and oppressed and who worked for human liberation. This was ignored. In fact, in the gospels his death resulted directly from his confrontation with the religious and secular authorities of his own time. The Jesus that was presented to the Asian converts was passive and obedient rather than active and liberating.

I mention these examples not to condemn the past, but to show the way in which Western religious and cultural forms can obscure the gospel and prevent the Church attaining true inculturation.

There will, of course, be problems linked to inculturation. How will the local Church avoid becoming a national Church? A national Church is always in danger of State control. A truly local Church runs the risk of being so encased in its own culture that it is not able to develop the facility of self-criticism. And how does the local Church retain communion with the universal Church? These are all important questions. The answers to them cannot be pre-determined in advance. At the present moment the Catholic Church runs no risk of splitting into local nationalist Churches. A strong sense of universal communion can be maintained through modern communication and frequent travel. The challenge before the Church today – and for the foreseeable future – is not the maintenance of universality but the development of true local Churches.

Karl Rahner has reflected on the future of the Church in his book *The Shape of the Church to Come* (1972). He is one of the greatest theologians of this century, so his ideas require consideration. The book was written for a synod of the West German Church, but its conclusions can be applied to the wider Church. Rahner says that the following realities will characterise the future of the Catholic Church. It will be a 'little flock'. By this he means that the Church will be no longer able to wield power in society in the old manner, it will not be able to look to the State to protect Christian values. Rahner insists that this does not imply a return to the ghetto, or retirement from participation in public events. It simply means a refusal on the part of the Church to use the civil arm. The implication is that Catholic 'action' will have to be more humble and less self-righteous. In Australia this would have serious repercussions, for Catholics certainly expect the civil arm – the government – to provide money for much of the education and hospital ministry of the Church. Rahner sounds a note of warning to those in the contemporary Church who advocate a remnant mentality. These are the people who say it does not matter how many are pushed out of the Church or are lost to it, as long as the remnant are orthodox and authentic Catholics. As one conservative put it recently: 'The Church would be better rid of self-indulgent neo-modernists!' Rahner responds:

Little flock does not mean the same as ghetto or sect, since these are not defined by numbers but by a mentality: a mentality which the Church can afford in the future even less than today . . . Where sectarian or ghetto mentality is propagated among us . . . it must be fought with the utmost severity in the name of true and authentic Christianity. If we talk of the 'little flock' to defend our cosy traditionalism and stale pseudo-orthodoxy in fear of . . . modern society, if we tacitly consent to the departure of restless, questioning people from the Church, so that we can return to our repose . . . we are propagating . . . a petty sectarian mentality. This is all the more dangerous because it shows up, not under its true name, but in an appeal to orthodoxy, church loyalty and strict morality. (*The Shape of the Church to Come*, pp 29-30)

Rahner says that the second characteristic of the Church to come will be 'non-simultaneity' – not every Catholic will be in the same place at the same time in their religious development. Previously most Catholics were from the same socio-economic group and their religious development reflected their social similarities. Now there are many different types of people in the Church at different levels of development and these differences must be respected. People will have to learn to live with each other, and for this compromises will be necessary. In the future the Church will be enriched by all these differences, but it will have to avoid the pitfalls of polorisation and the formation of parties. This is very difficult for right-wing Catholics. Their very position encourages a self-righteous conviction of orthodoxy and the temptation to act to 'expel' those whom they construe as unorthodox or insufficiently committed.

Thirdly, Rahner says that the Church of the future will be declericalised. He sees no need of a celibate priest if this is not the right choice for the particular community. He argues that there is no theological objection to the ordination of women; they have only been excluded for sociological reasons. The Church of the future will be concerned with serving – its purpose will be to serve others, not itself. The danger of self-serving will always be there: office holders and clerics particularly are liable to become 'ecclesiologial introverts'. The magisterium of the Church must be shown to be rooted in the gospel and not just imposed by authority. The Church must honestly abandon positions that are not part of her essential claims. Rahner maintains that in the area of ecumenism, union between the Churches cannot wait for the ironing out of all doctrinal differences. Nor should the Churches aim at institutional unity. It is by ministering together and being together that they will gradually come to accept each other. Even then different Church orders will remain. This will add to the richness and diversity of the Christian Church.

Rahner characterised the German Church of 1972 as 'dominated to a terrifying extent by ritualism, legalism and a resigned spiritual mediocrity.' This statement could easily be applied to the Australian Church of the late 1980s. The reason for this spiritual mediocrity is that so few who claim to be Catholics have opened themselves to the terrible risk of experiencing God. The word God remains an abstraction without meaning or content because God is sought in the wrong places. Conventional spirituality and religiosity are used as shields against the experience of the Ultimate. Rahner is particularly scathing on those who claim to preach God. The preacher's words, he says, are empty and lacking in conviction unless he has encountered God in a transforming way. The word God, he says, 'must constantly be divined afresh and suffered through all the heights and depths of human experience.' What an extraordinary phrase: 'suffered through all the heights and depths of human experience.' In other words, the person of genuine spirituality must enter the totality of life to discover God. As I mentioned, religion is often used as a shield against true spirituality. People become caught up in practices, laws, ritual, their own ideas and projections and then think that it is in these phenomena that one encounters God. So often all that is encountered are one's own projections.

I myself had to learn this the hard way. For the first 10 years after ordination I was a 'successful' priest. I worked in parishes, taught in the seminary and gave retreats to religious, priests and laity. I was a spiritual director (what an extraordinarily pretentious title!) and I even came to think that I 'knew' God. This was not a crass assertion of familiarity, but a subtle and pervasive assumption that underpinned my consciousness and ministry. My knowledge and ability to speak about spirituality reinforced this conviction. The trouble was that I only knew my own concepts and ideas, which immediately limited my possibility of entering more deeply into the mystery of God. The only way to experience this mystery more deeply was to break out of the straight-jacket created by the conventions of priesthood, ministry and my own unarticulated assumptions. I probably would have never done it myself unless precipitated by a whole series of circumstances, which I have now come to see as God's way of breaking down my own rock-solid arrogance. These circumstances were the human experiences of love and hate, loneliness and friendship, insecurity, fear and the dislocation of my 'career pattern'. Out of it all I have become more aware of the mystery and otherness of God. Paradoxically, at the same time, this awareness brings a profound sense of God's presence.

This excursion into autobiography is simply a way of saying that the quality of the future of the Church will be determined by the willingness of Catholics to allow themselves to seek the inner meaning of their human experience. Introspection, however, is not the way to attain this. What is important is the quality of one's experience and the ability to reflect on that experience. Through this reflection a pattern begins to emerge and the events of one's life begin to make sense. Introspection simply turns people inward, away from the tough issues of the real world. Introspective spirituality provides an escape from these intractable issues. Some people call this prayer but it is really a withdrawal from life. The challenge is out in reality.

In the future Catholics will have to integrate a spirituality that arises from a full life lived in the real world. Catholicism has always strived for – but rarely achieved – an integration of the life of the world and the life of the spirit. Human existence is an interlocking system in which individuals find themselves involved in a network of relationships with other persons, communities and with life itself. Our lives constantly interact with systems that involve us in a wide range of activities and responsibilities. We are never atomised individuals and our spirituality must reflect our essentially social nature. Yet the constant temptation is to introduce a split, a schizophrenia between religion and the life of the world. The Catholic of the future will have to achieve a delicate balance whereby life in the world and human activity assumes a new quality through the achievement of a genuine Christian humanism. Religion and spirituality are not separate from life in the world but an enrichment of it. It is only by entering the fabric of human life that one can discover the true mystery of God.

'Encountering God' naturally leads to a discussion of God's ultimate revelation – Jesus Christ. As Catholicism moves into the future it will need to focus increasingly on the person of Jesus as the normative figure in the history of Christianity. One of the signs of the health of Catholicism at present is the focus of many theologians on Jesus and on Christology (the study of Christ). For the Christian, Jesus Christ is normative. He is the pivotal point of Christianity. Christian life only takes meaning through him. Christ and the experience of the power of his personality can transform a person. St Paul is an example. The central experience of his life was the encounter with the risen Jesus on the road to Damascus. It transformed him from a narrow bigot to a man who reached out to the whole Roman world. The basic motivating force of his religious personality was his inner experience of Christ. For him, however, this could never be divorced from his ministry in the service of the Lord.

Hans Küng has pointed out in *On Being a Christian* (1976) that the fundamental characteristic of Christianity is that Jesus is 'ultimately decisive, definitive, *archetypical*' for a human being's relationship with God, others and society. Küng emphasises that the personality of Jesus is so mysterious that neither piety, dogma nor image can ever capture him fully. Most people – both Christian and otherwise – presume that they 'know' who Jesus is. But despite this assumption of familiarity, he remains a mystery. Every era in the Church must discover him afresh.

Jesus interacts with men and women in pain and in joy and he chooses companionship especially with those who are politically and socially oppressed. His identification with the marginalised and the lowest strata of society led to a confrontation with the politico-religious authorities and directly to his death.

Jesus' immersion of himself in human life was a response to his Father. His solidarity with us shows that God takes the world and the human condition seriously. St Paul expresses God's commitment to humanity in the extraordinary statement: 'For our sake God made the sinless one into sin, so that in him we might become the goodness of God' (*II Corinthians 5:21*). Jesus experienced all the consequences of bodily existence: physicality, frustration, joy, weakness, sexuality, anger, pain and the physical and psychological limitations of the human condition. When St Paul says that Jesus 'emptied himself' he means that Jesus clung to nothing of his divinity, that he entered into humanity totally. He did not use his divine sonship as a protection. There is a subtle temptation to think that Jesus' humanity was only an 'appearance' – that he only *seemed* to be like us. This is the heresy of docetism.

Christians are much more likely to deny Jesus' humanity than his divinity. This is because we do not take our own humanity seriously enough. Jesus immersed himself in our life and did not abandon his commitment to humanity, even when his own life was threatened. In dying his self-emptying was completed for he was stripped of everything. Jesus did not theorise about suffering; he suffered. He did not discuss life; he entered it to the full.

As the Church moves through this painful period of mutation it must discover Jesus afresh. This process has already begun in life and theology in Latin America, in the work of contemporary scripture scholars and theologians such as Edward Schillebeeckx, and among ordinary people as they read the gospels from the perspective of the late 20th century. The historical teaching about Jesus, enshrined in the Church's teaching, worship and piety, will continue to be of significance, but what will be most important will be the discovery of Jesus' unique relationship to men and women of today.

St Paul says that we discover 'the glory of God in the face of Christ' (*II Corinthians 4:6*). The face is the most expressive part of the person and it tells us most about them as a human being. The face distinguishes one person from another and gives us the essential clue to their humanity. We speak of a person with a kind face, a hard face, a smiling face, a sad face. The face is profoundly human. It is the face of Jesus that is the ultimate manifestation of God. It is this face that the Church must constantly seek to discover.

I end where I began by asking: does the Catholic Church have a future? Of course it does. But the price of that future will be profound change. This process has already begun. It can be slowed down, short circuited and opposed, but it cannot be stopped. Catholicism has emerged as one of the most creative and positive forces in the world today. Vatican II was the beginning of a mutation from which a profoundly renewed Church will eventually emerge. It will, of course, be deeply rooted in its history and experience. Tradition, in the full Catholic sense, does not mean finding answers in the past or retreating into an unreal world which no longer exists. Tradition means the ability to be able to look to the present and the future on the basis of the enormous experience of the past. Only a person or community with a deep sense of historical continuity has the foundation for a contemporary radicalism. The Catholic Church certainly has a history. I have no doubt that it also has a future.

BIBLIOGRAPHY

Balasuriya, Tessa, *Jesus Christ and Human Liberation.* Centre for Society and Religion Publications. Colombo. 1976.

Bausch, William J., *Traditions Tensions Transitions in Ministry.* Twenty Third Publications. Mystic, CT. 1982.

Beeson, Trevor, *Discretion and Valour. Religious Conditions in Russia and Eastern Europe.* Collins/Fount. London. 1982.

Blazynski, George, *Pope John Paul II: A Man From Krakow.* Sphere Books. London. 1979.

Broccolo, Gerard T. and Larkin, E.: *Spiritual Renewal of the American Priesthood.* US Catholic Conference. Washington, DC. 1973.

Buhlmann, Walbert, *The Coming of the Third Church.* St Paul Publication. Slough. 1974.

Buhlmann, Walbert, *God's Chosen People.* Orbis. Maryknoll, N.Y. 1982.

Bull, George, *Inside the Vatican.* St. Martin's Press. New York. 1982.

Burrows, William R., *New Ministries: The Global Context.* Dove Communications. Melbourne. 1980.

Campion, Edmund, *Rockchoppers: Growing Up Catholic in Australia.* Penguin. Melbourne. 1982.

Castelli, Jim, *The Bishops and the Bomb: Waging Peace in a Nuclear Age.* Image Books. New York. 1983.

Clark, C. M. H., *Occasional Writings and Speeches.* Collins/Fontana. Melbourne. 1980.

Coleman, John, *An American Strategic Theology.* Paulist. New York. 1982.

Conway, Ronald, *The Great Australian Stupor: An Interpretation of the Australian Way of Life.* Sun Books. Melbourne. 1971.

Conway, Ronald, *The End of Stupor? Australia Towards the Third Millennium.* Sun Books. Melbourne. 1984.

Dahm, Charles, *Power and Authority in the Church: Cardinal Cody in Chicago.* University of Notre Dame Press. South Bend. 1981.

Digan, Parig, *Churches in Contestation: Asian Christian Social Protest.* Orbis. Maryknoll, New York. 1984.

Durkheim, Emile, *Elementary Forms of the Religious Life.* Allen and Unwin. London. 1915.

Fox, Matthew, *Original Blessing: A Primer in Creation Spirituality.* Bear. Santa Fe, NM. 1983.

Granfield, Patrick, *The Papacy in Transition.* Gill and Macmillan. Dublin. 1981.

Harris, D., Hynd., Millikan, D. (eds), *The Shape of Belief: Christianity in Australia Today.* Lancer. Homebush West. 1982.

Hayes, Victor C., *Toward Theology in An Australian Context.* AASR Publications. Adelaide. 1979.

Hebblethwaite, Peter, *The Runaway Church.* Collins/Fount. London. 1975.

Hebblethwaite, Peter, *The New Inquisition? Schillebeeckx and Küng.* Collins/Fount. London. 1980.

Hebblethwaite, Peter, *Introducing John Paul II: The Populist Pope.* Collins/Fount. London. 1982.

Hebblethwaite, Peter, *John XXIII: Pope of the Council.* Geoffrey Chapman. London. 1984.

Hebblethwaite, Peter, *Synod Extraordinary: The Inside Story of the Roman Synod, November-December 1985.* Darton, Longman, Todd. London. 1986.

Hostie, Raymond, *The Life and Death of Religious Orders: A Psycho-Sociological Approach.* CARA. Washington, DC. 1983.

Huizing, P. and Walf, F., *The Roman Curia and the Communion of Churches.* Concilium/Seabury. New York. 1979.

Jedin, Hubert and Dolan, John, *History of the Church.* Volume IX. Crossroad. New York. 1981.

Kaiser, Robert B., *Pope, Council and World.* Macmillan. New York. 1963.

Keneally, Thomas, *Three Cheers for the Paraclete.* Angus & Robertson. Sydney. 1968.

Keneally, Thomas, *Schindler's Ark.* Penguin. Melbourne. 1983.

Kung, Hans, *On Being A Christian*. Doubleday. Garden City, NY. 1976.

Lodge, David, *How Far Can You Go?* Penguin. London. 1981.

Lewins, Frank W., *The Myth of the Universal Church*. Australian National University Press. Canberra. 1978.

Marc, Gabriel, *The Institutional Church in the Future*. Pro Mundi Vita Bulletin No 82. 1980.

Martin, Ralph, *A Crisis of Truth: The Attack on Faith, Morality and Mission in the Catholic Church*. Servant. Ann Arbor. 1983.

Milosz, Czeslaw, *Native Realm*. Doubleday. New York. 1968.

Mol, Hans, *The Faith of Australians*. George Allen and Unwin. Sydney. 1985.

Moorman, John, *Vatican Observed: An Anglican View of Vatican II*. Darton, Longman, Todd. London. 1967.

Muller, Robert, *New Genesis: Shaping A Global Spirituality*. Doubleday. New York. 1982.

Nolan, Albert, *Jesus Before Christianity: The Gospel of Liberation*. Darton, Longman, Todd. London. 1977.

O'Farrell, Patrick, *The Catholic Church and Community in Australia*. Nelson. Melbourne. 1977.

Pomian-Srzednicki, Maciej, *Religious Change in Contemporary Poland: Secularisation and Politics*. Routledge and Kegan Paul. Boston. 1982.

Pro Mundi Vita, *Dossier on Australia*. Pro Mundi Vita. September, 1980.

Ranaghan, Kevin and Dorothy, *Catholic Pentecostals*. Paulist, New York. 1969.

Rahner, Karl, *The Shape of the Church to Come*. Crossroad. New York. 1974.

Rynne, Xavier, *Letters from the Vatican City*. Faber and Faber. London. 1963.

Rynne, Xavier, *The Second Session*. Faber and Faber. London. 1964.

Rynne, Xavier, *The Third Session*. Faber and Faber. London. 1965.

Rynne, Xavier, *The Fourth Session*. Faber and Faber. London. 1966.

Sheed, Frank, *Theology and Sanity*. Sheed and Ward. London. 1946.

Suenens, Leon. J., *A New Pentecost?* Darton, Longman, Todd. London. 1975.

Trevor, Meriol, *Pope John*. Macmillan. London. 1967.

Van Kamm, Adrian, *A Psychology of Falling Away From the Faith*. Franciscan Herald Press. Chicago. 1966.

Ward, Russell, *The Australian Legend*. Oxford. Melbourne. 1966.

Wilson, Bruce, *Can God Survive in Australia?* Albatros. Sutherland. 1983.

Williams, George H., *The Mind of John Paul II. Origins of His Thought and Action*. Seabury. New York. 1981.

Wojtyla, Karol, *A Sign of Contradiction*. St Paul Publications. London. 1978.

Wojtlya, Karol, *Love and Responsibility*. Collins. London. 1981.

Yallop, David, *In God's Name. An Investigation into the Murder of Pope John Paul I*. Corgi Books. London. 1984.

INDEX